ELEMENTARY SCHOOL
ART
FOR CLASSROOM TEACHERS

Happy is the man that findeth wisdom,
and the man that getteth understanding.

For the merchandise of it is better
than the merchandise of silver,
and the gain thereof than
fine gold.

—*Proverbs 3:13, 14*

ELEMENTARY SCHOOL
ART
FOR CLASSROOM TEACHERS

John R. Sawyer

PROFESSOR OF ART EDUCATION AND FINE ARTS
Kutztown State College

and the late

Italo L. deFrancesco

Harper & Row, Publishers
New York, Evanston, and London

CONTENTS

PART FOUR. APPENDIXES

PREFACE

The provision of art education is one of the vital functions of education, and an elementary school art program is the logical starting point.

In most elementary schools, the responsibility for guiding the children's art experience devolves upon the classroom teacher. In one-half of the remaining classrooms, the classroom teacher has the help of an art teacher.[1] With these facts in mind, *Elementary School Art for Classroom Teachers* has been written as a "package-in-hand" text intended specifically for the undergraduate student preparing to become an elementary school classroom teacher. Nevertheless, elementary school teachers in service and students preparing to be art teachers or special education teachers will also find the book useful. The basic focus of this text is on understanding and teaching the "whole" of art; in its overall aims, therefore, it is intended for anyone who is teaching art or who plans to.

[1] *Music and Art in the Public Schools*, Hazel Davis, Project Director, Research Monogram 1963-M3, Research Division, National Education Association, Washington, 1963, p. 25.

Art education in the school program has undergone many transformations of emphasis since art was first taught in 1873.[2] Today another transformation appears to be taking place, from teaching the "whole" child to teaching the child as an "artist." There are many different viewpoints on the relative importance of specific means and ends in art education. In general, however, those who are involved in education and psychology are becoming increasingly aware that experience with art in the early years nurtures the development of visual perception and knowledge of visual art and that this stimulates the potential for further learning.

Whatever the means used in teaching art, behavioral or cognitive, there is evidence from developmental psychology that visual artistic behavior occurs in sequences and takes time. The volume of literature in art education amply indicates the importance of frequent and progressively more difficult challenges for the child within his potential, challenges that are drawn from all of the related aspects of art: behavioral, affective, cognitive, social, symbolic, and historical—the whole cloth of an art involvement.

In writing the book, I have been guided by the questions classroom teachers most often ask about teaching elementary school art:

· Why teach art, anyway?
· Why are there so many ways to teach art?
· What is art?
· What is to be learned and how is it to be learned?
· What is the way to teach an art lesson?
· What should children's art work be like?
· How should children behave when working?
· Can children who are handicapped do art work?
· How can I grade art work?
· Is art necessary in the elementary school?

The development of an art program in the elementary school is the responsibility of the special art teacher. He should design the art program to fit the conditions within the particular school system he

[2] Frederick M. Logan, *Growth of Art in American Schools*, New York, Harper & Row, 1955.

serves. His role is to coordinate the art program with the total educational program of the school. In such cases, the role of the classroom teacher is to support and cooperate with the special art teacher so that the children's total art experience will have purpose, balance, continuity, and qualities of art evident in the learning process.

The classroom teacher is even more challenged, however, in the majority of art situations; these are in the schools where there is no art specialist in the program, where, obviously, no cooperation is possible. Although not specially trained to teach art, the classroom teacher is well equipped to rise to this challenge. He best knows the immediate interests, needs, and experiences of the children; even the fact that his own artistic ability may be limited can also help him in teaching art—he has an empathic understanding of the challenges the children face in their art behavior. (The art specialist, if there is one, can supply special art qualities.) To do the job *well,* however, the elementary school classroom teacher should have an adequate understanding of the background and direction, means and ends, and the program of elementary school art in terms of their relationship to the goals of general education. He should be aware of the contemporary aims of art education in the elementary school—to educate the child in the "whole" of art experience. He should have some understanding of art behavioral goals in terms of the qualities of art, in terms of the typical experience of the artist in production, and in terms of discrimination and the heritage of art. He should have some understanding of the strategy of creative art teaching and the characteristics of children's art in terms of their maturity and ability level. He should be able to assist in providing a learning environment that will stimulate children to think and to formulate their ideas with art materials into art works.

It must be evident that I do not believe children should be taught art only by an art specialist. At least they should not be taught by a specialist under the system now used in a very few schools—the sort of "vending" arrangement by which an "itinerant" specialist visits a number of schools in an area at specified intervals. The main point is that art, no matter who teaches it, should be taught in a realistic atmosphere where artistic experience—producing and responding to art—takes place.

The classroom teacher is, as I have indicated, eminently capable of providing such an atmosphere, if he has certain kinds of understandings and knowledge. This book is intended to give the future elementary classroom teacher this background. Exactly how the book goes about fulfilling its function becomes apparent in the following summaries of its chapters and appendixes:

Chapter 1 discusses basic principles related to art education consistent with the principle of equal educational opportunity for all; art in the elementary school is projected against this background. The chapter also introduces the reader to a specialized vocabulary of art.

Chapter 2 presents directions which a number of viewpoints and theories seem to suggest for contemporary art education. To align practice with the contemporary thinking of art educators, a creative-evaluative approach is suggested—the strategy involves cooperation by the elementary school classroom teacher and the elementary art specialist.

Chapter 3 provides a rationale for a strategy of creative-evaluative teaching. This is reinforced by contemporary psychology and the emphasis on heuristically oriented teaching in respect to affective, behavioral, and cognitive goals for learning. Three teaching environments based on psychological learning theories are discussed: the academic, activity, and experience approach; they relate, respectively, to conditioning, behavioral models, and affective-cognitive structures. It is recognized that in creative-evaluative teaching all these approaches have some place, with the greatest initial emphasis on the experience approach.

Chapter 4 deals with the specific application of creative-evaluative processes to the teaching of an art lesson. The aim is to make clear, through the use of examples, the nature of the processes. Sample art lessons are presented, intended as instructional aids

in the context of their relation to the overall unit and to curriculum planning.

Chapter 5 discusses the child's involvement in the art lesson. Involvement comes about through opportunities for choice concerning possible ideas, materials, processes, and achieving a final product. It is a visual dialogue typical of the behavior of an artist. Some warnings about devices, contests, and competition at the elementary level complete the chapter.

Chapter 6 presents a way to understand children's art in terms of the relationship between age-grade level and stages of creative visual development and in terms of behavioral characteristics, interests, needs, responses, and the progression of artistic behavioral development expectancies.

Chapter 7 deals with teaching art to exceptional children. The problem of teaching such children, ranging from the gifted to the multiplicity of limited types, including the environmentally disadvantaged child, is recognized as a vital one for art education. It involves creative-evaluative teaching of art within the degree of the potential of the child and viewing successful attempts as the therapeutic by-products of art.

Chapter 8 probes the problem of evaluating children's growth in art. The objectives of the evaluation program are considered, and behavioral characteristics are identified. Mental, emotional, social, physical, aesthetic, perceptual, and creative growth characteristics are discussed as they are evidenced in art work. A number of techniques for evaluating children's art and teaching effectiveness are presented.

Chapter 9 orients the reader to the elementary art program as the foundation of the art curriculum and discusses its function and what to teach; qualities of art are described and keyed to the appendixes. The scope and sequence of the art curriculum and the contents a teacher may expect to find in a curriculum guide are treated. Finally, valid recommendations based on the expected artistic behavior of the child are made to guide the classroom teacher.

Chapter 10 describes and discusses the development of art units, using three possible types: subject-centered, behavioral activity-centered, and experience-centered. Examples of units representing two of these types of organization are included.

Chapter 11 discusses the environment that nurtures art. Three types of classrooms are described, along with conditions that nurture creative visual art learning. Educational aids and resource materials are included.

Chapter 12 views the roles of the elementary school classroom teacher in relation to varied practices and recommends a cooperative relationship between the art specialist and the elementary classroom teacher for the most effective atmosphere for teaching art.

The six appendixes, which are keyed to the text, are included specifically to aid the elementary teacher in preparation as he plans art experiences for teaching.

Appendix I provides the teacher in preparation with suggestions that extend the broad needs presented in Chapter 5 to more specific content areas related to the problem of "what to teach" in Chapter 9 (see the explanation at the end of this appendix).

Appendix II gives an example of a delimitation of the categories of specific needs and interests, listed sequentially by grade levels. Each category could be adapted to many modes of expression: painting, drawing, graphics, modeling, sculpture, construction, crafts.

Appendix III is a list of suggested art materials sequentially organized by grade levels and in relation to the stages of creative visual development presented in Chapter 6. Each section of this list includes suggestions for working with and shaping the materials.

Appendix IV is a resource guide to art materials intended to help the prospective classroom teacher gain a greater depth of understanding of the many approaches to working with such art materials.

Appendix V gives a glossary of basic design terms in order to provide a background for guiding children in developing aesthetically pleasing forms for their art products.

Appendix VI lists art materials needed for a basic program in an elementary classroom.

The appendixes are not intended to give detailed directions for teaching art; their purpose is to provide a reference source for both students and in-service elementary classroom teachers. The information in the appendixes should help the classroom teacher to plan art experiences for elementary children with greater assurance and teach the lessons with greater opportunity for creative visual learning.

The purpose of this book, then, is to prepare the prospective elementary school teacher to guide the art experience of the children in his classroom. To this end, the following beliefs are emphasized:

1. Every child's life can be enriched through a whole experience with art, typical of a producer or consumer of art in the context of contemporary culture, art criticism, and art heritage.
2. Every child should have the opportunity to express his own ideas with art materials, within the disciplines of the materials, at his level of maturation, and to the best of his ability.
3. Developing each child's creative ability to its highest potential is best done through a creative-evaluative teaching-learning atmosphere.
4. The classroom teacher, in cooperation with the special art teacher, plays an important role in coordinating art education with the total educational program.
5. To fulfill his important role, the classroom teacher should receive the best possible preparation for teaching art, preparation that involves the child, the processes, and the products.

·   ·   ·

In the initial planning phases of this text, Dr. Italo L. deFrancesco worked with me in the formulation of the original outline for the book. His unexpected death made it necessary to complete the text without his able editorial assistance in preparing the manuscript.

Let this book, and the thoughts it may engender, be dedicated to the memory of Italo L. deFrancesco. His life was dedicated to education and to art.

JOHN R. SAWYER

ACKNOWLEDGMENTS

I am indebted to many individuals who encouraged and supported my work on this book. I am grateful to Dr. Lawrence M. Stratton, President, and to Dr. Cyrus E. Beekey, President Emeritus, both of Kutztown State College, for their encouragement and, as I have said, to the late Dr. Italo L. deFrancesco, who collaborated editorially in the initial formulation of the manuscript and contributed to it.

For their significant contributions, I am indebted also to Dr. Herbert Burgart, Dean of the School of the Arts, Virginia Commonwealth University, Richmond, who made suggestions on the strategies of teaching; Dr. Ivan E. Johnson, Professor of Art Education, Florida State University, Tallahassee, who reviewed the final text; and Miss Helen Cynthia Rose, Director of Art Education, Richmond Public Schools, Richmond, Virginia, who gave her constructive attention to every page of the manuscript.

I wish to express my gratitude and respect to these professors who have affected a great many of the ideas presented: Dr. Kenneth R. Beittel, Professor of

Art Education and Research, Pennsylvania State University, University Park; Dr. Wayne S. Koch, Professor of Education Emeritus, University of New Hampshire, Durham; and Dr. Edward L. Mattil, Dean, College of the Arts, St. Cloud State College, St. Cloud, Minnesota.

I am grateful also to the many teachers and pupils with whom I have worked in my years of professional teaching experience.

It is my privilege and pleasure to be associated with members of the staff of the Art Department at Kutztown State College. Miss Mary Grace Wible, one of these colleagues, made suggestions in connection with the formulation of the manuscript, and I wish to express my personal appreciation to her.

Assisting me by faithfully supervising the correspondence related to this volume was Mrs. Ruth B. deFrancesco. I owe personal gratitude to Mrs. Nancy N. Roberts, Mrs. Harriet H. Nichols, Mrs. deFrancesco, and Mrs. Jean B. Sawyer for typing the original manuscript, revisions, the final manuscript, and the *Instructor's Manual*. To my devoted wife, Jean, I am deeply indebted also for her encouragement, attention to many details, and editorial assistance.

Many other people made valuable contributions to this book for which I am grateful: Mr. David Lehman and Mrs. Virginia Schatz, Allentown, Pennsylvania; Mr. Richard L. Micherdzinski, Baltimore; Dr. Roy Brown and Mrs. Susan Schneider, Bethlehem, Pennsylvania; Mrs. Sandra Lee Fulmer and Mr. Harry I. Gilbert, Boyertown, Pennsylvania; Mr. Walter Trott, Garden City, New York; Mr. Albert H. Sarkas, Hazleton, Pennsylvania; Mr. Stanley I. Yamamoto, Honolulu; Miss Mary Dell Buford, Jackson, Mississippi; Miss Rosemary Beymer, Kansas City; Mrs. Stephannie Barbour, Miss Christina Bluhm, Miss Mary Burkett, Miss Gretel Findeisen, Mr. Rodney Fogel, Mr. Harry Herring, Miss Rebecca Jones, Mrs. Janice Kulp, Mr. Allen McCurdy, Miss Kathy Snyder, and Mrs. Adelyn Van Gilder, Kutztown State College, Kutztown, Pennsylvania; Mr. Richard L. Tooke, Museum of Modern Art, New York; Mrs. Alice Smith, Oley, Pennsylvania; Dr. Harry Bentz, Mrs. Anna Lee Boyer, Dr. Ralph C. Geigle, Mrs. Vivian Manzella, Mrs. Olive Merritt, and Mr. Gene Wilkins, Reading, Pennsylvania; Miss Marilyn A. Gardner, Stratford, Connecticut; Mr. Howard Dierlam, Toronto.

Finally, I wish to express my appreciation to Mr. Voras D. Meeks, Mr. Lane Akers, Mrs. Pamela Forcey, and Mrs. Dorothy Obre for their editorial counsel and to Mrs. Rita Naughton, the designer of the book.

J.R.S.

PHOTOGRAPH CREDITS

FIGURES

1.2 Reading (Pennsylvania) School District / **1.3** Yvonne Freund / **1.4** Boyertown (Pennsylvania) Area Schools / **1.5** Rickenbach Research Learning Center, Kutztown State College / **1.6** Columbia Broadcasting System, Inc. / **1.7–1.9** Photographs by the author / **1.10** Fritz Henle from Monkmeyer / **1.11** Photograph by the author / **1.12** Collection of the author / **1.13–1.19** Photographs by the author

2.1 Carl A. Hess / **2.2** St. Louis Public Schools / **2.3** Baltimore City Public Schools / **2.4** Bethlehem (Pennsylvania) School District / **2.5–2.6** Kansas City Public Schools / **2.7–2.8** Jackson (Mississippi) Public Schools

3.2 St. Louis Public Schools / **3.4** Madison (Wisconsin) Public Schools / **3.6** National Education Association (Carl Purcell) / **3.7** Gregor from Monkmeyer

4.1 National Education Association (Carl Purcell) / **4.2** Vinard Studios / **4.3** National Education Association (Joe Di Dio) / **4.4–4.10** Collection of the author

5.1 Collection of the author / **5.2** Rickenbach Research Learning Center, Kutztown State College / **5.3** St. Louis Public

Schools / **5.4** Sybil Shackman from Monkmeyer / **5.5** Camera-Craft, Seattle / **5.6** Pittsburgh Public Schools / **5.7** Baltimore City Public Schools / **5.8** Reading (Pennsylvania) School District

6.1–6.8 Collection of the author / **6.9** Bethlehem (Pennsylvania) School District / **6.10** Rickenbach Research Learning Center, Kutztown State College / **6.11** Collection of the author / **6.12–6.13** Boyertown (Pennsylvania) Area Schools / **6.14** Oley (Pennsylvania) Area Schools / **6.15** Baltimore City Public Schools / **6.16** Honolulu Academy of Arts / **6.17** Toronto Board of Education / **6.18** Kansas City Public Schools / **6.19** Hazleton (Pennsylvania) Area School District / **6.20–6.21** Toronto Board of Education / **6.22** Baltimore City Public Schools / **6.23** Honolulu Academy of Arts / **6.24** CBS-TV / **6.25** Bethlehem (Pennsylvania) School District / **6.26** Collection of the author

7.1–7.7 Collection of the author

8.1 Kansas City Public Schools / **8.2** Honolulu Academy of Arts / **8.3** Rickenbach Research Learning Center, Kutztown State College / **8.4** Botwick from Monkmeyer / **8.5** Collection of the author / **8.6** Ford Foundation (William R. Simmons) / **8.7** Honolulu Academy of Arts / **8.8** Collection of the author / **8.9** Educational Services, Inc. / **8.10–8.11** Bethlehem Pennsylvania) School District / **8.12** Toronto Board of Education

9.1 Hazleton (Pennsylvania) Area School District / **9.2** Collection of the author / **9.4** Baltimore City Public Schools /

9.5 Collection of the author / **9.6** Baltimore City Public Schools / **9.7** Collection of the author / **9.8** Honolulu Academy of arts / **9.9** Baltimore City Public Schools / **9.10** Bethlehem (Pennsylvania) School District

10.1–10.6 Photographs by the author / **10.7– 10.8** American Airlines

11.1 Carl A. Hess / **11.2** Blythe Forcey / **11.3–11.4** Kansas City Public Schools / **11.5** Rickenbach Research Learning Center, Kutztown State College / **11.6** Peter C. Forcey / **11.7** Baltimore City Public Schools

12.1–12.2 Bethlehem (Pennsylvania) School District / **12.3** Allentown (Pennsylvania) School District

PLATES

VI Richmond (Virginia) Public Schools / **VII** Collection of the author / **VIII** Reading (Pennsylvania) School District / **IX** Bethlehem (Pennsylvania) School District / **X** Richmond (Virginia) Public Schools / **XI–XIV** Jackson (Mississippi) Public Schools / **XV** Stratford (Connecticut) Public Schools / **XVI–XVII** Reading (Pennsylvania) School District / **XVIII** Bethlehem (Pennsylvania) School District / **XIX–XX** Collection of the author / **XXI** Stratford (Connecticut) Public Schools / **XXII** Bethlehem (Pennsylvania) School District / **XXIII** Hazleton (Pennsylvania) Area School District / **XXIV–XXV** Reading (Pennsylvania) School District

Part One
BACKGROUND AND DIRECTION

Chapter 1
RELEVANT UNDERSTANDINGS
FOR TEACHING ART

This introductory chapter discusses (1) the implications for art teaching of the American democratic principle of equality of educational opportunity for all children; (2) the importance of starting a child's art education at the kindergarten and elementary school levels; (3) the meaning and implications of some of the special terms commonly used by art teachers and art administrators, terms that may be unfamiliar to the classroom teacher.

IMPLICATIONS OF DEMOCRATIC PRINCIPLES FOR ART EDUCATION

The goal of education in a democracy is to provide equal educational opportunities for all, with the limit of educational achievement determined solely by individual ability. This goal implies the general principle that all children should be encouraged to develop their abilities to the fullest extent. In relation to art education, this goal implies the following specific principles.

1. Art education is generously available for all the children of all the people.
2. Art education has a major responsibility to develop individual creative potential through experience with art, personal visual expression possessing qualities of art, and, ultimately, an aesthetic attitude toward art in the individual's environment and in art heritage.
3. Art education should foster in the individual visual aesthetic qualities in response to art in living in relation to his personal needs and to his social group.
4. Art education should occur in an atmosphere of creative-evaluative reflection and processes, within which the individual has the opportunity to formulate visual expressions in relation to his own ideas, at the same time recognizing that the boundaries of his freedom are established by the rights of his fellows.

These principles impose certain conditions on art education:

1. The belief that art expression with the whole quality of art is for all must be central to the philosophy and practice of elementary school art teaching. Every child should be afforded an art education at all levels to help him grow to his fullest potential in all of the qualities of art; naturally, no limitations that relate in any way to race, color, or creed should be imposed. Psychology indicates that what is done for a child at the beginning of his educational life is more significant than what is done for him as he advances to full maturity. It follows that art teaching in the *elementary* school classroom has a special responsibility—its function in the total process of art education is particularly vital.

2. The abilities and skills of all children must be developed. Art is a purposeful transaction between a child and his artistic environment. The elementary school teacher must act to develop qualitative art expression in each child toward the goal—a product of a total art quality—that, as an individual, he may assume some role as a doer or user of art in the culture of the society. At the elementary school level, attention to the special talent of a particular child should be subordinate to the nurturing of the full growth of the potential art ability of all the children. Psychologists point out that in-dividuals differ considerably from one another. Acknowledging that these differences exist resolves the paradox in democratic education: equal opportunity for all and at the same time divergent guidance for the individual. Individual differences exist because biological inheritance determines the capacity for art expression and because environmental forces and psychological influences may either inhibit or promote creative capacity. In a favorable atmosphere, with motivating direction and evaluative guidance and encouragement, a child can develop educationally to his fullest potential.

3. Children must learn to live and work harmoniously with their peers as they develop competency for artistic influence in their social group. They must share ideas and accept responsibility. They must examine the points of view of others and evaluate fairly, so that all may benefit from the experience. Planning, making decisions, and allocating work according to ability and personal interest are components of the democratic way. Art that functions in the solution of qualitative problems that relate to art in life and learning is valuable in the full education of children. A balanced art program has the essentials of art quality. It includes developmental art activity such as the artist experiences. It is correlated with, but not subservient to, learning in other subject areas as a means of stimulating artistic growth and reflective thinking.

4. Art results from personal imagination guided by perceptual awareness of ideas for visual forms and content. It is an instance of a child's artistic sensing and thinking in action. Meaningless manipulation or aimless action and expression in the name of spontaneity and freedom has little relation to art. Art education in the elementary school must develop in the child an understanding of freedom consistent with the qualities of art in a context of creative-evaluative judgments.

THE IMPORTANCE
OF ELEMENTARY SCHOOL ART

The question "Why should art be taught in the schools, particularly the elementary schools?" is asked not only by the public, but also by some teachers and school administrators. It is indeed a fundamental question. The answer lies in the unique contribution art can make to the child's artistic growth and development and to the total educational program; this contribution has seven major aspects: ~~that have been previously been stated.~~

1.1. *This acknowledged masterpiece of art in sculpture form is Constantin Brancusi's* Bird in Space *(1927?), the sixth stage of the artist's* Bird in Space *(1923). The bronze, a unique cast, is 54 inches high. (Collection, The Museum of Modern Art, New York.)*

1. The art experience promotes the sensitivity to, and appreciation of, visual art that enrich an individual's life. By art is meant in this context not only the acknowledged masterpieces of painting, drawing, sculpture, and architecture, but also the aesthetic aspects of the small things that make up the everyday world—the streamlined simplicity of a stainless-steel coffeepot, the harmonious colors of a girl's dress, the graceful lines of a chair, the pleasing type design of a book. Aesthetic awareness adds an extra satisfaction to living.

2. The art experience allows liberation of the creative impulse. The urge to create is universal and very strong. Involvement with visual experience gives the child an opportunity to express his innate creative urge and to discover his own potential in the satisfaction of completing a drawing or a clay form of which he can truly say, "I did it; it is mine."

Plates I–V

Figure 1.1

Figure 1.2

1.2. *These sculpture figures by a fifth-grader are not, of course, acknowledged masterpieces of art. Obviously, however, they should not be judged on the level of mature acknowledged masterpieces. When they are accepted as the art of a child, the action, spirit, and form can indeed be called masterful. Whether a Brancusi or a fifth-grade child, the urge to create is universal. Equipped with plaster of Paris and gauze, this child was able to express his ideas, discover his potentials, formulate his own work—in other words, satisfy the urge to create. In terms of experience, these sculptures are art.*

3. The art experience promotes the development of independent artistic judgment. It is an experience in discrimination, evaluation, and problem-solving. When a child draws a picture to express an idea, he undergoes an evaluative experience as he makes decisions about what idea to express, what image to invent, what materials to use, how to formulate the expression. The completed work represents the problem solved—a picture, a pot, a construction, etc. (*Figure 1.3*). The process involves choosing; the product is not only an art work, but an array of understandings whose content is related to the whole visual experience.

4. Artistic creation is a constructive response to stress in living. The process of growing up is at least as stressful as the condition of being an adult, and the child has fewer constructive outlets for frustration and anger and apprehension. Artistic creation offers an outlet for pent-up feelings which can be of great value to the child and can later serve the adult.

5. Artistic creation provides a sense of achievement and self-confidence. Mastering a task is one of the basic drives of life, and achieving mastery is a basic need. When the child is able to complete an art product that expresses his idea, he realizes great satisfaction in the achievement and gains confidence in his *own* ability.

6. Art permits communication at a symbolic level (*Figure 1.4*). To the young child especially, this is important because it enables him to invent and express symbolically ideas and emotions he cannot yet verbalize (*Plate VI*). Symbolic representation is his natural form of visual communication, and visual communication is universal.

7. Art education nurtures the child's social and personal growth in the context of his culture and his heritage. When art education is carried on in close relation to the rest of the educational program, the child becomes aware of art as an integral part of his life and of his personality (*Figure 1.5*).

Art is important in life—in the life of the child and in the life of the adult. If art is to be an integral part of living, aesthetic awareness, understanding, and appreci-

1.3. A sixth-grader finds great satisfaction as she works with the potter's wheel. When her clay pot is completed, it will be a problem solved—an art experience that will increase the girl's confidence in her own ability.

1.4. *The classroom teacher asked, "What do you think could be under this rock?" and a kindergarten child in the presymbolic stage responded by inventing an image of a "family" of insects.*

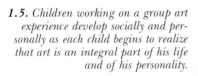

1.5. *Children working on a group art experience develop socially and personally as each child begins to realize that art is an integral part of his life and of his personality.*

However,

ation must develop with all the other dimensions of a child's growth. To ignore art education in the elementary school learning processes and offer an art appreciation course in secondary school is no more useful than to ignore arithmetic in elementary school and offer algebra in secondary school. The education a child receives in elementary school is the foundation on which all the rest of his learning must be built.

THE MEANING OF TERMS
USED IN ART EDUCATION TODAY

The following definitions and explanations are included to acquaint the elementary school classroom teacher with the specialized vocabulary of the art teacher and the art administrator.

Art

Although some writers assert that to have a theory of what art is contradicts the very nature of art as well as the creative process that gives it existence,[1] others do not hesitate to define it. These definitions[2] emphasize the properties essential for the creation of a work of art: the stimulus of the world apart from art, imagination, intelligence, emotion, form, spirit, technique, perception, inventiveness, organic structure, or unity. Here are two sample definitions:

Art is an intellectual and an emotional recording of an attitude or an experience presented in a personal manner. The visual arts—painting, sculpture, architecture, and other related arts—are concerned with the creative handling of lines, textures, shapes, colors, and space in materials such as paint, stone, and wood. "Creative" implies bringing into existence new constructions through a personal arrangement of existing or new elements.[3]

Art is a quality of doing and what is done. . . . The product of art—temple, painting, statue, poem—is not the work of art. The work takes place when a human being cooperates with the product so that the outcome is an experience that is enjoyed because of its liberating and ordered properties.[4]

Art thus involves action; however, it is not the product of action alone, but of the quality of experience the pupil undergoes in the process of doing—the *interaction* among the doer, his idea, and his material. The meaning for this text is that the interaction is a visual dialogue.

Creative experience

Dewey considers experience to be the result of the creative urge. He defines experience as "the result, the sign, and the reward of the interaction of organism and environment which, when it is carried to the full, is a transformation of interaction into participation and communication."[5]

The creative experience is dynamic. It is a purposeful transaction between a person, a whole being, and his environment, a whole context. The process of creation is like a field of magnetic action in which the creator's entire being is stimulated by a new challenge to his present state of well-being (a stimulation), his perceiving of ideas to meet the challenge (individuating possible solutions), his evaluation of possible solutions (interaction), his processes of decision-making (dialogue between self and solution), and his art work (final visual solution). In terms of art in the elementary school the child-creator in the process of visual expression is drawn from a state of satisfaction by a condition of perceptual awareness to recognize another condition contrasting with his satisfied state, to a new and larger state of visual satisfaction through the experience of solving a visual problem creatively. In terms of art teaching the definition suggests that art is living through a stimulating feeling, and sensing through insight the "whole" action of visual experience.

As one understands the dominant role of emotions in the creative act, it becomes clear that the spontaneity and vitality found in children's art result not from mere manipulation of a brush, but from thought-out creative

[1] Elliot W. Eisner and David W. Ecker, *Readings in Art Education,* Waltham, Mass., Blaisdell, 1966, p. 55.
[2] Ibid., pp. 50–56.
[3] James A. Schinneller, *Art: Search and Self-Discovery,* Scranton, Pa., International Textbook, 1961, p. 2.

[4] John Dewey, *Art as Experience,* New York, Minton, Balch, 1934, p. 214.
[5] Ibid., p. 22.

expression. Such excitement, skillfully guided by the teacher, leads to the successful completion of the creative experience.

Creative expression

Expression is a need of the living organism. But not all expression is creative—for example, yelling is not creative, but singing is; jumping is not creative, but dancing is; smearing paint to give vent to anger is not creative, but applying paint to compose a pattern is. Creative expression is the result of reflective action on a medium. It results from a process involving curiosity, questioning, inquiry, searching, manipulating, experimenting, and formulating ideas into objects. It occurs when past and recent experiences, insight, and concepts of art are purposefully brought to bear on the materials and tools of expression typical of an artist's behavior. Such expression makes use of the creator's whole array of understanding and knowledge, not only in the area of art, but in all the other areas of life. It is thus a unifying force of great potential value in all education.

Creative learning
and creative-evaluative teaching

Art is a process of modifying behavior in relation to the aesthetic aspects of visual perception. *It is the thesis of this book that because art is creative, and experience results from the creative urge, art teaching should guide the child to have an art experience typical of that of an artist.* Creative teaching involves stimulating the child to become interested in a particular aesthetic aspect of visual perception and guiding him toward discovery and understanding through an art experience as a producer or user.

There is a sound basis, both in theory and in research findings, for the superiority of creative over directed teaching. This is discussed in Chapter 2. Here we shall only define briefly what is meant by creative learning and creative-evaluative teaching.

Creative learning involves interaction and discovery in the process of an experience that leads to some solution, an art work. When a stimulating situation is structured by the teacher in the lesson presentation, the learner is motivated to evaluate the contrasting and comparable qualitative elements of the conditions the teacher sets up; that is, the learner interacts with the elements in a private dialogue, which, in the case of art, may involve trying out various ideas and materials in relation to the contrasting elements; then, through evaluation evoked by the teacher's questions, the learner reaches a solution. In this transition, the products are new understanding, related subject matter regarding content and form, and, in the visual arts, a completed art work. In the light of this new understanding of facts, the learner reformulates his ideas. The process is, essentially, one of evaluating alternative possible ideas, choosing an idea, selecting materials in relation to it, exploring the materials, and finding a means of shaping the material to produce an art work.

Creative-evaluative teaching capitalizes on the immediate needs and interests of the child by constructing a qualitative problem related to art (a situation composed of two or more comparable but contrasting art qualities or elements) that is closely related to ongoing classroom learning experiences. The structured condition related to art subject matter in terms of children's needs and possible behavior stimulates interest on the part of the learner and consequently the desire to evaluate the contrasting elements. There follows a double interaction—between the teacher and the pupil and between the pupil and his ideas. This process transfers from an interaction between the pupil and his ideas to an interaction between the pupil and processes and art work. The teacher asks questions that will stimulate the child to think reflectively about the problem; the child evaluates his ideas in relation to the problem and, with continued evaluative guidance from the teacher, is led to conceive a possible solution and thus to achieve an art work and new understanding.

Attention

Getting attention is the prerequisite to perception in the learning experience. Fundamentally, the control the teacher has in the learning process is the control of the child's attention. The teacher is concerned with changing the behavioral tendencies that she is able to control through the child's environment. When the child comes to the classroom without art understanding and leaves with art understanding, as observed in the way he thinks and acts, learning in art has taken place.

The degree to which the child has developed ideas of his own and the quantity and quality of his understanding directly reflect how well the classroom teacher has been able to hold his attention in the learning situation. His attention span may be increased either by forced means, that is by repetitive exercise, or, far better, by stimulation that creates in him an intrinsic desire to repeat and pursue, over a period of time, an idea that interests him—until he finds a solution. The attention span, then, is a function of the stimulation-motivation process. It is increased or decreased in relation to the process. More mature children who are intrinsically involved appear better able to acquire long-range motivation. In the absence of desire, forced, directed, and too simple art activities merely produce boredom and fatigue.

Stimulation

If learning is structured so that the learning situation and conditions themselves induce the child to be interested in the structure of the art content, the child will learn. In art, this occurs through the senses which affect the child. The affective experience leads to understanding. For example, the classroom is a social situation as well as a physical atmosphere; it includes child-child, teacher-child, and child-environment involvements. Using things the child can see, hear, or move, the teacher is able to affect the child with them through contrasting situations he develops. Integrally, the interactions of the children which result from a stimulation by the teacher produce conditions which intrastimulate children within the social situation and the physical atmosphere. This interaction in an art stimulation proceeds from the affective to evaluative to cognitive experience, to an art work. It is typical of the way an artist proceeds in action to produce a painting, a sculpture, etc.

Stimulation differs from motivation in that the known interests, needs, purposes, and goals that rest deep in the pupil need to be aroused to the point where the child recognizes the impulse and is ready for action. Here is the teacher's role in creative teaching. The child must be ready for the stimulation, and it must be so structured that it is not only challenging but also meaningful. Also, it must energize intuitive as well as analytical thinking.

Affective-cognitive faculties of knowing

The term "affective" is associated with the sensory and expressive areas of experience. It means knowing through intuition (feeling) rather than through reason, and thus involves the nondiscursive elements of art experience. The term "cognitive" is associated with the thinking-analytical-knowledge areas of experience. It means knowing through reason (factual knowledge)—knowledge and understanding of the form and content, as well as the techniques and skills of art—and hence involves the discursive elements of art experience. In every aspect of a creative work of art—stimulation, motivation of action, the doing, the analysis of the complete product, as well as in the appreciation of other works of art—these two faculties of knowing—affective and cognitive—interact and assist each other. In the classroom the feeling-sensory-expressive areas of art experience work hand in hand with the thinking-analytical-knowledge areas. Creative visual experience progresses from affective to reflective to cognitive experience. Thus both kinds of experience—affective and cognitive—are a part of creative visual expression.

Motivation

Motivation is indicated by an increase in the level of a child's response in a learning situation. It is intrinsic and extrinsic. The self-desire to pursue learning for its own sake is intrinsic. The desire to pursue learning for reasons outside the learning experience itself is extrinsic. As might be expected, creative learning usually results from intrinsic motivation.

Art motivation is related to increasing inherent interest in visual experiences structured for learning in the elementary classroom. Motivation results from stimulation of an active interest in art experience. Thus the classroom teacher should aim to arouse the child's desire to attend to and then have active interest in a situation in the classroom. Motivation is the intrinsic desire and interest of the child aroused through a stimulation in the learning situation. It is essential to creative learning. For this reason, the teacher in the creative teaching process tries to (1) relate the stimulation for the lesson to the learner's immediate interests, (2) make the circumstance inherently interesting enough so that related subject matter can come to his attention, (3) gear the lesson to the child's level of understanding.

Visual perception

Perception has been defined as "the embodiment of meaning derived from an individual's prior experiences and retained for future sensory reception."[6] Perception is selective, organized, and based on change. The individual responds to differences in his environment, he selects a particular aspect of it to give his attention to, and he responds to new things that he sees in terms of what effect his environment has had on him in the past. Perception is often the result of cooperation between several senses; in fact, seldom does one sense alone reveal all about an object.

One of the oldest claims of art teaching has been that there is no difference between the object and the image received by the viewer.[7] It resulted in the belief that the purpose of art was to "represent" and that artistic merit could be achieved by one's ability to reproduce naturally the world of nature. This is consistent with the definition given to perception by stimulus-response (S-R) associationist psychologists.[8] In view of the diversity of styles in art, it is obvious that this conclusion is open to question.

Another widely accepted view is that children draw what they know more than what they see. This is a popular view and has some basis of agreement with cognitive-field theories of perception.[9]

Arnheim relates art to the way the general nature of an object is seen.[10] He believes that objects are seen as the senses make them appear. The child expresses in his work the overall qualities of things—their general characteristics and their parts—for example, the roundness of a head, the straightness of the limbs, and the natural sameness of the sides of the body. This means that the child will draw simple structural shapes, often appearing geometric. Children see more than they draw. However, when a child is drawing a head, he invents a shape that has the general characteristics of the head. The circle embodies the visual qualities of the whole head. The circle is not given to the child—he invents it to represent the head after continually trying to express the roundness of the head.

Children find that the properties of particular materials seem to lend themselves best to express various invented shapes. This developmental process proceeds through a sequence of stages. The development of structural forms relates directly to the neurophysical system, with minor modifications caused by cultural and individual differences. In early childhood, especially, the child finds no need to assess what comes first, the content or the form. Each will emerge naturally.

A teacher who imposes on pupils predetermined ways to draw or insists that the child's picture look just like the object will inhibit the visual-perceptual development of the child. A child invents shapes in relation to his exposure to and knowledge of his environment. He does so within his perceptual ability to select from it generalized impressions for which he creates a form symbol. As he grows perceptually, he modifies his shapes by giving greater attention to the details and likeness. Later, as a mature artist, he uses his inventions to express in a simple way his reactions to his world, visually or emotionally, and, again, abstracts and simplifies.

Figures 1.6–1.11

[6] Manuel Barkan, *Foundations of Art Education,* New York, Ronald Press, 1955, p. 132.

[7] Eisner and Ecker, op. cit., pp. 85–96.

[8] Morris L. Bigge, *Learning Theories for Teachers,* New York, Harper & Row, 1964, pp. 74–75.

[9] Eisner and Ecker, op. cit., pp. 85–96.

[10] Rudolph Arnheim, *Art and Visual Perception,* Berkeley, University of California Press, 1954, p. 128.

These six pictures show how a mature artist perceived his world, visually and emotionally, using photography as his medium. He observed overall qualities and then simplified his perceptions by abstracting details. **1.6.** This is a visual-real *view of the CBS Building in New York, but in* **1.7** *the patterns produce an* emotional-abstract *impression of another building.* **1.8.** *Again this is a* visual-real *view, of Niagara Falls, but in* **1.9,** *darkness, lights, and a different viewpoint transform the Falls into an* emotional-real *experience. At the seashore the artist abstracted details in two ways.* **1.10.** *He saw the rocky beach and the surf in an* emotional-abstract *way. Then he focused on some of the stones in* **1.11,** *a* visual-abstract *impression of the beach.*

Transfer of learning

Transfer of learning means the carrying over of concepts, generalizations, understandings, skills and abilities, and attitudes and appreciations achieved in earlier learning experiences. It is basic to the whole process of education and is facilitated by creative-evaluative teaching. It is influenced by the structure of the learning circumstances as they relate to the subject matter and by the readiness of the child to learn. The learning conditions should be planned so that affective responses to stimuli and understanding of subject matter evolve in a logical sequential manner. Thus basic understandings are gained first as the foundation (frame of reference) for advanced learning. In other words, the emphasis should be on understanding principles and ideas because such knowledge facilitates transfer of learning. The teaching should, of course, be geared to the child's level of understanding, but this means that it should also be based on ideas that can be expanded, through the use of increasingly sophisticated materials, as the child's ability increases. All the child's past learning thus constitutes his frame of reference; his current learning occurs within this frame of reference and expands it and is expanded by it.

Ideas, concepts, insights

An idea is the product of mental reflection. A concept is an idea that includes all that is characteristically associated with or suggested by a term. Insight is the discernment, often intuitive, of the relations between ideas and concepts and of their meaning.

All three are involved in creative learning. When the pupil thinks about a problem, he sorts out pertinent ideas and concepts. His insight suggests which ideas will be useful in solving the problem. He experiments with these ideas, evaluates their usefulness in solving the problem, and accepts or rejects them accordingly.

Art education is education in affective and cognitive (intuitive and analytical) thinking related to visual experience. The production of an art work involves thinking, evaluating, and finally acting.

Integration

In the context of art education, integration means the harmonious unity of the various components within the individual—the oneness of the student's outlook as he relates art to the rest of the educational program, to his total environment, which includes people, things, and situations, indeed, to the whole of his life. Personal outlooks are the result of this integrative process, which is compounded of knowledges, concepts, and insights. The total effect is ultimately observed in the harmonious working of mind-body-emotions. This is itself an example of integrated behavior. Integration becomes a real potential for art because it shares and is inherent in the creative visual experience.

The purpose of art education is to foster the development of the components of a child's being—physical, intellectual, emotional, social, aesthetic, perceptual, and creative—and integration of them into a harmonious unity.

Aesthetic awareness

Children are aware of beauty if and when they are involved with it. Involvement does not always mean simply being in direct contact with a collection of imposed ideas, materials, and the "how" to use them. Often, it means being in contact with paintings and painters, pots and potters, buildings and architects, and culture and its history. The child, when in contact with

1.12. Children must learn to look for—and see— the existence of natural order in all sorts of nature forms.

What do you see when you climb a mountain?
1.13. *Perhaps you concentrate on the lines of the trees and the shapes of the rocks. Perhaps your attention is caught by the pattern of the farm land far below. Is your overall impression of a feeling of great height? Whatever you particularly notice, do you just look, or do you* see *art forms in nature?* ***1.14.*** *While you are on the mountain, do you step back and look around nearby? You can no longer see the valley below, but you see a tree with a distinctive shape. And you sense the many aesthetic relationships in the patterns of the rocks.*

aspects of the creative process, will be aware of the influence of the art forms around him. The creative process produces aesthetic relationships; therefore, when involved with it, the child will be aware of these aesthetic qualities in art forms around him. He can be exposed to and enjoy seeing and sensing them.

Children must learn to look. They must learn to see the existence of natural order in all sorts of nature forms. They must learn to see the aesthetic relationships in the art forms man has created. With his natural urge to create, the child also has an urge to share his experience. He communicates it to others through his awareness of the aesthetic relationships of line, form, and color that he sees in natural things and the reality of living. As Hurwitz puts it, the teacher should aid the child in this search for essentials in the aesthetic aspects of his environment.[11]

The child can be encouraged to look, and seeing will follow if a creative teacher opens the child's eyes. Seeing results when comparisons are made between two or more visual stimuli, with words serving only as the energizers of creative action. When a child has opportunities to see relationships in beautiful things around him, he has an experience in aesthetic awareness.

Figures 1.12–1.14

Figures 1.15–1.19

[11] Elizabeth A. Hurwitz, *Design, A Search for Essentials*, Scranton, Pa., International Textbook, 1964, chaps. I–II.

15

1.15

At the seashore you can be almost overwhelmed by the variety of possible aesthetic experiences. Often you gain in awareness by simplifying your perceptions. Then each experience becomes vivid, and they all begin to fall into a natural order. **1.15.** Do you see the beach? Or do you see the edge of the expanse of the ocean? **1.16.** You walk from the beach to a rocky point and look down. Do you see rocks jutting into the sea? Or do you see patterns in the foaming surf and the turbulent water? **1.17.** Step closer and look down again. Do you see lines and shapes and colors in the natural formations of the rocks and the water? Do these lines and shapes still look like rocks and water? **1.18.** There is even more to see. Look into the water. Are you aware of the beauty there? Just as you are having an experience in aesthetic awareness, so may children have such experiences when they are given opportunities like this. **1.19.** Look even more closely. Those stones under the water are beautiful!

16

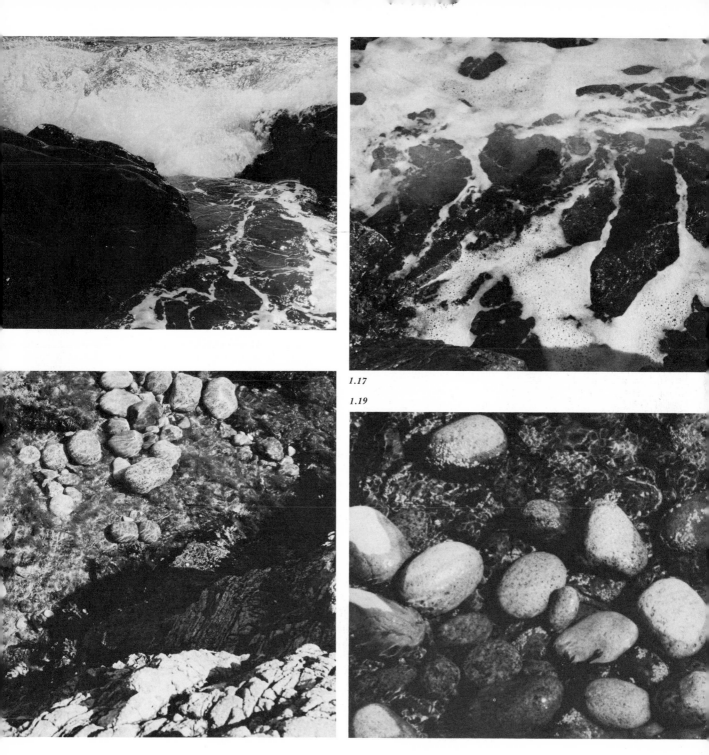

1.17

1.19

An art work

The artist is a doer; he paints, draws, models—the result is an art work. He evaluates, shapes, and reshapes his art object and enjoys both the activity and the result. This result of his doing is an art work.

Artistic quality

Every art work has some degree of artistic quality in terms of how it is made and of what is made. It is the ability of the artist to express his meaning for himself or for others, related to the content and form of the art work, which establishes the degree of quality. Quality is a condition of the artist or observer to be sensitive to the meanings and the aesthetic relationships of the content and form of the art work. Generally, the artistic quality commonly experienced is that experienced by the observer who is sufficiently aesthetically knowledgeable to make independent artistic judgments. The artist's judgments are more generally intuitive and subjective.

Determining artistic quality involves the observation and judgment of an art work in terms of its content and form. Content is the "thingness," or characteristics, of what is being expressed in terms of the qualities of the experience: sensitivity to mood, textures, and materials; ways of expressing; and intrinsic judgments that make it seem like the "thing." For example, clay can be modeled so that it has the "kitty" qualities of a kitten. On the other hand, form is a focus on systems of order, structure, and design elements: line, rhythm, shape, color, pattern, and style. Artistic quality is the achievement of "thingness" with "formness" that make the art work look, feel, and seem like the "thing."

Art appreciation

Art appreciation in the context of art education is the act on the part of the noncreator (the user, or consumer) of evaluating, understanding, and experiencing art through identification with the artist (the creator, or doer) with regard to his subject matter and his means of expression. It involves the total response of the noncreator—an integrated response to the work of art in which the whole being is involved. Art appreciation does not develop through prescribed "standards." It cannot be formally taught but, rather, is developed by the visual learning experience; the fact is that it is an effect of the evaluative process that results from creative-evaluative teaching.

SUMMARY

The democratic goal of equal educational opportunity available to all children implies that art education should (1) be provided for all children, (2) develop individual potential and personal visual expression as a doer and user of art, typical of the experience of the artist and the consumer, (3) foster a wholesome aesthetic relationship between the individual and the social group while improving the art environment, and (4) take place in an atmosphere of freedom, but within the boundaries of the disciplines of art, typical of the dialogue of an artist's experiences.

The art experience is important because (1) it promotes the sensitivity to, perception of, and discrimination and appreciation of the visual qualities of art that enrich the life of the individual and his social group; (2) it allows expression of the creative impulse; (3) it promotes the development of independent artistic judgment; (4) it offers a constructive response to stress in living; (5) it provides a sense of achievement and self-confidence; (6) it permits communication at a symbolic level; (7) it nurtures the child's social and personal growth through experience with the production, use, evaluation, and heritage of art.

Art education should begin in the elementary school so that the child's aesthetic awareness, understanding, and appreciation can develop as the rest of his life develops.

Definitions and explanations are provided for the following terms used in art education: art; creative experience; creative expression; creative learning and creative-evaluative teaching; attention; stimulation; affective-cognitive faculties of knowing; motivation; visual perception; transfer of learning; ideas, concepts, insights; integration; aesthetic awareness; an art work; artistic quality; art appreciation.

AIDS TO UNDERSTANDING

For discussion

1. These are two primary educational principles in a democracy: provide equal opportunity for all; accept individual ability as an educational limitation. How can you reconcile them?
2. What is the difference between the contributions made by art education in the total elementary school program and those made by programs in reading, writing, mathematics, science, and physical education?
3. Are the viewpoints about art held by Schinneller and Dewey essentially the same? In what respect?
4. What is the difference between creative experience and creative expression?
5. How can one be stimulated to sense the whole action of a visual experience?
6. What is the difference between yelling, jumping up and down, or smearing paint on paper and singing a song, dancing interpretively, or painting a picture?
7. When the classroom teacher uses his idea for the lesson, why do the drawings of all the children look alike?
8. A teacher remarked, "I didn't show the children how to draw a thing, and now look, they haven't painted anything that looks real." How would you respond?
9. What is the relationship between stimulation and motivation?
10. How do you account for the fact that a boy from the country didn't seem to know what he should draw in his picture after his trip to the city?
11. How do you account for the fact that a child in fifth grade could not transfer his understanding gained by working with clay to new experiences in painting?
12. What is the relationship between insights, concepts, and ideas?
13. What takes place within the individual as he integrates his visual learning experiences?
14. What is the difference between perceptual awareness and aesthetic awareness?
15. It is said that art experience is an affective area of learning and that cognitive understandings result from this experience. What is your reaction to this viewpoint?
16. Appreciation is a product of an art experience. How would you respond to this statement?
17. Describe conditions which encourage children to work to the limit of their ability in an art lesson.
18. Write your own definitions of the following: art, creative, transfer, concept, harmonious unity, aesthetic, affective, art appreciation.

For involvement

1. Observe some elementary classroom situation and report how the children were affected by art in some of the following ways:

   a. Did the children have an urge to create?
   b. Did the children have an opportunity to exercise their own judgment when selecting materials, or were they told to use particular materials?
   c. Did the children express their own ideas, or did they want the teacher to show them what to do?
   d. Did the children make realistic things, or did their drawings look like symbols?
   e. Did the art experience cause the children to be enthusiastic about their work, or not?

2. With a group of colleagues, prepare a panel discussion on this topic: "To ignore elementary school art and later teach secondary school art appreciation is like ignoring elementary school arithmetic and later teaching secondary school algebra."

For in-service teachers

With another teacher, take your classes on a field trip to some place of interest (fire station, playground, boiler room, etc.). Using the field trip as a resource for a lesson stimulation, teach an art lesson to one class, stressing that the children make the objects look like those they saw. Have the other class draw pictures of those things that interested them most on the trip. Compare the pictures of each class in terms of the following: (1) The time the children took to start working. (2) The characteristics of the final drawings. (3) The amount of space they used on the paper. Compare the behavior of the children in terms of the following: (1) The kinds of questions they asked. (2) The confidence the children seemed to have. (3) How they liked their pictures.

Chapter 2
FOUNDATIONS OF CREATIVE ART TEACHING

There is a sound theoretical basis for the practice of creative and evaluative teaching. In this chapter we shall discuss some theories about art and art education and note the elements that give direction to art education today. We shall then describe two contrasting methods currently used to teach art—the directed and the creative-evaluative approaches—and discuss the need for revising the practice of art education where it is necessary.

THEORIES AND RESEARCH IN ART EDUCATION

Some of the many theories and pertinent research about how art should be taught are briefly outlined below. Although the theories and research are many in number, they are not wholly divergent. Several elements bring into focus a direction they suggest for teaching art.

ART AS FUNCTIONAL Some time ago Ziegfeld and Smith, on the basis of a study which indicated that all

Figures 2.1–2.2
(right column)

people, in some way, use art in the satisfaction of some daily need, said they believed that all phases of art should be included in a functional program; that the art program should establish relations between various modes of art expression and other subject fields; that in planning the art program, the interests of the pupils should be central; and that in art education, it is important to develop expression without overemphasizing technique.[1]

[1] Edwin Ziegfeld and Mary Elinore Smith, *Art for Daily Living: Story of the Owatonna Art Education Project*, Minneapolis, University of Minnesota Press, 1944.

THE INDIVIDUAL AS CREATOR According to D'Amico, every child is a potential creator endowed with those sensibilities that characterize the artist, although not every child will become an accomplished artist.[2] He views art, not as performance or product, but as a way of living—as the means of enjoying and enriching life through creative expression. He recognizes the child's need to develop certain values and techniques at appropriate stages in his maturation. He advocates life experiences rather than fictitious, precon-

[2] Victor D'Amico, *Creative Teaching of Art*, rev. ed., Scranton, Pa., International Textbook, 1953.

"Every child is a potential creator endowed with those sensibilities that characterize the artist." These two children obviously are deeply involved in creating.
***2.1.** A first-grader works with crayons.*
***2.2.** A sixth-grader completes the design for a mask to be used in a class play.*

ceived programs as the source of art activities. He proposes arranging the art program to provide the growing child with experience in all media. The child is central; the teacher a continually stimulating guide.

THE CREATOR–CREATION–CREATIVE RELATION To Lowenfeld and Brittain creative development and expression are closely related to self-expression, self-adjustment, and self-identification in terms of intellectual, emotional, social, perceptual, physical, aesthetic, and creative growth. They emphasize the importance of (1) understanding the creative process and its effect on the child, (2) identifying the child's creative type (visual or haptic), (3) extending the child's frame of reference, (4) encouraging the child's self-identification with his work.[3]

A RELATIONAL VIEW DeFrancesco presents three propositions that should be considered of equal importance in a philosophy of art education: (1) every child is

[3] Viktor Lowenfeld and W. Lambert Brittain, *Creative and Mental Growth*, 5th ed., New York, Macmillan, 1970. "The visually minded person is one who acquaints himself with his environment primarily through the eyes and feels like a spectator. The person with haptic tendencies, on the other hand, is concerned primarily with his own body sensations and subjective experiences, which he feels emotionally. Most people fall between the two extremes." (Ibid., p. 234)

endowed with a will to create and has some degree of plastic sensitivity; (2) art experience must be presented in terms of the needs and interests of the child; (3) the created object must have worth for the creator and/or his social group.[4]

THE PERCEPTION-DELINEATION THEORY McFee assigns to the classroom teacher the function of raising

[4] Italo L. deFrancesco, *Art Education: Its Means and Ends,* New York, Harper & Row, 1958.

the level of elementary school education through the study of art. She considers the production and appreciation of art as forms of human behavior and emphasizes the response of the individual child to his art. Her theory involves four progressive stages of an individual's communication of his ideas in response to his surroundings through art. The stages are (1) readiness—the overall preparation of a person to respond to what he sees in his environment; (2) psychological environment—the influence on a child's feelings in encouraging or discourag-

ing his ability to draw things he sees; (3) information-handling—the child's ability to think and sort out the details of the things he sees; (4) invention—the selection of symbols to be arranged visually to make story-telling pictures of the child's surroundings.[5]

INTERACTION APPROACHES Barkan stresses the need for purposeful interaction between teacher and pupil.[6] Burkhart thinks of creative experience as a process of interactive learning.[7] He indicates that the function of the teacher is to stimulate, through his contacts with children, an awareness of problems real to them so that they will try to interact with their problems and find solutions. In an interactive dialogue between the teacher and pupil which stimulates a similar dialogue between the pupil and his problem, the child learns through guided self-discovery of problem solutions by progressively relating his ideas in the learning situation.

DIVERGENT AND SPONTANEOUS WAYS OF VISUAL LEARNING Beittel and Burkhart have identified two ways of learning related to visual art: spontaneous and divergent.[8] In the spontaneous way of learning, an individual gets an idea through some stimulation and sets a goal to be achieved. He tries many processes and materials in his effort to achieve it. As he pursues the goal, he gains knowledge related to his own ideas, and through his efforts an art work evolves which becomes his "finished" product. In this method, the goal is relatively fixed and the procedure is fluid. In the divergent method, the procedure is relatively stable, and the goal is changing: the parts that are added to the art product transform the idea, and an art form emerges as the final

2.4. *This was the result when a class of second-graders displayed the pots they had made. Look closely and you will see that though each child used essentially the same method in making his pot, no two are alike. Each child has expressed his own individual creative impulses.*

product. The final art work may be quite different from the artist's original goal. (The author believes after many years of teaching elementary school children that they work these ways.)

QUALITATIVE PROBLEM-SOLVING Following Dewey's[9] lead, it is Ecker's contention that careful study of what the artist does and says when ordering artistic "means and ends" provides insight into methods of teaching related to artistic production.[10] These "means and ends," Ecker calls "the qualities artists manipulate, orchestrate, modify, and create in solving problems." He suggests (1) that the artist thinks with qualities—lines, colors, planes, and textures; (2) that he thinks of construction of further qualities—the qualitative problem; (3) that he solves artistic problems in the medium—design possibilities with materials; (4) that he is aware of prospects within the range of qualities with regard to

[5] June King McFee, *Preparation for Art*, Belmont, Calif., Wadsworth Publishing, 1961.
[6] Manuel Barkan, *Through Art to Creativity*, Boston, Allyn & Bacon, 1960.
[7] Robert C. Burkhart, *Spontaneous and Deliberate Ways of Learning*, Scranton, Pa., International Textbook, 1962, chap. 6.
[8] Kenneth R. Beittel and Robert C. Burkhart, *Effect of Self-Reflective Training in Art on the Capacity for Creative Action*, University Park, Pennsylvania State University (Cooperative Research Project No. 1874, Office of Education, U.S. Dept. of HEW), 1962–1964.

[9] John Dewey, *Art as Experience*, New York, Minton, Balch, 1934.
[10] David W. Ecker and Elliot W. Eisner, *Readings in Art Education*, Waltham, Mass., Blaisdell, 1966, pp. 57–68.

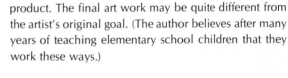

2.3. *When a 5-year-old painted "Our Class," she gave her classmates only the most rudimentary indications of body parts. Still, don't we all think of other people mostly in terms of their faces?*

2.5. This is a 7-year-old child's early symbolic impression of Columbus discovering America.

Figure 2.5 (right column)

some intended order, end-in-view, or pervasive quality; (5) that the means for resolving qualitative problems are component qualities; (6) that verbal ability to describe a qualitative problem is not necessary to establish that the artist has one; (7) that judging is selecting among alternative actions and qualities—selecting among alternative means-ends and methods.[11]

TYPES OF CREATIVE BEHAVIOR   Through the analysis of the art work of children and adults, Eisner has identified types of creative behavior. The behavior is based upon the various qualities and characteristics that have an art heritage and have been considered creative in the visual arts in terms of the treatment of form, of selection of subject matter, of new handling of known customary styles, and of innovating new directions. Four creative types were identified: (1) boundary pushing—"an ability

to attain the possible by extending the given"; (2) inventing—"an ability to employ the known in order to create an essentially new object or class of objects"; (3) boundary breaking—"the rejection or reversal of accepted assumptions and making the 'given' problematic"; and (4) aesthetic organizing—"the presence of objects of a high degree of coherence and harmony, conferring order and unity of matter."[12]

OTHER CURRENT FINDINGS   Current findings of research in art education seem to indicate clearly (1) the fact that children inherently learn creatively; (2) the characteristics of creative teaching—fluency of ideas, flexibility of thinking, originality, sensitivity to problems, productive thinking, divergent thinking, etc.; (3) the process of creative learning as discovery through problem-solving; (4) the process of beginning and develop-

[11] Ibid., pp. 323–335.

[12] Ibid., p. 62.

ing works of art as artists do; (5) the need to ask questions that have divergent power; (6) the value of teaching art in depth; (7) the development of social-cultural conditions that stimulate creative growth and learning; and (8) the importance of involving children with the qualities of art.[13]

With the demand for developing creative talent in our democratic society, there is the challenge to teach art in a creative manner in terms of the whole of art. The more recent theories and research findings point to directions for art teaching today.

CURRENT DIRECTIONS IN TEACHING ART

Current directions in teaching art are as follows:

1. Belief that all human beings have some type of natural creative endowment and that they all need artistic expression.
2. Concern with the individuality of the learner and his artistic development as it relates to his needs and ideas about art in life.
3. Belief in the equality of opportunity of the learner commensurate with his ability and with expectation that his performance will be different from others'.
4. Belief in the need for developing aesthetic sensitivity and artistic judgment within the child's behavioral potential.
5. Belief that children's artistic growth progressively develops and is limited only by the level of maturation attained and the degree of ability.
6. Belief that art experience involves subject matter structured in terms of the production, response to, and heritage of art, and is basic to expression.
7. Belief that readiness for and an interest in visual learning based on art qualities are essential.
8. Recognition that art needs to be taught in context with the child's contemporary culture and artistic heritage.
9. Recognition that the child's art experience should be consistent with the experience of the artist.
10. Recognition that stages of visual growth, behavioral processes, and art qualities in products are the basis of evaluating art achievement.
11. Commitment to the provision of opportunities for freedom of choice within the boundaries of the disciplines of an art experience.

These directions positively indicate that elementary school art teaching should be creative and constantly evaluative in order to make available to all children a qualitative program of art in their educational life.

[13] W. Lambert Brittain, ed., ''Creativity and Art Education,'' *Studies in Art Education*, Washington, D.C., NAEA, 1964; Elizabeth A. Hurwitz, *Design, A Search for Essentials*, Scranton, Pa., International Textbook, 1964; E. Paul Torrance, *Education and the Creative Potential*, Minneapolis, University of Minnesota Press, 1963; Burkhart, op. cit., pp. 197–224; Edward L. Mattil, Kenneth R. Beittel, and Robert C. Burkhart, ''The Effect of Depth vs. a Breadth Method of Art Instruction at the Ninth-Grade Level,'' *Studies in Art Education*, Washington, D.C., NAEA, Vol. III, No. 1., Fall 1961, pp. 75–87; George Pappas, ''An Analysis of the Process of Beginning and Developing Works of Art,'' *Research in Art Education*, Jerome J. Hausman, ed., Washington, D.C., NAEA, 9th Yearbook, 1959, p. 123; George Pappas, *Concepts in Art Education*, New York, Macmillan, 1970; Paul R. Henrickson and E. Paul Torrance, ''Some Implications for Art Education from the Minnesota Studies of Creative Thinking,'' in W. Lambert Brittain, ed., ''Creativity and Art Education,'' *Studies in Art Education*, Washington, D.C., NAEA, 1964; Manuel Barkan, ''Curriculum Problems in Art Education,'' *A Seminar in Art Education for Research and Curriculum Development*, Edward L. Mattil, Project Director, Cooperative Research Project V–002, University Park, Pennsylvania State University, 1966.

THE PRACTICE OF ART EDUCATION

There is agreement among theorists, then, supported by current research, that art should be taught creatively in terms of the qualities of the experience of the artist. Nevertheless, in the day-to-day practice of art education, two diametrically opposed methods of guiding child art are still used. The older method, the directed approach, grew out of early research in the psychology of learning, supported to some extent today, which seemed to show that particular skills and abilities result from a particular stimulus. The newer method, the creative-evaluative approach, grew out of common agreement among art theorists concerned with teaching and out of the research previously described.

The directed approach

In the directed approach, the subject matter is presented in a logical, connectionistic manner related to particular conditions. The approach encourages set procedures for the production of art work. Art lessons are planned and almost totally directed by the teacher with the intention that the child should understand content and form of art properly and have a particular experience with art. The teacher determines that a particular material will be used in the lesson. A minimum of attention is given to the child's individual and social needs in terms of his personal behavior as an artist, and the child's art work when completed is very similar to the work of every other child in the classroom and looks just about the way the teacher had anticipated in his lesson plan.

This approach limits the child's initiative because it stifles his ideas, thinking, and individuality. He has little opportunity to think about what he would like to make or to select materials for it. He is not confident that what he has produced is his own. He memorized facts about art without being able to relate it to the structure of the subject matter. He can never say in complete honesty, "I did this drawing." The directed approach lacks flexibility and generally follows a repetitious pattern of thought—the teacher's, derived from previous years of teaching the same lessons over and over again. The subject matter is presented as a list of facts to be learned first by rote. Creative expression is almost totally inhibited, and little transfer of interest and little growth in visual arts result. Some unregenerated art teachers, a

2.6. An 8-year-old in the symbolic stage, painting "Birds and Flowers," showed several things in his picture.

number of elementary school classroom teachers, and many parents accept this approach as effective teaching of art because the child is able to bring from the encounter a product about which the adult can say, "Now that really looks like something." The criterion for an art product is that the viewer can tell what the picture represents.

The creative-evaluative approach

In the creative-evaluative approach the teacher stimulates the child to bring forth his own ideas by structuring an evaluative situation related to his needs and the qualities of art. Then the teacher interacts with the child through questions in a natural, cooperative learning environment. In the presentation of the lesson the questions bring out the differences in the situation, are open in nature, and have divergent power. (See Chapter 3 for a detailed description of open questions with divergent power.) Toward the end of the lesson, as the structure of knowledge becomes evident and the teacher evaluates the child's progress in terms of his understanding, the questions are more specific and factual. The individuality, thinking, and development of the child, typical of the artist's experience, are paramount; he is not forced to conform to "average" standards or to be limited by the teacher's idea. The child has a complete experience in the visual arts; his initiative is stimulated; he discovers new aesthetic relationships in terms of himself. He has the opportunity to select materials, to express his ideas, and through evaluative experimentation he comes to understand techniques in the process of formulating his own product, which constitutes a unique and qualitative visual expression. Because the learning atmosphere is natural and cooperative, an understanding of the structure of subject matter in terms of content and form of the visual arts results from the child's art encounter.

The creative-evaluative approach is: pervasive, interactive dialogue between people and conditions; structured subject matter; internally stimulating; natural in terms of a typical artistic experience. Each child can confidently say of his art work, "This is my drawing."

THE NEED TO ALIGN PRACTICE WITH THEORY

The superiority of creative-evaluative teaching over directed teaching is clear. The need is to bridge the gap between teacher-dominated practices and creative directions in teaching. Under the leadership of professional art organizations, art educators have clarified directions, defined objectives, and described the art process and product. Research has pointed the way to creative-evaluative teaching that is qualitative art education, and the personnel who administer art programs have interpreted the concept of qualitative teaching for elementary school art. Further alignment of practice and theory of art teaching in the elementary school depends on cooperation between art and classroom teachers. The classroom teacher occupies a central role because he best understands the needs and interests of the children. The classroom teacher who clings to stereotyped practices, who uses too few visual, sensory, and literary resources, who possesses only a meager background in understanding the psychology of learning pertaining to art, or who lacks updated training can inhibit creative art education. The well-informed, interested, resourceful, cooperative elementary classroom teacher can advance it—so too can the art teacher.

*Figure 2.6
(left column)*

To fulfill his role in providing qualitative lessons of creative art experience for the children, the elementary school classroom teacher needs a strategy for teaching. This is not to suggest that he should learn or follow a prescribed program for teaching art. On the contrary, the essence of art learning requires creative teaching that has individuality and flexibility, that encourages artistic involvement, and that makes constructive use of the unforeseeable discussions and occurrences that make up a school day. Each child, each teacher, each class is unique; so, too, *within the concepts of art qualities, each art program should be unique.* Such a strategy is developed over a period of time, beginning with undergraduate courses in elementary school art teaching and continuing with graduate courses, with in-service training under the guidance of special art teachers, through an understanding of the whole curriculum structure, and

*These watercolors were both done by fifth-graders. They both give an impression of lightness, even gaiety, but the differences are striking, also. **2.7.** In "Kittens in the Garden," the kittens seem real, but not in an adult sense. **2.8.** In "Beach Balls," the child has conveyed the emotional quality of fun on the beach. He has done this partly by exaggerating the balls, which, like the kittens, seem thus even more real, though not realistic.*

through the day-to-day creative-evaluative experience with the children in the classroom. It comprises an awareness of the contemporary aims of art teaching, a knowledge of the sequence of children's visual development, knowing the processes with materials, knowing and recognizing art qualities in art works of children, and understanding of creative-evaluative means of stimulating children's creative visual art experience. All this is discussed further in Chapter 3.

It is important for the classroom teacher to develop a strategy for teaching art creatively because in art education, as in general education, the elementary school program is the foundation for all future learning. The initial learning experience sets the tone for all the rest. If the start is established creatively and is of quality, the child is influenced toward an effective education. If

the start is repressive, regardless of the child's abilities or shortcomings, his subsequent education suffers unless remedial steps are taken. In other words, the effectiveness of the elementary school classroom teacher as a participant in stimulating the child's visual learning experience profoundly influences the child's later educational and personal life.

SUMMARY

A number of theories about art and art education are briefly described. The theories and research provide the 11 directions in teaching practice in art education that are listed. These directions constitute the basis for the strategy of creative-evaluative art teaching at all levels.

Theorists, supported by the results of research, agree that art involves creative expression and should be taught creatively in a way typical of the experience of artists. Nevertheless, in practice today two very different methods of art education are used—the directed approach and the creative-evaluative approach. The evidence clearly indicates that creative-evaluative teaching is a superior strategy for achieving effective, qualitative art education.

The need now is to revise the practice of art teaching in terms of the creative-evaluative approach. This requires cooperation between art and classroom teachers. The latter play an important role because they best understand the needs and interests of each child. The special art teacher understands the qualities of art. To fulfill this important role, the elementary school classroom teacher needs to understand the strategy for creative-evaluative teaching.

AIDS TO UNDERSTANDING

For discussion

1. How do the elements common to all the theories about how art should be taught relate to current findings of research in art education?
2. Compare the fundamental differences between two theories of teaching art.
3. What are the significant unique contributions of the following: Ziegfeld and Smith, D'Amico, Lowenfeld and Brittain, deFrancesco, McFee, Barkan, Burkhart, Beittel, Eisner, Ecker?
4. How does an interactive theory of teaching art differ from a functional theory?
5. What is the significance of self-identification in an art experience? Develop an example.
6. As you understand the three propositions of the relational view, how do they align with a democratic philosophy of living?
7. How does a creative approach to teaching art differ from a directed approach?
8. How do you account for the gap between educational theory and the practices of teaching art? How may an alignment take place in an elementary school art program?
9. What are some of the conditions that foster a strategy for teaching art creatively?
10. Suggest how the goals of the elementary school program differ from those of the middle and secondary school programs.
11. What is the relationship of contemporary qualitative problem-solving and creative-evaluative teaching?

For involvement

1. Observe an entire art lesson taught in an elementary classroom and report conditions that support a directed or a creative teaching approach.
2. Write a critical analysis of a theory of teaching art in terms of the elements that are common to all theories of teaching art.
3. Develop your own synthesis from a deeper study of the theories prevalent today about how art should be taught. Test its validity in relation to the general criteria related to current findings of research.
4. Arrange a debate among your classmates on the proposition, "In a democratic society, there is a challenge to teach visual art in a creative manner."

Chapter 3
A STRATEGY FOR CREATIVE-EVALUATIVE ART TEACHING

In education generally the emphasis today is upon creative teaching. Classroom work in English, science, social science, and mathematics is largely heuristic, that is, designed to guide the pupil in an involvement with learning experiences leading to his discovery of new understanding and affects in the solutions to problems. In other words, learning is stimulated by setting up situations that challenge pupils to seek solutions to the problems. Creative learning in art provides affective experience on the sensory, or expressive, level while promoting understanding of the fundamental structure,[1] principles, and ideas of a subject and encourages the retention of subject-matter details on a cognitive level. It fosters the application of reflective and affective learning techniques to the correlating of the whole educational climate and thus facilitates continuity between elementary and advanced education.

It was shown in Chapter 2 that in the visual arts as

---

[1] Jerome Bruner, *The Process of Education*, Cambridge, Mass., Harvard University Press, 1965, pp. 17–32.

Figures 3.1–3.2
(right column)

well there is a firm theoretical basis for the superiority of creative-evaluative teaching over directed teaching and that the practice of teaching art needs to be revised in terms of the theory. It was also pointed out that the classroom teacher has an important role in the teaching of art in the elementary school and that to fulfill this role he should develop a strategy for creative art education. In this chapter, such a strategy is described in terms of the question, "How can art be taught as an experience?" To answer the question, we shall discuss briefly the three educational environments common today, indicate the relation of creative teaching to these environments, and then develop an approach that fosters a creative visual experience for the child through evaluative teaching.

CONTEMPORARY EDUCATIONAL ENVIRONMENTS

There are three fundamentally different theories about how learning takes place. In the 1930s they were termed connectionism, purposeful behaviorism, and the field concept.[2] In the 1960s the terminology was revised to reflect new thinking about learning, and the theories were renamed conditioning, model identification, and cognitive restructuring.[3]

From these learning theories have developed the three teaching environments characteristic of contemporary education: the academic, or subject-matter approach (developed from connectionism, or conditioning), the behavioral activity approach (developed from purposeful behaviorism, or model identification), and the experience approach (developed from the field concept, or cognitive restructuring). The characteristics of these three teaching environments are shown in Table 3.1.

It is important for the elementary school teacher to understand all three approaches because his strategy for

Figures 3.3–3.4
(right column)

creative-evaluative teaching will find a use for each. Creative-evaluative teaching is individualized teaching, and no single method will be effective for all children or for all situations.

The academic approach

The academic approach to teaching generally tends to indoctrinate traditional subject matter, to limit thought to a particular area of a subject, to present the factual aspects of a subject as they are known by the teacher, to converge upon goals pre-established by the teacher, to limit the child to the teacher's frame of reference, and to emphasize the teacher's role in planning. At first glance this approach appears to ensure good teaching. But what happens if the teacher is wrong or does not keep his knowledge up to date? If the teacher's knowledge were encyclopedic, this approach would be ideal; if the children were all very limited, the approach would not frustrate creative thinking. Since this type of teaching converges narrowly toward the scope of the teacher's mind and experience, the pupil's thinking mirrors the teacher's. This is not effective education, for the purpose of education is the development and modification of the child's own individuality. This approach is especially prevalent at the secondary level of teaching but is apparent at all levels.

The behavioral activity approach

The behavioral activity approach to teaching analyzes the way people behave in daily living and establishes a series of educational activities or model situations in which the child acts out roles. With a grade level of pupils in mind, the teacher plans the pattern of experiences which makes up the total education of the child within the grade. Emphasis is placed on participation in the activity of role-playing. For example, in first grade, children might "play store" to learn how to count to 100, how to tell about an incident, how to write simple stories about stores. The stimulation for the activity would be a trip to a store. From the activity, the children would find out about the place where they buy things and would produce imitatively a model of a store in the corner of the classroom which for a long time would be

[2] Nelson B. Henry, ed., *The Psychology of Learning* (Forty-first Yearbook, Part II, of the National Society for the Study of Education), Chicago, University of Chicago Press, 1942. This yearbook and the one cited in the next footnote contain detailed and valuable discussions of learning theories.

[3] Herman R. Richey, ed., *Theories of Learning and Instruction* (Sixty-third Yearbook of the National Society for the Study of Education), Chicago, University of Chicago Press, 1964.

Table 3.1 CHARACTERISTICS OF THE ACADEMIC, BEHAVIORAL ACTIVITY, AND EXPERIENCE APPROACHES TO TEACHING

CHARACTERISTICS	ACADEMIC APPROACH	BEHAVIORAL ACTIVITY APPROACH	EXPERIENCE APPROACH
Psychological basis	Conditioning	Behavioral models	Cognitive structures
Planning principle	Part to whole	Matrix of behavioral activities	Whole to part
Nature of teaching	Convergent	Organizing activities	Divergent
Teacher's role	Teacher-directed	Teacher-pupil plans	Teacher-stimulated
Emphasis of motivation	Facts of subject (art)	Model activities of art in life	Qualitative solving of art problems
Content of subject matter	Facts direct the art experience	Behavioral activities of art	Knowledge is the product of a problem-solving experience
Goal direction	Structure of the subject matter	Organized behavior patterns of art	Concepts of art-oriented goals
Achievement	Teacher-established	Assumed behavioral ends	Evaluative processes

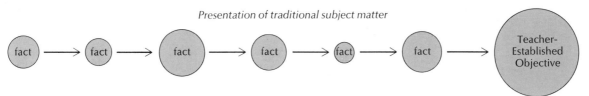

Presentation of traditional subject matter

fact → fact → fact → fact → fact → fact → Teacher-Established Objective

3.1. The academic approach. This diagram, showing a synaptic connecting together of a series of facts, indicates what happens when the teacher presents subject matter based on his background, knowledge, and experience. The subject matter is pointed toward an objective established by the teacher. This approach limits the child according to the teacher's ability and background.

3.2. This child undoubtedly enjoys helping decorate her school for Christmas. Nevertheless, as far as art education is concerned, it is the academic approach: traditional subject matter directed by the teacher is being used, and the child has no opportunity for creative thinking.

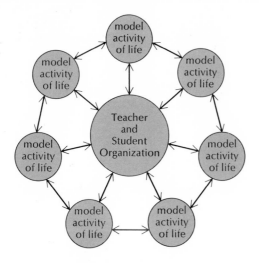

*Figures 3.5–3.6
(right column)*

3.3. *The behavioral activity approach. This diagram shows an organization of activities of life based on model activities (behavioral patterns) typical of most people's daily living. It is assumed that if children "role play" these model activities of life, they will learn. One problem with this approach is that learning is assumed. Also, unless the teacher is careful to analyze life situations thoroughly, the child may be deprived of vital learning experiences; that is, the total pattern for learning may be weakened because some activities of life are not included.*

the center of most of the activity for learning in the classroom. The assumption is that the child learns how to act in a real situation by participating in a staged one. However, exposure to life experiences does not ensure cognitive learning, and the weakness of the approach is that learning is assumed. This approach is most prevalent at the elementary level of education, where it is felt that children like to play in the course of learning; however, the approach is apparent at all levels of teaching.

The experience approach

The experience approach to teaching encourages reflective thinking on the part of the learner, and ideas result from structured stimulations involving comparable contrasting circumstances which the learner can evaluate. The child is oriented to a "whole" situation, and smaller "parts" are separated out for solution in relation to the whole situation. The problem (the whole) develops, which is as large or as small as the learner's ability allows. The problem is real in relation to the learner. The child discovers a solution through dialogue with the teacher. The process is divergent because there are no prescribed boundaries of knowledge while there are a great number of possible goals related to needs of life in terms of artistic behavior and qualities of art con-

3.4. *The drama is certainly an activity of life, and it is common—and rewarding to all—to relate art education to all aspects of dramatic productions. This child, who made the puppet, obviously takes great pleasure in endowing it with "life." The teacher who directs such a behavioral activity, however, should be sure that he does not assume that a genuine art experience will result.*

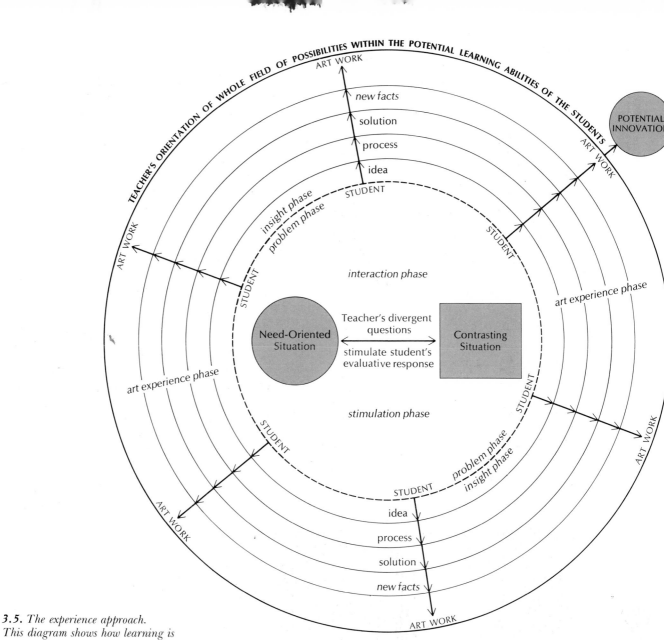

3.5. *The experience approach.*
*This diagram shows how learning is
stimulated when a need-oriented situation is
altered by some contrasting situation (disequilibrium)
that enters the learning environment. The occurrence stim-*
ulates interaction between the two conditions. It also presents a problem for the learner. In helping the learner resolve
the problem, the teacher guides him to a number of alternative actions through questions of divergent power. Thus he
leads the student to evaluate the condition and state the problem *as he sees it. The child can then separate out*
(individuate) a possible action he could take to solve the problem. First he achieves insight, *then an* idea, *then a*
process, *which leads him to a* solution; *the solution, combined with necessary* new facts, *results in an art work.*
For the child learning, the art work is a creation. It is new to him. The outer scope of the large circle is, initially, the
teacher's total orientation in relation to his students. The teacher's initial presentation (orientation of the problem
situation) provides the potential for many ways for each pupil to achieve a new state of growth. Thus, in a reciprocal
way, the outer scope also represents this new state for each student, which may become as large and as unique as each
individual learner is able to make it. As can be seen, this new state contrasts greatly in size with the original need-
oriented situation. This change is evident in the modification of the child's behavior. Therefore, he has learned.

3.6. *While these children look at the pussy-willow branches, the teacher encourages reflective thinking: "Is there any pattern in the way the buds are arranged?" "How would you paint the buds' fuzzy look?" "Do you think the buds should look fuzzy?" As the children answer, each begins to have his own insight. Each is on the way to his own total art experience.*

tent and form. The emphasis is on the student's thinking, ideas, and frame of reference; the teacher is the interacting agent. The teacher structures a situation related to concept-oriented needs of art in life. The situation has contrasting conditions that stimulate the learner to think and respond. The facts learned about art are the products of the experience, and the acquisition of facts extends the child's knowledge of art. This, with experience in affective areas of visual art, provides a total art experience. In the words of Dewey, the learner has "an experience."[4]

RELATION OF CONTEMPORARY EDUCATIONAL ENVIRONMENTS TO CREATIVE-EVALUATIVE TEACHING

The author believes that creative-evaluative teaching is most closely related to the experience approach and that such teaching, through the stimulation of affective qualities of art experience, provides behavioral experiences typical of the artist and an understanding of the structure of subject matter, the goals of the academic and behavioral activity approaches. Certainly there are times when a teacher needs to "tell" a fact or a student needs to participate in role-playing; however, these times occur in the total art experience. In general, however, to teach creatively—to promote in the pupil reflective thinking—the teacher must give the pupil an opportunity to be involved in the whole process of learning art and to realize that he has had a part in the formulation of his art work. Visual learning is a cognitive and affective experience in the course of which the child sees and evaluates conditions, links together ideas, and participates in "an experience." Learning is a dynamic process of change that must occur in the child if his behavior is to be modified.

The dynamic process of learning is initiated when the child is stimulated by a need to change his circumstances because some contrasting idea or event occurs to alter his state of well-being. This condition for learning is set up by the teacher, who orients the child to a set of circumstances which indicates that a problem exists.

[4] John Dewey, *Art as Experience*, New York, Minton, Balch, 1934.

Through use of questions that cause the child to gain insight into a solution to the problem, the child is led to interact with possible ways of solving his problem. He separates out a course for his solution and proceeds toward a goal that he has established under the teacher's guidance. When the goal is achieved, he has more factual knowledge, more affective experience, and a different concept of things related to his original problem. A new state of well-being emerges.

In the circular figure, the outer circle represents the child's new "whole" state that has resulted from his growth. Note that it is much larger than his original state, the need-oriented situation. As this process continues through his total educational experience under the teacher's guidance, the child establishes a pattern of experience (the goal of the behavioral activity approach) and he learns facts (the goal of the academic approach). Most important, the child can grow as large as he is able and can achieve his own individual potential.

Figure 3.5

A STRATEGY FOR TEACHING ART CREATIVELY

The creative-evaluative teaching of art involves (1) setting up a situation composed of comparable but contrasting elements about which the child can have ideas, (2) stimulating him to evaluate the contrasting elements by asking questions about the situation which can be answered in a number of ways that are relatively correct, and (3) guiding him in evaluating the elements so that he discovers for himself a fact which is new *for him*.

Setting up the learning situation

The first process in a creative teaching episode is setting up a situation in which the child can learn. In the art lesson, the situation is composed of two or more comparable but contrasting elements—for example, three squares of the same size but of different colors, or two identical cardboard figures, one painted with vertical and the other with horizontal stripes.

The situation should be closely related to the child's immediate interest and environment, growing naturally out of ongoing classroom activities. The facts that the child will be helped to discover should be within his ability to grasp but sufficiently difficult to identify so that he is not bored. The situation should challenge, but not overwhelm him. It follows that the situation should be tailored to each child's individual level of ability. For the limited child, the teacher would structure a simple situation composed of only two, rather obviously different elements, for example, a blue triangle and a blue circle. For the gifted child, he would set up a fairly complicated situation, perhaps adding a figure with diagonal stripes to the vertically and horizontally striped ones. For the "average" child a suitably complex situation would be somewhere in between.

Asking questions to stimulate ideas and perception

The second process in the creative-evaluative teaching of art is asking questions that will lead the child to evaluate the elements in a structured situation. Particularly important is the form of the question and the flow of the pattern of questions. When the situation has contrasting elements children will be able to perceive differences. When questions establish differences in a situation children will respond to them in relation to their perceptions, their interests, and their needs. Effective questions are those that mature aesthetic sensitivity and at the same time cause understanding to evolve and, ultimately, facts. Questions should relate to both the affective and the cognitive areas of visual learning experience through the child's response to structured situations built around visual circumstances that are comparable. Contrasting works of art can be shown, or contrasting elements of art can be set up.

For example, when the teacher has set up for the class a situation in which three same-sized but different-colored squares are to be compared, he might ask,

"Why, do you suppose, does one colored square stand out more than the others?" This question will allow each child to express his personal reaction to the three colors and will elicit ideas concerning brightness and dullness, darkness and lightness, as well as the actual differences in hue. The question might also provoke ideas concerning the effect of the viewer's position in the room or the position of the squares in relation to the light source on the perception of the intensity of colors.

Questions that stimulate ideas are termed "open" questions, or questions that have "divergent power." They are open because many answers are possible. They have divergent power because they elicit a great variety of responses that encourage further discussion, further questioning, and further diverse responses. It is possible that questions may be too open and general for some children whose backgrounds are limited. For this reason, a very open question that confuses is not a good question. The amount of open-endedness in form should be well-adjusted to the learning group.

For example, a question that is only somewhat open in form, yet open, would be, "What is the difference between the colored shapes you see before you?" This question tends to focus on the situation more directly for the child and yet involves him personally in a dialogue about the different shapes. For the less sophisticated student this kind of question is open enough, yet structured enough, so that it does not lead to doubt that he is really learning something.

In contrast, closed or factual questions (the kind used in directed teaching) must be answered by statements of fact, by "yes" or "no" or by "true" or "false." For example, using the artist's paintbrush as a topic, the directing teacher might ask such factual questions as, "What is the shape of the brush?" or "How is the brush made?" These questions elicit factual answers. The creative teacher would ask questions with divergent power such as "What would you be doing if you were not working with this brush?" or "How could you paint a picture without this brush?" These questions elicit ideas.

Questions of good form for relevant teaching tend to cause the child to focus openly on a comparable situation in which there are apparently relationships and some obvious differences. When the stimulating situation provides greater opportunities for choices, the question form may be more specific, as long as inherent in the stimulation there are great opportunities for choices.

A third type of question, the affective question, is used with divergent and factual questions. On some occasions, in beginning a lesson or in the process of teaching, it is necessary to ask questions that tend to stimulate children's reactions to an art work—a painting, a piece of jewelry, a color print, etc. Or, at times, it is necessary to get responses to a situation or to found objects in the surroundings. The teacher in these instances will use affective questions. For example, he might ask a child, showing him a work by Miró, "How do you feel about the colors in this painting?" A question of this type draws the child's response in terms of his feeling toward the work. His response, naive as it may be, gives insight into his artistic sensitivity and judgment. He may reveal his understanding of the work of others, his own art work, or even a cultural and linguistic development appropriate to his age. Follow-up questions of an affective nature—such as "Do the colors make you feel happy?" (or sad, irritated, quiet, etc.)—tend to encourage the child to express more of his personal feelings and attitudes. These questions lead into a dialogue between the child and the teacher and an interaction between the child and the condition to which he is responding. Questions of an affective nature coupled with divergent questions give the classroom teacher a very effective way to stimulate children's aesthetic and perceptual awareness by leading them to describe their awareness in relation to the affective aspect of learning —feelings and attitudes about art.

Additionally, questioning involves the condition of flow. Questions that emerge from the responding situation are said to have flow. When they seem to come from the background knowledge of the teacher from a

*Figure 3.7
(left column)*

3.7. This teacher stimulates ideas when he asks the children, "What is the difference between the textures of the trees and the barn in her picture?" (The boy seems to be pondering his answer with particular care!)

3.8. *In this diagram of a divergent strategy, the central circle symbolizes a dynamic stimulation, the evaluative situation. This is the orientation (presentation) by the teacher of a structured situation of contrasting conditions related to the needs and interests of the students. The outer broken circle symbolizes the extent of the teacher's frame of reference in relation to the situation. The arrows from the inner circle to the centers of the spirals represent the different ideas the students get from the stimulation. Each spiral illustrates the progress of the development of a student's initial idea. The open end of the spiral implies a readiness to accept new valid thinking in relation to the idea. As each child's idea expands and develops, it may include or become part of the idea of another child. It may result in an interaction between the idea and another child's idea or between the idea and the teacher's questions or comments, or both. The shaded areas, where all ideas overlap, include all the phases of the initial stimulation and all aesthetic learnings common to the particular art experience. Such a divergent strategy produces educational experiences that encourage and make possible unique and innovative actions—a measure of true creative-evaluative experience.*

3.9. *In this diagram of a convergent strategy, the same circle used in* **3.8** *again symbolizes the scope of the teacher's frame of reference. The inner circle represents an objective preset by the teacher—a goal predetermined for the students to accomplish. The small circles outside the larger circle symbolize individual students' ideas and thoughts, forced to focus toward the teacher's goal. In other words, each student is forced within the teacher's frame of reference, toward his idea for a solution to the objective. Thus the students are limited to the background and authority of the teacher. Such a convergent strategy causes the learner to conform to the teacher—it inhibits creative-evaluative experience.*

set content area or traditional information, they may interfere with flow. Question flow that stimulates is dependent upon the teacher's use of questions that grow from the structured stimulation and from the revealing responses of the students to it.

Two figures illustrate diagrammatically the difference between the divergent strategy characteristic of creative-evaluative teaching and the convergent strategy associated with directed teaching. Divergent strategy encourages unique and innovative action and nurtures creative-evaluative art experience; convergent strategy forces the pupil to conform to the teacher's background and inhibits creative-evaluative art experience.

Guiding the evaluative process

The third process in the creative teaching of art is guiding the child in evaluating the contrasting elements of the structured situation so that he discovers for himself a new fact and so that he may have an affective perceptual experience. In the art lesson, this involves allowing the child's ideas to interact with a group of materials provided by the teacher and selected for their appropriateness to the learning goals of the lesson and to the child's level of intellectual and manipulative ability. Through the use of questions with divergent power, the teacher guides the child to evaluate various materials in relation to his ideas, to evaluate his own ideas in relation to those of the other children and to the teacher's questions, and to achieve from the insight thus gained a piece of information that he did not know before.

Importance of the divergent question

The ability to ask questions with divergent power is the most valuable asset a classroom teacher can have. With this ability, he can encourage the creative artistic development of his pupils even in the most authoritarian educational milieu. He can activate a searching tone within the learning situation which will free the minds of his students for first evaluative, then reflective, then interactive, and finally creative action. Creative art education is possible in every classroom if the teacher's

questions stimulate evaluative and reflective thought through their divergent power. Any teacher can continue work in the same classroom in the same school and find each year of teaching different because each group of students respond differently to his creative teaching.

Figures 3.8–3.9 (left column)

SUMMARY

The rationale, presented in the previous chapter, for teaching art creatively is reinforced by present-day emphasis on qualitative and heuristic teaching in other educational areas.

The three teaching-learning environments common today have developed out of basic psychological learning theories. The academic approach has developed from connectionism, or conditioning; the behavioral activity approach from purposeful behaviorism, or model identification; the experience approach from the field concept, or cognitive structuring. All three approaches are useful and should be understood by the teacher. The experience approach is, in the author's opinion, most closely related to creative-evaluative teaching. This approach involves aspects of the academic and behavioral activity approaches in the total process, but in different relationships and emphases.

A strategy for creative-evaluative teaching of art involves (1) setting up a situation composed of comparable but contrasting elements of art qualities about which the child can have ideas, (2) asking questions with divergent power in order to stimulate the child to evaluate the contrasting elements, and (3) guiding the child's evaluation, by means of further questions with divergent power, so that he learns about art qualities that relate to his life and are new *for him*. This means the child should be guided to make independent artistic judgments within his ability while producing or responding to art work.

The ability to ask questions with divergent power is a valuable asset for the teacher; it allows him to generate a creative learning environment in the classroom.

AIDS TO UNDERSTANDING

For discussion

1. What is an art experience? What implication does it have for a strategy of creative-evaluative art teaching? How does it relate to qualitative problem-solving?
2. Compare the three different theories about how learning takes place presented in this chapter with respect to the nature of the learning environment which they generate.
3. What is the relationship of contemporary educational environments and creative-evaluative teaching?
4. How are the goals of the academic and behavioral activity approaches to teaching art fulfilled through creative-evaluative teaching or an experience approach to art teaching?
5. What is the difference between an open question with divergent power and a closed question?
6. What effect do questions that involve the condition of *flow* have on a learning situation?

7. Why are divergent questions important in the initial stimulation of a lesson and factual questions important in the closing assessment of the lesson?

For involvement

1. Set up a strategy for creative-evaluative teaching of art.
    a. Develop the learning situation.
    b. Design questions which stimulate children's perception.
    c. Plan questions that tend to guide the child to evaluate conditions in the learning situation so that he discovers for himself things that are new for him and from which you as the teacher may develop new concepts, ideas, and facts.
2. Write a question that is open in nature and that will cause children to respond with a number of possible directions of thought.

Part Two
MEANS AND ENDS

Chapter 4
TEACHING AN ART LESSON

In the preceding chapter we discussed a strategy for the creative-evaluative teaching of art; in this chapter we shall describe the specific application of creative-evaluative processes to the teaching of a lesson. The purpose is not to set down a prescription for teaching an art lesson: creative-evaluative teaching is, by definition, flexible and adaptable and cannot be formulated into a "standard procedure." The aim of this chapter is to make clear, through the use of examples, the nature of the creative-evaluative procedure in the process of teaching a lesson. Sample art lessons are presented that are based on the structure and procedure of a creative-evaluative strategy for teaching.

RELATION OF THE ART LESSON TO THE ART CURRICULUM

The individual art lesson is a part of the overall elementary school curriculum. The curriculum is discussed in Chapters 9 and 10, but will be explained briefly here. The art curriculum is developed in terms of the educational objectives to be attained at the different grade levels. The areas of art experience based upon needs of the individual and of society comprise the educational objectives for art. The individual units within each grade are developed in relation to the areas of art experience, the overall objectives. This series of units within the grade make up the scope of learning experiences within a grade. This organization is carried out for each grade. Collectively, all of the units organized as such for each grade are the curriculum. The individual units of the curriculum correlate each learning goal with the child's ability at each grade level. Each unit progressively organized from kindergarten to Grade 6 according to an area of experience comprises a sequence of learning experiences related to one of the educational objectives for art. It is called sequence of learning in art. The art unit is thus a teaching plan organized to help the child at a particular level of ability to achieve his potential in terms of a particular goal in relation to a fundamental area of art experience based upon a need for art in his life. The general objectives of the unit are subdivided into more specific objectives, each of which (or several combined) is an objective of the art lesson. These relationships are indicated in a sample unit that will be used in the following discussion of an art lesson.

SAMPLE ART UNIT

Unit Title: The Need for Art in the Daily Life of Man and in the Community in Which He Lives: Grade 6

I. General objective: To understand the design problems involved in achieving a well-planned wardrobe and the desirability of such a wardrobe for effective personal living

A. Specific objectives for individual lessons

1. To understand the need for consideration of personality in the selection of a wardrobe
2. To understand that clothing design can seem to effect a change in stature
3. To understand that the color of a costume affects an individual's complexion
4. To understand that a costume is selected in relation to the time and place it is to be worn
5. To understand that designs of clothing may contribute to better health
6. To understand that a well-designed wardrobe can be selected within a limited allowance

THE LESSON PLAN

For his own use, the teacher should prepare a plan of the lesson, based on an outline similar to the following one:

OUTLINE OF LESSON PLAN

I. Objectives

List the learning goals of the lesson in terms of the related understandings to be gained, abilities and skills to be developed, and attitudes and appreciations to be acquired.

II. Scope of subject matter   CONTENT

List the factual knowledge you expect to include within the lesson experience.

III. Presentation PROCEDURE

A. Stimulation motivation

1. Decide what situation, composed of comparable but contrasting elements (visual preferably), you will set up for the children to evaluate.
2. Decide what questions with divergent power you will ask to stimulate the children to think about ideas related to the learning objective.

B. Activities

1. List, in the order in which you expect them to arise, ideas that children may gain from the stimulation.
2. List activities that are possible with art materials in relation to the list of ideas.
3. Note the nature of the progress which you may expect from the particular group of children.
4. List further questions with divergent power which you can ask to stimulate the formulation of ideas by the children in the process of working with art materials.

IV. Evaluation

Decide when and how you will guide children in the self-evaluation of their own work in relation to the specific objectives of the lesson. Again, this requires questions with divergent power. However, as the children's thinking comes into focus on a particular set of facts, questions of a factual nature are in order, as a product of the learning experience in art will be facts as well as affective sensitivity to art.

V. Resource materials and references

List the pictures, visual aids constructed particularly for this lesson, slides, movies, models, tape recordings, records, books you want to use in teaching the lesson.

VI. Art materials

List the art materials you want the children to use or select from in the activity part of the lesson.

VII. Clean-up

Decide how much time will be needed to clean up after the procedure you intended to employ is completed.

*I. Pieter Brueghel, the elder (c. 1525–1569), Children's Games, detail.
(Kunsthistorisches Museum, Vienna; Art Reference Bureau, New York)*

*Five acknowledged masterpieces of art
are shown on these four pages.*

4.1. *Clean-up may be uninspiring to all, but it is important to allow enough time for it.*

VIII. Time budget

Outline a tentative time guide to help you teach the lesson within a reasonable time allotted for art experience.

In addition to outlining the probable course of the lesson, the teacher should make sure his lesson structure meets the following criteria:

1. The lesson should be appropriate to the children's experience level.
2. The lesson should permit sufficient variety of interpretations to satisfy each child's inner vision.
3. The materials and tools of expression should be appropriate to the children's manipulative and mental ability.
4. The lesson should lead to further self-development of the children.
5. The objective of the lesson should be worthwhile in terms of healthy mental and behavioral growth for the children.

The teacher should realize that an art lesson does not always go as planned. This happens because children are individuals and, even though basically similar

"The lesson should be appropriate to the children's experience level." What kinds of differences do you think there were in the lesson plans used by the teachers of these two girls? 4.2. A first-grader starts in on her modeling with enthusiasm. 4.3. This sixth-grader's teacher is helping her evaluate her own work.

in a given school grade, are sufficiently different to be unpredictable, and because the conditions of the teaching-learning situation cannot be entirely foreseen. Two of the important qualities of creative teaching are its flexibility and individuality. The creative teacher should be enterprising enough to pursue unanticipated activities that will lead the children to the desired learning goals. The more experienced the teacher, the better he is able to utilize constructively the unplanned-for occurrences. For the less-experienced teacher, the lesson plan provides an opportunity to build flexibility and individuality into the art lesson and to prepare himself as much as possible to cope constructively with the unanticipated.

Later in this chapter three sample lesson plans are given; for one of them, the transcript of the actual teaching session is included for comparison.

THE LESSON PRESENTATION

We shall illustrate the presentation of an art lesson in terms of the objectives specified for the sixth-grade art unit outlined earlier. The lesson is based on the first four specific objectives. Thus, the learning goals are:

1. To understand the need for consideration of personality in the selection of a wardrobe
2. To understand that clothing design can seem to effect a change in stature

ers, and simple sporty dresses when they went shopping. Now her closet was filled with these, and yet her wardrobe seemed very limited. She pushed these clothes aside and pulled out a fluffy dress her mother had made her buy so that she would have "something to wear to a party." She had never liked this dress, and anyway it wasn't suitable for this particular party. She threw it on the bed. Another selection and still another produced the same response. Now that she saw her clothes all together, she realized that all her dresses were sporty and that the gaily colored blouses and sweaters didn't go with her loud skirts. There seemed to be some justification for her reputation as a tomboy.

Anne wished that instead of the three or four sporty dresses that now didn't seem suitable, she had a more expensive outfit in a good material and with good lines. Finally, she settled on a full-skirted dress made of a soft blue material which was a little sporty. After looking at it a moment, she realized that it really was not that much different from those she had rejected, but seemed nevertheless to be more appropriate. After dressing, she turned to her shoe rack. Here, too, many of her shoes were in bright colors and sporty in style. One by one she discarded them until only a pair of ballerina slippers remained. These were suitable in style, but they would have been much better if they hadn't been bright red. As Anne put them on, she wondered if she should even bother to go to the party at all.

About this time, she phoned her friend Jane, who was in the same class, to find out if she thought the party was really worth going to. Jane was filled with excitement about the party and what she was going to wear. She said she was glad that she had listened to her mother's advice about what styles and colors were becoming to her small stature and olive skin, even though she thought some of her mother's ideas were old-fashioned. Jane had had no trouble choosing an outfit for the party from her limited number of carefully selected dresses and shoes. She would wear a pretty red dress, and she had neutral green accessories to go with it that made a stunning combination. She would wear her new mesh stockings, and one of her three pairs of shoes matched the outfit perfectly. So Jane was all set, she said, exclaiming to Anne on the phone, "See you there." Anne didn't get a word in, but she was sure now that she must go to the party because Jane was going.

3. To understand that the color of a costume affects an individual's complexion
4. To understand that a costume is selected in relation to the time and place it is to be worn

Stimulation

As the first part of the presentation process, the teacher structures the following situation (many episodes are possible):

Anne, who is taller than most children her age and who has a pale complexion, went to her closet to pick an appropriate dress to wear to the sixth-grade class party. She had teased her mother to let her buy brightly colored blouses, skirts, sweat-

As the second part in presenting the lesson, the teacher asks a question to stimulate the children's thinking about the situation: "Why was Jane very happy about her clothes while Anne was very unhappy about hers?" In the ensuing discussion, the children produce a number of ideas. The teacher asks more stimulating questions, and more ideas are produced. The ideas are listed on the blackboard and become the objectives of the lesson.

If the structured situation and the stimulation have been well-planned, the ideas produced by the children and accepted by the class as the objectives for the lesson will be related to the learning goals found in the teacher's original lesson plan and unit.

In this illustration, the situation about which the children are encouraged to think is pertinently structured by the teacher in relation to the desired learning goals. Built into the structure (the plan) are the following contrasting elements:

1. Jane and Anne have different personalities.
2. Jane and Anne have different statures.
3. Jane and Anne have different complexions.
4. Jane and Anne are going to the same party and their wardrobes are different.

The ideas produced by the children grow out of the contrasting situations structured by the teacher under her guidance; they are not accidental. At the same time, the structured situation and the stimulating questions are sufficiently open to permit the development of more ideas than the teacher could possibly contrive and thus give the children an opportunity to identify learning goals for additional lessons. For a gifted child, particularly, this is important because it frees him from the limitations of the teacher's ability, frame of reference, ideas, and background and allows him to extend wherever his own ideas lead him.

Process activities

When the children have expressed their ideas and these have been translated, under the teacher's guidance, into learning goals for the lesson, the class is ready for the process activities of the lesson presentation. The teacher will develop with the children, on the basis of the ideas that have evolved from the stimulation, what activities will best lead to the learning goals. He will guide children in the selection of art materials that will be suitable both to their individual activities and to the children's intellectual and manipulative abilities. These

materials should be readily at hand, perhaps spread out on a table. The teacher should *not* distribute the materials and instruct the children formally in a step-by-step manner in their use. Neither should he allow each child to use just any material he wishes and do whatever he wants with it. Rather the teacher should guide the children to try out various materials in relation to their ideas and compare those that prove suitable for the ideas with those that prove unsuitable. The pupils should be allowed to experiment, not merely for fun, but as a learning experience. The "fun" will be experienced anyway because a creative experience with ideas and materials is inherently satisfying and enjoyable.

Again we shall use the story of Anne and Jane as an illustration. One of the objectives of this lesson is to understand that clothing design can seem to effect a change in stature. To stimulate thinking about this, the teacher might use two identical cardboard dolls, prepared for this stimulation as a visual aid, and swatches of different kinds of fabrics, including vertically striped material and a horizontally striped material. He would allow the children to try out the different fabrics on the doll figures to see how various colors, textures, and patterns affect the doll's appearance. By asking questions with divergent power, citing differences among the fabrics, the teacher would guide the children to see that the vertically striped fabric seems to make the dolls appear taller and the horizontally striped fabric to make them appear shorter.

Some educators argue that the importance of tools and materials in the art experience should be de-emphasized lest children's creativity be hampered by teachers who stress manipulation. In the author's opinion, however, the educational advantages of allowing children of this age to experiment (try out) with the art materials related to their ideas outweigh the danger of overconcern with technique. By trying out the related art materials—paper, cardboard, paint, crayon, chalk, clay, whatever may be the need—children learn what are the possibilities and limitations of each and derive greater satisfaction from the art experience as well as build a foundation for future use of the materials.

SAMPLE LESSONS

To illustrate some of the problems involved in planning and teaching an art lesson, three sample lessons (evolved by students working with the author) are given here. For Lesson 1, the teacher's plan for the lesson is followed by the transcript of a tape recording of the actual teaching procedure; the strengths and weaknesses of this lesson are then discussed. For Lessons 2 and 3 only the lesson plans are presented. These lessons have been chosen to illustrate how understanding of an art element, in this case the element of line, can be progressively developed over several grades.

LESSON PLAN 1 (Grade 2): Teacher's Plan

I. Objectives
 A. To understand that in many kinds of shelters the design is planned for those who live in them
 B. To understand that lines found in houses for people and animals make the houses so they can be lived in
 C. To understand that many kinds of materials are used to make houses
 D. To develop an awareness of straight and curved lines in our immediate environment—my room in my family's house

II. Scope of subject matter
 A. The lines in my family's house and in my pet's house are different because the way we live is different.
 B. Lines are curved and straight.
 C. Straight lines are most always man-made.
 D. Curved lines are most always found in nature.
 E. The two ends of lines can be bent or curved to meet and make shapes.
 F. When edges of shapes meet, a line is formed.
 G. Lines that go around things are outlines.
 H. Lines can be made to tell stories about our house, our family, and our friends.

III. Presentation
 A. Stimulation (an evaluative structure)
  1. Orientation
   Two different kinds of houses will be shown to the children. One is a model of a house in which people live. One is an actual house in which an animal lives (a snail shell). The children will be oriented to the characteristics of the houses by questions to which they respond.
  2. Questions
   Do these houses look like the houses in which you live? How are they something like your house? How are they not like your house? If you lived in this house (pointing to the shell), how would you get comfortable? How do you get into these houses? What kind of lines could be used to show other children what these houses are like? Do you have your own room in your house? Can you think of lines in your room which are straight? curved? How would a picture of your room look? Etc.
  3. Orientation of materials
   On the table there are many different materials in large boxes. A different material is in each box. There are drinking straws, yarn, chalk, and glue you have not used.
  4. Demonstration-experimentation
   Have the children try many things with the materials they selected from the boxes. Suggest that they choose the materials that will best tell the story about the lines in and around their houses. Give the children the opportunity to "show and tell" about their "tries." Cut, tear, sew, mark, glue, etc.
 B. Process activities
  1. Have children select their materials.
  2. Through visual materials, have children tell about the lines in their house and about the lines in nature around their house.

IV. Evaluation
 A. Children will come to the front of the class in small groups and point out the lines in their pictures—about the straight man-made lines in their pictures and the curved nature-made lines.
 B. Questions
  1. How can we see your picture lines better?
  2. What are important lines like?
  3. When you look at other children's pictures, can you tell what lines are more important?

V. Resource materials
 A. A model of a house (actual, slides, pictures, or movie)
 B. A snail shell (actual, slides, pictures, or movie)

VI. Art materials
 A. Assorted colored paper, 12 by 18 inches in size
 B. Vegetable glue
 C. Assorted yarn in varied lengths up to 18 inches
 D. Wax crayons. Boxes of 16 colors or assorted scraps.
 E. Colored chalk
 F. Assorted colored drinking straws

VII. Distribution and clean-up of materials
 A. The materials will be in six cardboard cartons measuring about 18 by 24 by 4 inches. (The cartons have been saved from the shipping room for school

supplies.) The boxes will be placed near the working area on a table.

B. The children will go to the boxes after the orientation and select the materials as they choose to use them. Twelve children working six on each side of the boxes at the table may select materials at one time.

C. At clean-up, six helpers will carry the boxes to the work areas, and materials will be placed in the designated box.

VIII. Time budget

A. Orientation: 15 minutes

B. Material distribution: 5 minutes

C. Activity period: 20 to 35 minutes

D. Clean-up: 5 minutes

LESSON 1 (Grade 2): Transcript of Lesson

T.—Teacher; *C.*—Child responding; *Ch.*—Children responding

T. We will take some materials to our desks so that we can start working after I have told you what to do. Miss A. will show you what you need. (*We sent children from two tables at a time to the supply table. Each child sat at a table; 20 children were in the class.*) Let's have this

group and this group go back to the supply tables for materials. (*Mr. M. pointed to a total of four children on five different occasions.*) As soon as they (*the first group*) come back to their seats, I want you to go and you to go. All right, next group go. Now, the next group. The last group may go back and get your art materials. (*The children were by now very excited.*)

T. Boys and girls, let's do this very quietly. (*The materials were placed in large low cardboard boxes. Each item was in a separate box. Items included colored straws; lengths of colored yarn; colored chalk; black, white, and colored paper; crayons; and tubes of glue.*)

T. When we all talk the room gets noisier and noisier. Don't worry about the number of straws you have because if you need more, you can get them at any time while you are working. So that will be no problem right now.

T. It is time for me to tell you what we will do in art today.

(*Stimulation begins.*)

T. Here is something I made. (*Mr. M. unveiled a model of an English Tudor-style house which he had made.*)

T. This is not what you are going to make.

Ch. (*Disappointed*) Oh!

T. This is a house, as you all can see.

Ch. How did you make it?

T. It is not quite like your house, is it?

Ch. No. It is better than my house. It isn't like my house. It is something like my house.

T. Well, it might be a little like your house. This is the kind of a house that people lived in a long time ago. We do not see very many houses just like it today. With boards like this and with grass roofs? But it does have some things like your house. What is it that this house has also?

Ch. Windows. Trees. A chimney.

T. Trees, shrubs, and a chimney for the smoke to go out.

C. Is there furniture in the house?

T. I think there would be if this were not just a model of a house.

C. A roof?

Ch. Every house has a roof.

C. A brown door.

T. It does have a door because every house has to have a door. What would happen if the house did not have a door?

Ch. We couldn't get out of the house.

T. We could get out if we crawled out of the windows.

Ch. (*Laughed at the idea of crawling out the windows.*)

T. I think this house, even though it is an old house, has some of the things that your house has because people of all times have needed the same things with which to live.

4.4. *This is the model of a house that Mr. M. showed to the class.*

4.5. This is the shell that Mr. M. showed to the class.

This model represents one kind of house. (*Mr. M. produced a large paper bag, reached into it, and began to take out something, as he said the following:*) I'm going to show you a real house. I have it in this paper bag. (*The children were all big-eyed with curiosity.*)

Ch. Can you get a house in that paper bag!

T. Oh yes. I have very special houses in this paper bag. (*At this point, Mr. M. removed a shell from the paper bag.*) You probably know who lives here.

Ch. (*in unison*) A snail!! Oh! Ah! A snail. It's a snail!

T. Yes. This is a house. Do you think it is a house?

Ch. Yes. It is a house.

T. It is the only house a snail has. So, we now have two different kinds of houses here.

Ch. Yes, we have.

T. They are not too much alike are they?

Ch. No.

T. They have something about them that is alike.

Ch. They are both houses. They both have doors.

T. What other things are the same?

Ch. They have roofs.

T. Could you live in this house? (*Mr. M. pointed to the shell.*)

C. (*Laughingly.*) Someone would step on it.

T. That is one thing to think about. This house is not as strong as your house. (*Mr. M. handled the shell in his fingers very gingerly.*)

Ch. (*Many comments about the shell house of the snail.*)

T. Why do you think a snail would not like to live in your house?

C. The snail might be stepped on as he was walking around my house.

T. Because of all the traffic in your house, someone might step on him.

C. There are no cars in my house. That's silly.

T. I mean people traffic; not car traffic. (*Still handling the shell.*) Do you think you would be very comfortable in this house?

C. No.

T. How would your body fit into it?

C. My finger couldn't even get into it.

T. Would your body be comfortable?

C. I'd be all bent up in it.

C. I might get an earache. When you put a shell to your ear, it makes a noise.

C. I'd be all uncomfortable.

T. The reason I brought these two houses today was so you could see if there is a difference between two houses. Who made this house? (*Mr. M. pointed to the model.*)

C. People.

T. Who made this house? (*Pointing to the shell.*)

C. The snail.

T. The snail didn't use boards and nails. So, we can say there is a big difference between this kind of house and this kind of house. (*Mr. M. pointed to each of the examples of houses.*) There is something about the lines of the houses that is different. If you were to draw the houses, you would use two different kinds of lines. What kinds of lines do you see in the two houses? How is this house like this shape? (*Mr. M. drew a shape with straight lines on the board.*) How is the shell like this shape? (*Mr. M. drew a shape with curved lines on the board.*) What kinds of lines are these? (*Pointing to the straight lines.*) What kinds of lines are these? (*Pointing to the shell.*) (*Then, pointing to the curved lines on the blackboard.*)

C. This line goes like this. (*Making a straight line up and down motion with his fingers.*) This kind of line is like this. (*Making a curved motion with the tip of the finger.*)

T. We call these straight lines. (*Motioning with finger and pointing to the line on the blackboard.*) We call these curved lines. (*Similar gestures related to curved lines.*) Many of the things people make have straight lines. That is not the way it is with houses that snails make. They have curved lines.

Ch. No. It isn't.

T. Do you know why? What do you use when you make straight lines?

C. I use a rule.

T. How about snails, do they use rules?

Ch. No! (*With an amused look on their faces.*)

T. Animals are not as smart as we are. What we are going to do is to make drawings today. We are going to think about the two kinds of lines. Since we have been talking about houses, let's think of your house. Let's think about your room in your house. What is in your room or around your house that has curved lines? What is made up of all straight lines? Most things that are made by man have straight lines in them. Most things that are made by animals or which you find outdoors are made of curved or crooked lines. So, I'm going to give you two things which you can use to glue. One is straight. One can be used to make curved lines. How can we get them to stay on to a surface like paper? (*Assorted straws, yarn, chalk, colored paper, crayons, and glue.*)

C. Paste them on.

C. Glue them on.

C. Tape them on.

T. You will be getting different kinds of paper. One paper is white while the other paper is black. Which drawing do you think that you will do with the black paper?

C. I'll do one with straws. They'll show up on the black paper.

T. Then we can see the drawing better. This is going to be a drawing of straight lines. On the white paper, we are going to do a drawing of curved lines. We can use our curved lines. We can make any curved lines we wish to make. We have lots of kinds of yarn. If you need more you will be able to go back to the supply table and get it. Think very hard about what you would like to draw. Curved lines will probably come from nature and

Figures 4.6–4.9
Plate VII

straight lines will be used in things that are made by man. Now, these straws are round and will roll. How can you make them easier to paste down?

C. Make them flat by pushing them in.

T. What if they are too long to make what you wish to make in your picture?

C. Cut them so they will fit.

T. We can also keep a straw in one piece. What I want you to do is to make your drawing with the straight lines first. After we have bent and glued down our straight-line drawing, we will work on our curved-line drawing. Then, when the glue is dry we can go back and work with chalk in our picture. Think of something to draw which is inside or outside your own home.

C. I have made a swing already.

C. I am making a robin. It has curved lines.

C. I am making a fish.

T. I will now give you each some glue in a squeezer. As soon as you have your glue, you may go to work. If you use one finger for glue, you will not get all glued up and messy. Shall we try not to be a messy class?

Ch. Yes.

C. May I use cutout paper in my picture?

T. You may if you want to use it with your other materials.

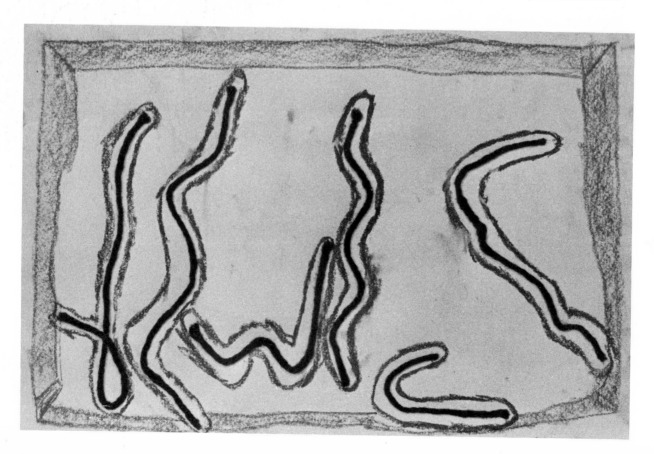

Five pictures that three of the children in Mr. M.'s class made are shown here, on the next page and in Plate VII. Note that though the teacher exhibited a house and a shell, these children did not portray houses. They seemed to be responding more to his rather casual suggestion to "think of something to draw which is inside or outside your own home." Should he have made this suggestion at all? **4.6.** *Douglas first used chalk and yarn in a manipulative way to create symbolic figure forms (presymbolic stage).* **4.7.** *Then Douglas thought of his own house and, looking down like a bird, he saw the street, lawn, and driveway. Is that form in the yard a see-saw, a swing, or what? In any case, it is a presymbol for play that he wished he were involved in.*

These two pictures were done by another child in Mr. M.'s class who also used chalk and yarn and then straws. **4.8.** Laura portrayed the hills and a winding stream near her house. In this presymbolic stage, she kept changing symbols. **4.9.** Then Laura also turned to her yard, as Douglas did, showing what is apparently a jungle gym.

C. I would like to, also.

(*At this point in the stimulation, every child was working. Mr. M. and Miss A. went around the room working with the children individually.*)

T. We can cut, and bend, and flatten things. Try to do these things with your materials.

EVALUATION OF LESSON PLAN 1 AS PLANNED AND TAUGHT

Weaknesses

1. Materials were distributed before the children had developed any ideas. In this way, the materials to be used by the children were predetermined by the teacher.
2. The teacher, in general, told and directed the children rather than orienting them and permitting them to think and present answers. For example, the teacher said: "We will take some materials to our desks so that we can start working after I have *told* you what to do." "It is time for me to *tell* you *what* we will do in art today." "Here is something I made." "*This is* a house, *as you all can see.*" "Most things that are made by man have straight lines." This directed teaching is apt to occur when the time allotted for the lesson is short. It is encouraged by rigid schedules.

3. Questions with divergent power were asked at the end of the stimulation, and factual questions at the beginning. The reverse of this practice would encourage the students' ideas and responses.
4. Although the use of a model and a shell set up an evaluative situation, the use of a third kind of house, such as a bird's nest, would have provided another type of house with an observably different structure. This structure could have been related to the use of straws as materials and would have given an understanding of the technique to which straws and yarn lend themselves.
5. The stimulation was prolonged beyond 15 minutes.

Figure 4.10

Strengths

1. The structure for the orientation developed a contrast and comparison which, with the use of a question with divergent power, gave children an opportunity to evaluate in terms of ideas that the question stimulated.
2. Materials used in the lesson included some which the children had already used and understood as well as new materials to expand their frame of reference of art techniques.
3. The lesson was developed within the ability level of the children and was related to their personal environment.

4.10. This is a typical bird's nest that might have been shown to contrast with the house and the shell. Notice the line qualities and how they are similar to both straws and yarn.

LESSON PLAN 2 (Grade 4): Teacher's Plan

I. Objectives
   A. To understand line as it relates to form and movement through an awareness of the gesture of the human body
   B. To understand that feeling may be expressed through line
   C. To understand that various characteristics of line may be combined to express the qualities of objects

II. Scope of subject matter
   A. Action may be created through line by use of vertical, angular, curve, and horizontal line directions.
   B. Linear movement is present in forms.
   C. Lines can express speed, height, tranquillity, dignity, etc., through straight, zigzag, short, long, broken, unbroken, or flowing lines.

III. Presentation
   A. Stimulation
      1. Orientation
         Play two contrasting excerpts from Tchaikovsky's *Nutcracker Suite:* "March" and "Waltz of the Flowers." The classroom will be darkened and the children, holding penlights in their hands, will create various movements to the music.
      2. Questions
         If we took pictures of the class moving their penlights to the music, what would the light lines look like?
         (Pictures are taken with a special camera that produces direct prints in the camera quickly. These prints are looked at carefully by the children.)
         How do the light lines in the picture showing movements to the "March" differ from those in the picture showing movements to the "Waltz of the Flowers"?
         What would the lines be like if we drew them to describe the entire body moving to the music? Let's try this with some of the materials on the table.
   B. Process activity
      After the stimulation, children select from the materials on the table and make drawings in which lines suggest the gestures of children posing and moving to the music being played. The children will be guided to seek a wide variety of line movements with their drawing materials. Following this, the children will see slides of drawings by contemporary artists in which they have used line in many interesting ways.

IV. Evaluation
   A. Look at your drawings and compare the differences in line, rhythm, etc.

   B. Question examples: "What are the lines like in the images we made while the selection 'March' was playing?" "Are they different from those in the drawings made while the selection 'Waltz of the Flowers' was playing?" "What do the lines seem to tell you?" "Do you have any lines that seem fast?" "Slow?" (etc.)

V. Resource materials
   A. Recording of *The Nutcracker Suite*
   B. Drawings and prints by contemporary artists
   C. Polaroid camera, film pack (black-and-white film)

VI. Art materials
   A. American white drawing paper, 18 by 24 inches
   B. Crayons (wax)
   C. Thick black pencil
   D. Cut paper
   E. Chalk
   F. Scissors
   G. Paste or rubber cement

VII. Clean-up
   A. Children will return materials to boxes in front, sides, and back of the room.
   B. Children will wipe their desks clean with damp towels.

VIII. Time budget
   A. Orientation and stimulation: 15 minutes
   B. Selection of materials: 15 minutes
   C. Activity: 25 minutes
   D. Clean-up: 5 minutes

LESSON PLAN 3 (Grade 5): Teacher's Plan

I. Objective
   To understand that aural stimuli to the emotions can be translated into line and movements expressed in the edges and surface of three-dimensional form

II. Scope of subject matter
   A. Experience in deriving mood from a piece of music and using it as inspiration in creating a form in carved sand core, soft wood, plaster of Paris, etc.
   B. Spontaneous creation of a form based on the musical inspiration.
   C. Line is observed in the edges and surfaces of three-dimensional form.

III. Presentation
   A. Stimulation
      1. Playing of portions of Stravinsky's *Rite of Spring*.
      2. Question: "How does this music make you feel?"
      3. Active evaluation of mood, for example, showing body positions inspired by music and discussion of feelings.
      4. Transfer of ideas into small sand-core forms, wood

forms, or plaster forms, etc., either abstract or figurative, as the student senses it.

    5. Question: "How can you carve the materials into a shape that shows your sense of feeling about the musical selection?"

  B. Process activity

    Carving of three-dimensional materials. Some children may prefer to model the form first with clay, papier-mâché, etc. Some may prefer to model only and not carve. Others may sense a feeling of form by working directly in the materials for carving or sculpting.

IV. Evaluation

    The student will be asked to describe the feeling he gets from the edges and surfaces of the carved or modeled materials. What do edges do? What do surfaces do? Where do the forms make lines?

V. Resource material: Record—*Rite of Spring*

VI. Art materials

  A. Sand core, soft pine, balsa wood, plaster of Paris, modeling clay, etc.

  B. Carving instruments: spoons, knives, sticks, pieces of metal, wood-carving tools

  C. Shellac

  D. Brushes

  E. Newspaper

  F. Paste

VII. Clean-up

  A. Each child will carry his own work to the front of the room and roll up his own newspaper.

  B. Children will sweep the floor.

VIII. Time budget

  A. Orientation: 10 minutes

  B. Stimulation using record, body movements, discussion: 15 minutes

  C. Process activity time: 1 hour or more

  D. Shellacking (may be done in another period of time, later): 15 minutes

  E. Clean-up: 10 minutes

SUMMARY

This chapter does not attempt to prescribe the "right" way to teach an art lesson. In any case, there *is* no one right way to teach art. What this chapter does do is use examples to try to clarify the nature of the creative-evaluative procedure in the actual teaching of a lesson.

The art lesson is part of the overall elementary school art curriculum. It is based on the specific objectives of the art unit.

For the teacher, the initial step is to plan the probable course of a lesson to achieve a direction with the children toward a learning goal. This includes structuring the stimulation from which children's ideas may be generated toward the learning goal, assembling art materials that may lend themselves to the children's probable ideas and to the children's level of ability and skill, amassing the resource materials to be used in the lesson, and allotting appropriate time to each phase of the lesson.

A lesson that stimulates many ideas in children will usually not go according to a plan, because the essence of creative-evaluative teaching is its flexibility and allowance for individual involvement of children. However, the plan helps the teacher allow for the unanticipated and use it constructively.

Three sample lesson plans are presented.

In addition to structuring (planning) the lesson, the teacher should make sure that his proposed lesson meets the following criteria:

1. The lesson should be appropriate to the children's experience level.
2. The lesson should permit sufficient variety of interpretation to satisfy each child's inner vision.
3. The materials and tools of expression should be appropriate to the children's manipulative and mental ability.
4. The lesson should lead to further self-development of the children.
5. The objective of the lesson should be worthwhile in terms of healthy mental and behavioral growth for the children.

The teacher begins the lesson by structuring a situation composed of comparable but contrasting elements and asking questions with divergent power to stimulate the children to have ideas about the situation. Under the teacher's guidance, the ideas are developed to become the objectives of the lesson. If the structured situation and the stimulation have been well planned, these objectives developed from the children's ideas will be related to the learning goals set up for the lesson.

AIDS TO UNDERSTANDING

For discussion

1. How do you account for the fact that when a teacher applies a creative strategy for teaching art, the art activities and resulting art products will differ from classroom to classroom?
2. What is the relationship of the art lesson to the art curriculum?
3. What is the difference between the scope and the sequence of the curriculum?
4. How would the objectives of an area of art experience differ from an art unit and objectives for an art lesson? In what way are they similar?
5. With reference to the lesson developed in the chapter, how did the situations concerning Anne and Jane differ?
6. Would the situation relating to Anne and Jane be more effective as a stimulation presented visually or verbally? Suggest three possible ways in which either could be done.
7. Constructively respond to the author's evaluation of strengths and weaknesses of Lesson 1 presented in this chapter. How does your evaluation agree with the author's? How does it differ?

For involvement

1. Write an objective for an area of art experience.
2. Write an objective for a unit related to the previous area of art experience (see item 1).
3. Write a series of specific objectives related to the objective developed for the previous unit (see item 2).
4. Develop a series of lesson plans related to the specific objectives already developed (see item 3) as follows:
   a. Objective
   b. Scope of subject matter
   c. Presentation
      (1) Stimulation
      (2) Activities
   d. Evaluation
   e. Resource materials and references
   f. Art materials
   g. Clean-up
   h. Time budget
5. Using the objective of Lesson Plan 2, Grade 4 (or Lesson 3, Grade 5) in this chapter, develop a plan completely different from the one presented.

Chapter 5
CHILDREN'S INVOLVEMENT
IN THE ART LESSON

The presentation of the art lesson is the function of the teacher. This has been discussed in the previous chapter. If the stimulation is relevant, in terms of the visual aids used and the content, the lesson will be both interesting and understandable for the child. Too frequently, the teacher does not recognize the child's part in the art lesson. His involvement begins when he gains ideas through the teacher's stimulation related to his needs and interests. This is a process of motivation which leads to processes of art activities relevant to the child.

In the field of art, there are hundreds of right answers, all dealing with individuals in their own way. Related answers come about when a child has opportunity to gain an idea, select materials in relation to it, explore the materials, and, ultimately, find a means of shaping the material or combined materials to express in some visual way his own idea.

It is the purpose of this chapter to show how the child becomes involved in the art lesson. His involvement comes about through opportunities to be stimulated, to choose an idea of his own, to select materials, and to formulate materials into things that have meaning for him.

CHOICE OF IDEA THROUGH RELATED INTEREST AREAS

Below are listed 27 general categories of needs and interests that may be the basis of areas of art interest and experience that, when used effectively in stimulations for art lessons, will elicit ideas from most children.

1. Everyday needs of life
2. Special events
3. Transportation
4. Visual communication
5. Responsibilities at home
6. Having animals as pets
7. Recreation through play
8. Stories children know and tell
9. Visits to interesting places
10. Acting out a character
11. People children know
12. Family
13. Neighborhood friends
14. Shelter
15. Dreams and wishes
16. Providing protection
17. People at work
18. Happenings that bring security
19. Clothing
20. Audiovisual experiences
21. Imaginary situations
22. Exploring new or unusual materials
23. School events
24. Community social groups
25. Helping others
26. Religious life and customs
27. Ideals of living

The teacher can use some of these general categories as the basis for stimulation and eliciting ideas from the children and for allowing each child to choose within some general area a subject that appeals to him. Examples of how some of the broad areas can be broken down into specific content are shown in Appendix I.

SELECTION OF MATERIALS

Each child should be involved in opportunities to select materials in relation to his ideas. In this chapter we shall discuss the manner in which this comes about.

The child needs to experiment to learn what possibilities are inherent in art materials. He needs to reflect on the many problems of using them. Experimenting with art materials also includes comparative situations as does the lesson stimulation. The child can evaluate two more or less different materials and, as a result, select the more appropriate way to use the materials in relation to his idea. When the teacher is asking questions with divergent power, teacher-pupil interaction is involved. When the child has direction, this is a personal dialogue. This is part of the whole art experience. If it is neglected, the child's understanding of art materials is jeopardized.

A resource guide to art materials, presented in Appendix IV, is designed to assist the elementary school teacher in guiding children in the techniques of working with art materials and handling related tools. It is hoped that the teacher will use this appendix to set up comparative situations relating to the various materials and en-

5.1. *The child needs to experiment with materials. One sixth-grader tried out several methods of printing, including the pie-plate silk-screen printing shown here. Ultimately, she decided to use this technique for a picture that began to evolve in her mind.*

5.2. *This is one of the many types of printing techniques that can be used in involving children in art. The fourth-grader is absorbed as he prepares to use a screw press.*

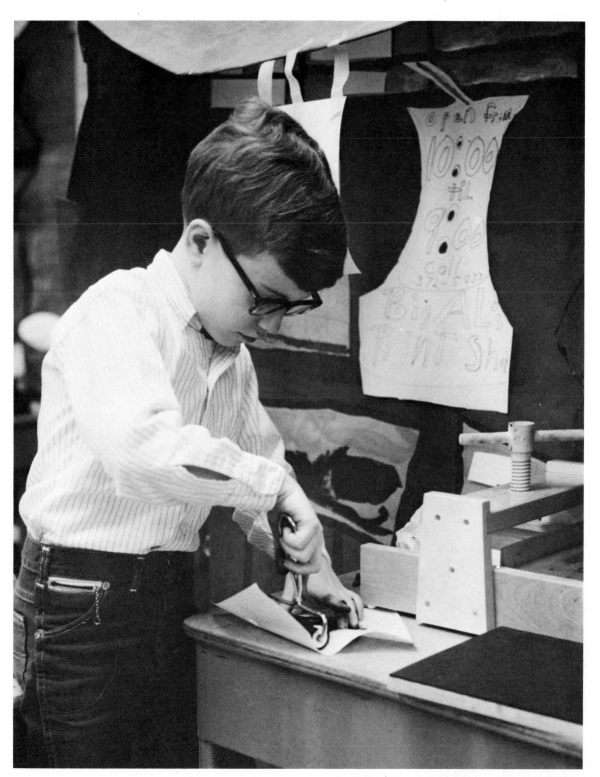

5.3. *Four children experiment with making compositions by rolling printer's ink of different colors directly onto the paper with brayers. As they work, they share their experiences with one another. They are likely to come up with different effects they can compare. This kind of interaction during an art activity can be very stimulating, not only to the children but also to the teacher.*

courage the children to explore and experiment with them in a reflective manner. Thus, they will learn the characteristics and limitations of the materials.

It is essential, therefore, that the teacher alert the children to the possible uses of art materials through demonstrations involving the children, through observation of materials, and through visual aids which *Figure 5.3* show two or more conditions the children may compare. The conditions should apply to the child's idea. For example, if as a result of a stimulation by the teacher, the child decides to create a pot, a film

showing the various possibilities of building clay by coil, slab, or pinch techniques gives him an opportunity to select from among the procedures. If the child has an opportunity to try out each approach in a simple way, he can evaluate his tries and decide which approach is most suitable to his idea.

In another situation, the teacher can demonstrate working with clay to small groups or to the entire class. In this demonstration the teacher should bring out, through the children's observation of his working with clay, that the clay may be too wet or too dry or just damp

5.4. *Papier-mâché is messy, but it is fun! One boy was so eager to begin that he forgot to roll up his sleeves—the teacher is remedying the situation. The other boy holds a roll of newspaper destined to become the backbone of a fierce tiger.*

Figure 5.4

enough to be plastic. He should be careful to ask questions that focus the children's attention on the condition of the clay and the different ways of working with the clay. He should avoid telling the children what they are obviously observing. Through this kind of orientation, the teacher guides the children in exploring, experimenting, and evaluating the material so that each can select a material that best fits the requirements of his idea for a visual product. A creative approach to the children's involvement with materials is essential to creative art experience for the children.

As the child is challenged through this kind of evaluative guidance, the shape of his materials will develop into the shape of his ideas. From this point, the teacher should tackle in a similar creative-evaluative manner the problems of design that arise in the process of the formulation of the visual product. The result will be that the child will create *his own art work* in terms of *his own needs and interests* and in relation to *his own situation*. The product that results will be his. It is important that the elementary school classroom teacher understand that the child's art product is not to be evaluated by adult standards. He must accept the idea that with continued creative-evaluative orientation to art materials, the child's knowledge of materials and techniques will develop as he progresses from experience to experience through each grade level.

SAMPLE LESSON IN TEACHING TECHNIQUES WITH MATERIALS

LESSON PLAN 4 (Grade 6): Teacher's Plan[1]

I. Objectives
   A. To understand the relief process in creating visual expression
   B. To understand that materials determine to a large degree the nature of a design
   C. To understand that good design is the basis of good art quality

II. Scope of subject matter
   A. Positive and negative relations are basic to good design.
   B. To develop an awareness that emotional quality results from limiting colors.
   C. To understand the effect of materials on the product in size, simplicity, use of space, color, quality of line, etc.

III. Presentation
   A. Stimulation
     1. Display four or more contrasting relief prints.
     2. Display four or more prints of contemporary paintings directly beneath these prints.
     3. Question: "What comparison can we make in terms of the media between the prints and the reproductions of the paintings?" (*Color—the prints were in one and two colors and the paintings were done in many colors.*)
     4. Demonstration: The children will carve marks on linoleum and soft pine wood scraps, ink the surface of these materials with a brayer, and print "tries" on various kinds of scraps of paper. Questions: "What is the difference between printing from a block and painting?" (*Children have done much painting in their past art experience.*) "Which of the modern paintings would seem to make the more successful relief print?" (*Some were very complex in detail and others were of varying degrees of abstraction.*) "Why would the painting you selected be more suitable?"

Figures 5.5–5.8 (right column)

(*Size, interest, simple design quality, limitations of the relief process of printing.*) "What are the differences between printing and painting?" "What are the advantages of the printing process?" (*Reproduction of many similar products.*)
   B. Process activities
     1. Distribute tools and blocks for the children's "tries."
     2. Children will cut marks on the block, ink, and print.
     3. Each student will select a variety of paper to "try." This will be followed by an evaluative discussion.
     4. Children will draw directly on their blocks with crayon, felt-tip pen, or india ink.
     5. The white space will be cut away, and the blocks inked and printed.
     6. The student will select his preference of paper from many and will be able to select a number of colors of ink.

IV. Resource materials
   A. Collection of paintings or lithographic reproductions of paintings
   B. Collection of artists' prints

V. Art materials
   A. Linoleum, soft pine wood
   B. Assorted paper (white, colored, newspaper pages, textured paper, colored pictures from magazines, etc.)
   C. Felt-tip pens, crayons, india ink
   D. Brayers and cutting tools
   E. Slabs to roll printer's ink on
   F. Printer's ink

VI. Clean-up
   A. Each student will keep his own area clean.
   B. Two students will clean the areas designated for inking and printing. They will take turns.

DESIGN: SHAPING THE MATERIALS TO RELATE TO THE IDEA

As the child continues to be challenged, the shape of the material should evolve from his idea. When the child shapes something visually that results in a satisfying statement, he has participated in a design experience. Designing is a process of arranging plastic elements according to basic design principles. In designing, the child explores the nature of the art material, makes independent artistic judgments, and is aware of the relationship of his visual product to his social environment—his own surroundings.

When visual form is satisfying to the child, it is his product. In the process of achieving it, the child has

[1] Courtesy of Rodney Fogel, student of the author at Kutztown State College.

5.5. Making rugs satisfies the need children feel at times to produce something. These sixth-graders are at various stages on their latchet-hooked rugs.

many aesthetic experiences with his product. He decides that it is too large or too small, too bright or too dull, too thick or too thin, and too light or too dark. This dialogue is an experience of visual sensitivity. The design is complete when the child senses that the elements seem to belong together—to unite. Every art object when it seems to be complete has unity. If an idea is beautiful or ugly, it is an art form when the final visual object expressing it has unity. Generally, beautiful forms are the more satisfying; however, ugly forms, although not always aesthetically satisfying, may be very expressive in terms of the thinking of the child and have a quality of unity.

In the early years the process of creating a form and the satisfaction of having shaped it into a final product are of primary importance in the development of the child's consciousness of unity. As the child's frame of reference expands in art, the quality of the design of the product becomes more and more important.

To help the classroom teacher in understanding terms and relevant understandings of design Appendix V is provided. Reference to a specific source on design will provide the elementary teacher with greater understanding of design when he feels the need for it.[2]

CAUTIONS ABOUT TEACHING ART

Creation versus the use of devices

The first 10 years of life are the most vital in the child's

[2] Carl J. Heyne, Florence W. Nicholas, Margaret M. Lee, and Mabel B. Trilling, *Art For Young America,* 5th ed., Peoria, Ill., Chas. A. Bennett, 1967, chap. V.; Luise C. Kainz and Olive L. Riley, *Exploring Art,* New York, Harcourt, Brace & World, 1951, chaps. III, XI; Elizabeth Adams Hurwitz, *Design, A Search for Essentials,* Scranton, Pa., International Textbook, 1964, chaps. V, VI, VII (for understanding in depth).

5.6. *String and yarn are among the many simple materials that can be transformed by children who are involved in art. The children here are making constructions and pictures.*

that the use of workbooks produces regression in creative growth, stereotypy, and reliance on "crutches."[4] Patterns, ready-made posters to be colored, and "idea" books have similar ill effects. To wean the child from these "aids" is a difficult, if not impossible, task. Once attached to them, the child derives a great deal of false satisfaction from such "aids." After all, they are created by adult artists; thus the child feels that he is doing good work when he is coloring in the images. When the child then attempts to work at his own level, he is very much aware of the differences between his work and the coloring work and rejects his own as not being "good." Similarly, the common practice of allowing elementary school children to copy and trace pictures not only discourages creativity but encourages outright dishonesty. Teachers of art cannot sanction such practices.

To the classroom teacher who asks "What is there to replace these convenient and time-hallowed devices?" there is but one answer: "Let the child have opportunity to work with a creative teacher and develop naturally within his *own* potential abilities and skills." Children need only opportunity and encouragement to work in art as art. Enlightened specialists in other fields are becoming aware of the harm caused by devices and of the superiority of means that evoke thinking and original work on the part of the child.

Contests and competitions

Contests and competitions have many negative aspects at all levels of the public schools; however, they are most harmful in the elementary school because of the

creative development.[3] Personal independence, wholesome social attitudes, confidence, individuality, and other important characteristics of behavior are related to early experience at home and particularly in the elementary school. Over the years, certain damaging devices have appeared in the guise of educational aids for art classes. Among these are certain workbooks, coloring books, pattern books, holiday project books, numbered paintings, camp or playground craft kits, and instruction manuals. The irreparable harm these devices inflict on artistic growth and on the confidence of the child has long been suspected, and sufficient evidence has now been amassed to demonstrate the dangers inherent in the "aids." For example, a study has shown

[3] E. Paul Torrance, *Constructive Behavior: Stress, Personality, and Mental Health,* Belmont, Calif., Wadsworth Publishing, 1965, pp. 88–95, 99–113.

[4] Horace F. Heilman, "An Experimental Study of the Effects of Workbooks on the Creative Drawing of Second-Grade Children," doctoral dissertation, University Park, Pennsylvania State University, 1954.

When children are able to select materials
from many available types and when they
are challenged by questions with divergent
power, each one ends up with a solution—
an art work—that is right for him—and
therefore right for everyone else who sees
the work. These two examples illustrate
these points with particular effectiveness.
5.7. A fourth-grader portrayed a king
and queen in torn paper. **5.8.** When a
sixth-grader wanted to show life under
the water, she chose the medium of a wax
crayon on paper batik. This child is in the
stage of analytical realism.

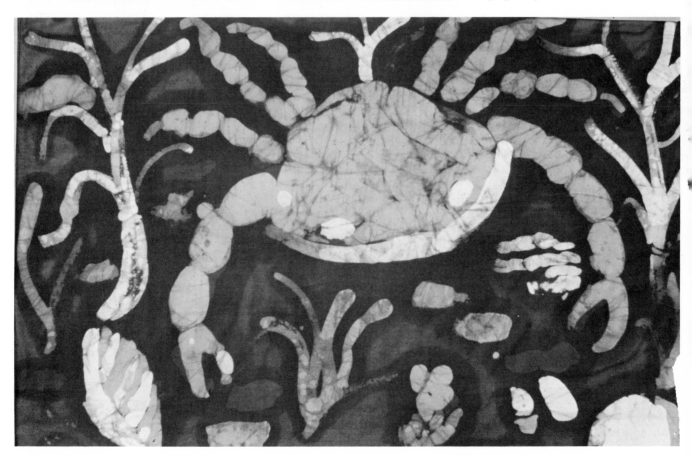

impressionable nature of the children. The National Art Education Association in a recent publication takes the following position on this subject:

The elementary program is related generally to individual growth and development. Children are expected to achieve in terms of their individual capabilities and at their own speed. Growth is measured on a personal basis. While one may contrast against this viewpoint the acceptance of the spirit of competition as a part of the American way of life, it seems inappropriate to permit competitive elements to enter the elementary art program. Rather, it is more appropriate to build on individual growth in creative expression, in developing healthy, positive attitudes towards art, in giving art significance as an important element in daily living. The elementary art program does not attempt to develop ''artists,'' while most contests and competitions tend to have this type of orientation—at least to the point that they identify and reward selected individuals for being more successful than others.[5]

The sum and substance of the objections may be summarized thus: work involved in competition is usually imposed, is irrelevant to children's interests, relies on forced technique for the sake of prizes, places a premium on cleverness rather than on creation, gives winners a false notion of their true abilities and losers a sense of futility and frustration. Is a prize worth all this?

Children can, however, be encouraged to take part in outside special activities when recognition is given to all who take part, and honors, in the form of ribbons or certificates, constitute recognition of participation in extracurricular art activities in the support of worthy community needs. A general award to a school is preferred, as the award emphasizes the participation of the group rather than spotlighting the achievement of an individual child.

SUMMARY

Children are involved in art in a very personal way. This chapter describes how the child becomes involved in the art lesson and the responsibility of the classroom teacher to bring about his involvement. It also cautions about the deleterious effects of certain devices used in

art classes and about the harm that can be done by contests and competition in which the individual is rewarded.

Involvement does not mean that the child discovers independently but rather that he discovers when the stimulation and questions with divergent power of the teacher cause him to be intrinsically involved. When motivated by a set of circumstances, the child is involved in his ideas, the selection of materials, the testing of materials, and the forming of materials into a satisfying art work that is his own. His involvement is a dialogue in terms of the goals of a lesson objective. At a point, it is a private affair, and the teacher enters the situation only to cause the child to extend his involvement in the dialogue.

So that the child's experience can be extended, the structured situation and the questions that stimulate the child should be geared to his level of ability and frame of reference. The child's involvement in the process of the art activities should also be so geared. In the total situation of the art lesson, the direction of the lesson should be interesting to the child and within the range of his experience and relevant to his needs and interests.

A number of general areas of needs and interests are listed which elicit ideas from most children, the process of selecting and working with materials is discussed, a sample lesson related to the presentation and orientation of art materials and techniques is given, and the process of selecting materials and creating a design that expresses the creator's idea to his satisfaction is described. The resource aids presented in Appendixes I, IV, and V are relevant to the content of this chapter.

Two cautions are voiced: (1) Allowing children to use devices such as workbooks, coloring books, paint-by-number kits irreparably damages their creative growth. (2) Awarding prizes in contests and competitions places a premium on cleverness, not creativity; the winner derives a false sense of his own ability, the loser a sense of frustration. It is better to have children take part in worthy art activities where all who participate are recognized, or a general award to a school is given for their community participation in art.

[5] Mary M. Packwood, ed., *Art Education in the Elementary School,* Washington, D.C., National Art Education Association, 1967, pp. 84–85.

AIDS TO UNDERSTANDING

For discussion

1. How do the teacher's stimulation of and the child's involvement in the art lesson differ?
2. Do you think that teaching begins with the subject of art, art behavioral activities, or the child's need for art as a producer or consumer?
3. How does a child's involvement in the selection of materials relate to the original teacher stimulation of the art lesson? Is this consistent with a definition of art and the actual experience of a creating artist?
4. Re-examine the approaches to teaching as they relate to theories of learning presented in Chapter 2. Discuss these as they relate to teaching art so that the child has a real involvement consistent with a definition of what art is: "the expression of one's idea with materials selected and formulated to convey the meaning."
5. Stage a debate on the following topic: In a creative-evaluative strategy for art teaching, the teaching of techniques of using materials and the designing of the materials and space around them are essential to the total art lesson.
6. How would selecting materials for an art lesson differ in these two types of classrooms: one in which the creative-evaluative approach is used and one in which the directed approach is used?
7. What might happen if a child's work were evaluated by standards for adults, particularly for professional artists?
8. What observable differences may exist between children's art products that seem to express qualities of design and those that do not?
9. As a child is involved with shaping material, he is involved in a dialogue that is an experience of visual sensitivity. How does such an experience differ from that of following a teacher's directions, copying another's work, tracing and coloring in predrawn imagery?
10. Is a prize won in an art contest or competition worth the negative feedback that might become evident later in the child's experiences in the classroom and in his life?

For involvement

1. Develop a list of general categories of children's needs and interests which may serve as basis of areas of art interest and experience for a particular elementary school whose educational conditions you have observed.
2. Prepare a breakdown of each of your general categories of needs and interests into specific content.
3. Select a specific need or interest of children suitable to a particular elementary grade level and develop a lesson plan of presentation in which a creative-evaluative strategy is employed in the stimulation, selection of materials, and shaping of the materials in relation to ideas stimulated.
4. Arrange for a planned visit to a school and observe how the teacher stimulates pupils, what type of stimulation is used, what types of questions are asked. Note whether children are motivated to gain personal ideas, how children select materials, to what shapes their products relate. Develop a constructive analysis of this lesson in terms of the three approaches to teaching presented in this text and in terms of your careful judgment of whether or not the children personally had an art experience or were following directions of the teacher.
5. List the strengths and weaknesses of the art lesson you observed.
6. Using the same objective of the lesson you observed, rewrite the lesson plan, showing evidence of the application of your constructive suggestions.
7. Compare the art products of an art lesson using a creative-evaluative strategy with those of one in which children followed the directions of the teacher. Which products exhibited original forms with a great variety of expression?

Chapter 6
UNDERSTANDING CHILDREN'S ART

To fulfill his responsibility for guiding the child's creative expression, the teacher must understand the relation between a child's level of growth and the stage of his creative visual development. Creative development in this context refers to the sequential emergence of artistic ability and perceptual awareness. Growth includes not only chronological aging, but also intellectual, physical, emotional, aesthetic, and social maturation. The relation between growth level and stage of creative development has been determined on the basis of psychological studies that show that *most children* of a certain age have developed particular artistic abilities and perceptions. A means of reference for relating growth to creative development, shown in Table 6.1, is the basis for the organization of this chapter.[1] (Tables 6.1 through 6.7 are included at the end of this chapter.)

Although a relation based on the growth and

[1] The system has been adapted from I. L. deFrancesco, *Art Education: Its Means and Ends,* New York, Harper & Row, 1958, p. 572.

behavior of the "average" child is inherently limited, it is nevertheless a useful basis for structuring an art program. It is valuable as a guide because children differ in the rate of their intellectual, physical, emotional, aesthetic, and social growth, so that, for example, one 8-year-old is more mature, and another less mature, than the average. It is useful because the teacher deals with classes of children within the same age group, and he can do so effectively if he is aware of the psychological findings about the creative visual characteristics, interests, and needs of the "average" child at the various age-grade levels. He can then develop his teaching on the basis of factors recognized as common to most children in a particular class and be prepared to deal separately with the individuals who are faster or slower than the "average" in achieving developmental levels. Such a procedure utilizes the teacher's time and energy effectively and still provides for special attention to the exceptional pupils.

In this chapter we shall discuss the development of creative expression through visual arts from early childhood through adolescence. While the chief emphasis is on the work of elementary school children, the characteristics of older children's and adolescents' art are referred to briefly to enable the teacher to recognize the work of gifted children. The text discussion concerns the characteristics of the child's art at each stage of creative visual development. Tables 6.2 through 6.5 list the major characteristics, interests, needs, and responses of the "average" child from nursery school through Grade 9; Table 6.7 lists these qualities for the teenager. These tables indicate possible means of stimulation which nurture creative visual development. The teacher should use them as guides in developing a visual learning atmosphere that nurtures children's creative art experiences. Table 6.6 summarizes how creative visual development can be expected to progress during the elementary school years.

6.1. A child 3 to 4 years old manipulates materials to gain control over them. Mostly, he scribbles, making crude, aimless movements as he ranges over the paper in front of him.

THE MANIPULATIVE STAGE (AGES 2–5)

In this early phase of creative visual development, the child manipulates the materials to develop control over them. He should be able to select different materials to try. Handling and grasping a crayon in different ways or thumping, squeezing, and forming a lump of clay are his chief preoccupations. As Hurlock points out, for a young child, owing to poor muscle coordination, activity with thick pencils, paints, and crayons consists mainly of scribbling, making crude, aimless movements over whatever space is available.[2] It is exploratory. A child of 3, 4, or 5 is happy when given a chance to create a riot of color on a large sheet of paper, and is ready to show some initiative in shaping it. The child usually forms the color into some indistinct shapes. Not until he is older does the child repeat many forms over the area of his paper. The child does not associate colors with real objects, but merely senses the difference among colors.

Figure 6.1

Plate IX

[2] Elizabeth B. Hurlock, *Child Development,* 4th ed., New York, McGraw-Hill, 1964, pp. 458–459.

6.2

Mastery comes with continued trying. In the manipulative stage, the child progresses from uncontrolled scribbles to purposeful scribbles. **6.2.** When the very young child scribbles, one blank space is as good as another. **6.3.** This scribbling is a little less uncontrolled there are random circles and up-and-down movements. **6.4.** There is a feeling of purpose in these curving arc-like lines. **6.5.** Finally, these mixed lines give an impression that the child had a definite purpose—that he was drawing "something."

6.3

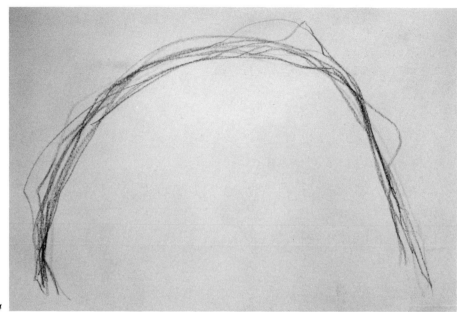

6.4

6.5

He should be allowed to choose them and work with colors that hold his interest. (See Table 6.2.)

Early in his life, a child needs opportunities to manipulate materials with his arms, hands, and fingers so that he is able to develop his physical coordination. Thus, the works produced by a young child fill a physical as well as a creative need. His scribbling is important; it involves his whole self; it should be encouraged, watched, and guided. Mastery comes with continued trying. As the child grows, the kinesthetic enjoyment continues; but from the developmental standpoint, it is the visual realization of what he has scribbled that interests him. He progresses from uncontrolled scribbles to purposeful scribbles; horizontal, up-and-down, random circles, and mixed-line movements, often in wide or long sweeping strokes. However, he does not yet name his images. At this stage the teacher should be careful not to discourage the child by asking thoughtless questions such as "Is it your toy?" or "Is that your house?" The child uses the same shape for a number of things and changes the meaning of the form to suit his mood. The teacher should also refrain from forcing the child to draw or paint specific things, but should stimulate the child in such a way that he is able to express himself freely.

At this age level the child enjoys manipulating clay and brushing colors over paper with abandon. His handling of these and other media parallels his progress with thick pencil and crayon drawings. Clay is a very suitable material for kinesthetic development and can be given to quite a young child. His initial pounding, pulling, and flattening attempts progress to spontaneous expressions of elemental form concepts. On the other hand, when he is painting, a very young child usually picks out a particular color. This is not so visually distracting as to interfere with his kinesthetic development. After the child has achieved motor control, he should be encouraged to use the primary colors—red, yellow, and blue. He is very curious when they mix together and make new colors—orange, green, and purple. This is one of his first exciting visual discoveries. He is interested in colors for this appeal rather than because they relate to anything.

Figures 6.2–6.5

Figures 6.6–6.8 (right column)

Plate X (right column)

Figures 6.9–6.15 Plates XI–XII (right column)

THE PRESYMBOLIC STAGE (AGES 5–7)

At this stage, the child is still concerned with developing control over his tools and materials, but has usually achieved sufficient skill to make his scribbling represent what he is thinking about at the moment. As the result is not generally recognizable as a real object, but is a symbol form, the teacher should not attempt to quiz the child, but should be interested in the shapes the child has depicted as simple visual expressions. The child has names for the symbols he creates—often "me," "my family," "my friends." Since he has not yet developed a clear concept of people and things in his environment, his drawings depict these elements in geometric or abstract shapes—a circle stands for the head, broad horizontal lines for the arms, broad vertical lines for the legs. Seldom are all parts of the body present, although especially precocious children may have fairly complete symbols for "me," "boy," "girl," "house," "tree," "dog," "cat."

The child usually begins to notice spatial relations; however, there is no orderly arrangement of background, foreground, or middle ground. His paintings often show a number of objects—which he can identify by name because of emotional relations—arranged over the entire sheet of paper. However, his work is not "composed" in the adult sense, and he is not aware of perspective.

The child at this stage of creative development needs abundant opportunities for personal experience. Since his chief interests are "me" and "my," his art experience should involve participation in events closely related to himself. (See Tables 6.2 and 6.3.)

THE SYMBOLIC STAGE (AGES 7–9)

By this time the child has acquired enough physical coordination to give him greater skill with art tools and materials. He has also gained experience and accompanying knowledge to augment his natural tendencies for visual expression. He has a clearer concept of people and things and begins to use more specific symbols to depict them. For example, he uses bent lines to suggest

MAN

6.6. *Evidence of a circle for the head may appear as early as 3½ years and as late as 5 years, depending on many individual factors.*

movement of the body and limbs of his figures. He still uses geometric shapes to portray his ideas, but adds, subtracts, or varies certain elements according to the subject he is depicting. The change relates to the importance the child attaches to the subject. The child's work is purposeful in the sense that the product has meaning for him. However, it is usually not representational, but rather expresses the child's feelings about the subject.

Also at this stage the child exhibits a sense of spatial relations—both an abstract concept of space and a sense of the position and direction of things in space. He regularly uses a base line in his pictures. At times he stacks up base lines to tell the whole story or draws the base line around the edges of his paper to show the whole scene. He also produces folded-over and X-ray pictures. In the folded-over type of expression, objects are arranged on both edges of the picture and the sky is in the center. In the X-ray type of expression, objects are shown in their actual physical, rather than their visual, relation because the child does not yet realize that when

The presymbolic stage merges with the symbolic stage. The age at transition depends on the individual child. 6.7. A precocious child only a little over 3 years old represents a fairly complete symbol for "me." 6.8. A first-grader paints his symbol for "cat."

IV. *Mary Cassatt (1845–*
1926), The Bath
(La Toilette).
(The Art Institute of Chicago,
Robert A. Waller Fund)

V. Pablo Picasso (1881–   ), First Steps.
(Yale University Art Gallery, gift of Stephen C. Clark)

6.9. *In the symbolic stage, a 7-year-old has a clearer concept of people and things and begins to use more specific symbols for them.*

several objects are viewed from one point, one object may partially conceal another. To the child everything is important and should be seen simultaneously. The child at this stage also lacks a realization of time-space relations and is apt to portray several events in one picture.

Color, used by the young child for its emotional meaning, for the older child begins to assume some significance in relation to objects. At first the child's feeling about the object determines the color he assigns it; later he discovers that various objects in his environment are differently colored.

Three-dimensional materials, such as clay and papier-mâché, provide useful art experiences at this stage of development, particularly for the child whose artistic sense is more kinesthetic than visual. The properties inherent in these materials allow him to discover the limitations as well as the possibilities of working with the media. (See Table 6.3.)

Plates XIII–XIV

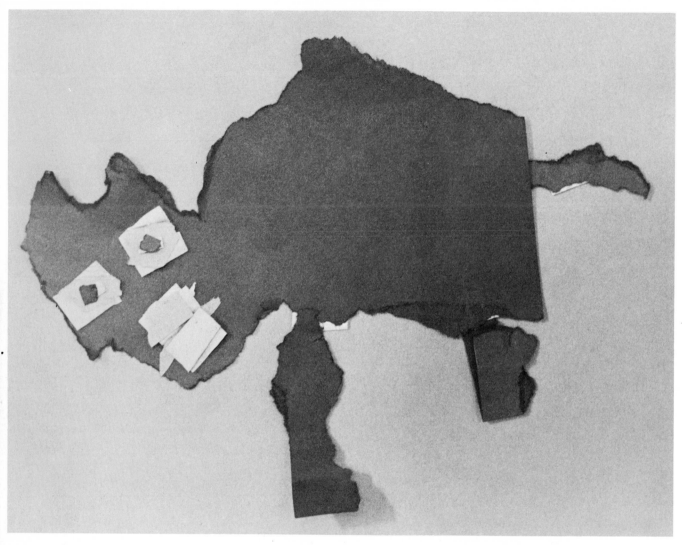

Tearing or cutting and then pasting pieces of colored paper is a process that lends itself to the geometric stage of symbolism. *6.10.* A first-grader made this cat of torn paper. *6.11.* In this composition of cut paper, notice the typical stick-like trees and the base line. The sky is not seen here, but it is felt, since the top line of the trees represents the sky line.

82

83

6.12, 6.13. These pictures show how two different children remember the clowns they saw at a circus. Each has invented his own geometric shapes to portray his clown, with very different results. There is one thing the two children definitely agree on, though: a clown is a happy guy!

6.14. *This child, aged 7, has a symbolic concept of space and a sense of the position and direction of things in space. Portraying Halloween night, he shows the sky "up there," the air "right here," and the ground "down there." The witch and the moon also are up where they belong. The people apparently disagree in their feelings about Halloween—they are symbolically both happy and sad.*

6.15. *A 9-year-old in the later symbolic stage uses the X-ray type of expression in this crayon resist. Note that virtually everything is shown whole, with little indication of depth.*

THE STAGE OF
REALISTIC AWARENESS
(AGES 9–11)

At this stage in his creative development the child becomes increasingly aware of his environment and perceives it with understanding as well as feeling. The symbols that have up to now sufficed to express his ideas are no longer adequate. He notices the characteristics of the parts of an object, as well as the whole object, and sees the relation of the whole and the parts. He notices that similar objects are different in detail. As a result of this increasing awareness, his artistic expression begins to become realistic rather than symbolic.

The child's sense of spatial relations continues to develop. Perspective replaces folding-over in his pictures. He tries to indicate background, middle ground,

Figures 6.16–6.17
Plate XV

6.18. A 10-year-old boy in the realistic awareness stage depicts a city in which objects overlap. The car overlaps the bus; the bus overlaps the buildings. Perspective is felt, and there is no X-ray feeling in the buildings or vehicles.

In the stage of realistic awareness, the child notices the characteristics of the parts of an object, as well as the whole object. He notices that similar objects are different in detail. 6.16. An 11-year-old boy who lives in Honolulu shows the characteristics of various types of people of the Hawaiian Islands. He has noticed the details of eyes, hair, and skin color that differentiate the people in a land of many races. 6.17. Studying dinosaurs, two children have noticed many details, which they carefully show in their clay models.

and foreground, and understands that because of their relative positions certain objects are partially hidden by other objects. People, houses, and trees are no longer anchored to a base line; they are related to space and ground, so that trees grow from the earth and rise to the sky. Objects lap over one another.

Figure 6.18

Colors at this period are recognized as qualities of light. The child now experiences color in terms of its visual quality, its emotional quality, and its symbolic value.

Design (that is, the initial conscious approach to surface texture and pattern) becomes significant at this stage of development. Designing offers the child a form of expression closely related to his desire to decorate himself and to his awareness that he can produce useful objects with his skill with art materials. The child's

Plates XVI—XVII

The child's interest in design extends to three-dimensional media of many different types. *6.19.* A mask, sculptures in paper and clay, and hand puppets—all were created and decorated by sixth-grade children. *6.20.* Two fifth-grade children used soft wire for these forms; one modeled a kangaroo, the other, a tricycle.

6.21. *In this emotional-type painting, a sixth-grader shows an awareness of spatial relations and details in the action and the uniforms of the players in a hockey game.*

growing interest in design parallels his increased sensitivity to visual pattern in his environment. In this connection, it is important that the teacher avoid propounding "principles" and "elements" of design. Rather, the teacher should provide the child with suitable materials (for example, a three-dimensional form which he has created to decorate, a linoleum block to carve and print, or textures of natural materials to arrange as a collage) and encourage him to work out for himself the relation of rhythm, balance, emphasis, thus creating a sense of unity that constitutes design.

The child's interest in design extends to three-dimensional media—cord, wire, soft metal, thin wood, clay, plaster. Experience in three-dimensional design

Figures 6.19–6.20

*The types of art expression can be broadly classified as visual and emotional. **6.22.** An advanced 9-year-old in the analytical realism stage did a self-portrait in chalks. In this visual representation, the boy depicts his own head as it looks to him. **6.23.** A 12-year-old in the same stage painted the head of a man. In this emotional representation, the child depicts the head according to how he feels about the man.*

helps him establish the relation between materials and objects, between the form of an object and its intended use. It allows him to realize for himself the principles of design. Creating his own new shapes and combining materials of different textures stimulate his imagination and thinking. (See Table 6.4.)

THE STAGE OF ANALYTICAL REALISM (AGES 11–13)

At this time the child is moving into adolescence, and the psychological and physiological changes that accompany this process affect his artistic endeavors as they do the whole of his life. This is the period when a child learns to reason, attempts to find causes, and analyzes things and situations. (See Table 6.5.)

In the area of art, the child's increasingly keen observation leads him to notice details as well as the general characteristics of people and objects. For example, he becomes aware of folds in a dress, of the effect of changing light on color, of the effect of different actions on the appearance of the figure. He notices spatial relations and perspective. He sees color, texture, form, space, and plane in terms of changes.

At this stage his art products are no longer merely spontaneous expressions: they are representations of subjects executed as more or less awkward but realistic images. Although they are not realistic by adult standards, their quality is evaluated by the child against *his own previous achievements* and against his observation of the original subject. Thus, the final art work and the technique of producing it assume an importance they formerly lacked. The teacher should encourage this new

interest in technique and artistic refinement, but should not do so overzealously, and should avoid imposing adult standards on the child.

By this time also the child has begun to develop a characteristic way of creating his art work. For classroom purposes, the types of art expression can be broadly classified as visual and emotional. Some

Figure 6.21
Plate XVIII
(left column)

Figures 6.22–6.23

children like to depict things according to how they look, others according to the emotions they elicit. It must be emphasized, however, that all children perceive both visually and emotionally; the distinction is that some tend more toward the former, and some more toward the latter, type of representation. It is the teacher's responsibility to guide the child in the direction of his preferred mode of expression. (See Tables 6.4 and 6.5.)

THE STAGE OF PERCEPTUAL REALISM (AGES 13–15)

Plates XIX–XX

The child, now adolescent, is subject to all the physiological, emotional, and social stresses that accompany the transition into adulthood. His perception of his surroundings and his artistic expression now becomes objective. He is perceptively aware of the reality around him and senses the contrast between it in nature and in the work of adults. These conditions cause him to be highly critical of his own work. (See Table 6.6.) If, through creative teaching guidance, the child has been encouraged to accept his own work as his unique expression and has gained confidence in his creative abilities in art, he is not likely to be discouraged. He can accept the fact that his work is usually somewhat different from the work of adults who are mature artists. He is also aware that his visual creations compare favorably with those of adults who have not matured as artists.

The creative teacher should help the teenager to realize that with continued experience in art he will mature in his ideas, abilities, and skill with art materials, so that his art products will gradually become more accomplished. The teacher should encourage him to understand his art imagery in terms of himself and thereby develop his self-confidence. The teacher should guide him to work in a number of media with which he has developed skill and to create in terms of whichever mode of perception—visual or emotional—he naturally prefers. (See Tables 6.5 and 6.7.)

THE STAGE OF CREATIVE RENASCENCE (AGES 15 AND OVER)

Having successfully passed through early adolescence, the youth finds new confidence and assurance. He is now capable of almost mature artistic expression and is

6.24. *The adolescent is subject to emotional and social stresses. He also is perceptively aware of the reality around him. In this sensitive painting, the girl shows herself in isolation, the kind of social isolation that is particularly poignant in a big city where the buildings full of people always loom overhead.*

confident of the merit of *his own* creative visual expressions. His teachers discovered, guided, and nurtured his innate creative ability to its full potential as a contribution to the integration of his visual creative learning with his total educational experience. (See Table 6.7.)

SUMMARY

Creative visual ability develops sequentially in parallel with physical, social, intellectual, and emotional maturation.

For practical purposes art is taught to groups of children of the same age-grade level on the basis of what has been found appropriate for the "average" child. The

6.26. *If the child has been nurtured in a creative-evaluative manner, he will be capable of almost mature artistic expression when he achieves the stage of creative renascence. He will find new confidence and assurance in his own visual expressions. This spontaneous drawing—a still life—shows these qualities.*

6.25. *A group of children in the perceptual realism stage enjoyed turning the glass panels at their school's main entrance into Christmas decorations. This simulated stained-glass window shows strong linear characteristics. The work is different from the work of mature artists, of course, but it certainly compares favorably with the work of adults who have not matured as artists.*

teacher must adjust his approach to accommodate individuals who achieve levels of growth faster or slower than the average.

Visual artistic ability progresses from manipulation without intent to represent a subject; to representation of various subjects, identifiable only by the artist, in terms of a few changing symbols; to the creation of special symbols for particular objects; through several stages of increasing awareness of spatial relations and of details that make objects different from each other; to more perceptive visual realism. This sequence of development as it relates to elementary school children is summarized in Table 6.6.

The child's creative visual development is characterized by greater awareness of the environment, wider concern with other people and their activities, increasingly conscious identification of himself with his creation, more effective application of his accumulated knowledge to his work, and growing ability to evaluate his own work. He progresses from emotional satisfaction in working with art materials to a more conscious (but emotionally satisfying) pleasure in the quality of his creation and interest in the techniques used to produce it.

To encourage this natural development, the teacher should *guide* the child in the processes of self-realization and self-discovery and not impose adult standards on him.

Two kinds of expression have been identified in the art of older children: the visual and the emotional. All children express themselves both ways at some time, but some tend in their art work to portray a subject according to how it looks and others according to how they feel about it.

AIDS TO UNDERSTANDING

For discussion
1. What characteristics are unique for each of the normative stages of growth in regard to the following: representation of the human figure, of space and form concepts, of color, proportion and design, and of meaning?
2. If the child is to create unhindered by adult influence, what is the function of the classroom teacher?
3. Since children differ widely among themselves within the visual stages of growth, what means can the classroom teacher use to provide for these individual differences? What practices inhibit creative visual development?
4. What value do you attach to the general behavioral characteristics of so-called average children? How does a knowledge of these aid the teacher? How do these characteristics influence the planning of the art curriculum, unit, lesson?

For involvement
1. Collect examples of art work which typify the characteristics of child art work in the manipulative, presymbolic, symbolic, realistic awareness, and analytical realism stages. If possible, begin a slide or colored photograph collection. Expand your examples of these five stages as you progress in the work of the course.
2. Observe a child in an art class in four grades (K, 2, 4, 6) over an extended period of weeks and write parallel case studies of the four children. Particularly, try to determine at what level of visual growth their visual development has progressed.

Table 6.1   RELATION BETWEEN AGE-GRADE LEVEL AND STAGE OF CREATIVE VISUAL DEVELOPMENT

AGE (YR.)	GRADE LEVEL	STAGE OF CREATIVE VISUAL DEVELOPMENT	AGE (YR.)	GRADE LEVEL	STAGE OF CREATIVE VISUAL DEVELOPMENT
2 3 4 5	Nursery school, kindergarten	Manipulative	11 12 13	Grades 6–8	Analytical realism
5 6 7	Grades K–2	Presymbolic	13 14 15	Grades 8–10	Perceptual realism
7 8 9	Grades 2–4	Symbolic	15 16 17 18 19 20	Grade 10 and above	Renascence
9 10 11	Grades 4–6	Realistic awareness			

Adapted from I. L. deFrancesco, *Art Education: Its Means and Ends,* New York, Harper & Row, 1958, p. 572.

Table 6.2   CHARACTERISTICS, INTERESTS, NEEDS, AND RESPONSES OF THE CHILD IN NURSERY SCHOOL, KINDERGARTEN, GRADE 1

CHIEF CHARACTERISTICS	MAJOR INTERESTS	SIGNIFICANT NEEDS	USUAL RESPONSES
1. Wide differences among children 2. Fear of unusual 3. Motor activity predominates 4. Attempt to relate art to reality; grows with individual 5. Self-identification strong; ego predominates 6. Frequent change of symbols; motion and sound 7. Proportion in relation to significance to self 8. Color choices to please self 9. Noisy, vigorous, alert 10. Clear purpose of own activities 11. Symbols become more definite as child grows 12. Relation to environment grows with individual 13. Realization of space is gradual 14. Realization of physical body is gradual but certain 15. Naming of symbol may occur as early as kindergarten	1. Self is most important 2. Possessiveness: "I" and "my" 3. Parents, later on brothers, sisters, neighbor children 4. Pets and toys 5. Teachers, schoolmates, playmates 6. The world about him is an ever-new experience: pleasing, surprising, sometimes frightening 7. Games 8. Art of any type 9. Singing rhymes 10. Rhythmic activities (dance, band) 11. Dramatics (make-believe) 12. Stories about children, animals, things 13. Making things, manipulation	1. Guidance of a "mother" sort 2. Love of parents and teacher 3. Freedom under patient guidance 4. Assurance that someone is watching 5. Encouragement by parents, teachers, older people 6. Praise when due 7. Firmness of guidance with clarity 8. Confidence in self as he moves, plays and accomplishes	1. Varied response as children vary 2. Interested in all new experiences 3. Fearful at first; later develops confidence 4. Eager to do and act largely through play 5. Enthusiastic; generally ready to respond 6. Imaginative answers, stories, activities 7. Spontaneous responses 8. Stereotyped tendencies 9. Reacts quickly to environmental stimuli as new experiences 10. Oblivious of adult world and concepts 11. Conclusions are reached in a child's manner, but definitely

Adapted from I. L. deFrancesco, *Art Education: Its Means and Ends,* New York, Harper & Row, 1958, p. 250.

Table 6.3 CHARACTERISTICS, INTERESTS, NEEDS, AND RESPONSES OF THE CHILD IN GRADES 2, 3, AND 4

CHIEF CHARACTERISTICS	MAJOR INTERESTS	SIGNIFICANT NEEDS	USUAL RESPONSES	EFFECTIVE STIMULATION
1. Buoyant, active, energetic; bodily movements more co-ordinated; conscious rhythm sought for pleasure 2. Realization of "adult" world and ways 3. Beginning of independence from teacher and parents 4. Imagination not as active as formerly 5. Sense of relation of form and space 6. More adequate sense of values, size, etc. 7. Heightened sense of realism 8. Emotional response high 9. Self-organization rapid and enjoyed	1. People, particularly schoolmates and playmates 2. Environment, particularly adjusting to it 3. Skills sharpened to communicate adequately	1. Art needs are many; needs help and counsel 2. How to adjust with little emotional disturbance 3. How to fit in with others 4. More technical interest	1. Degree of independence felt 2. Choice of groups and friends; "gangs" 3. Initiative improving 4. Emotions still very important 5. Seeks company of own sex 6. Self-confidence	1. Self-motivation 2. Group work and committee responsibility 3. Competitive activity for its own worth

Adapted from I. L. deFrancesco, *Art Education: Its Means and Ends*, New York, Harper & Row, 1958, p. 256.

Table 6.4 CHARACTERISTICS, INTERESTS, NEEDS, AND RESPONSES OF THE CHILD IN GRADES 5 AND 6

CHIEF CHARACTERISTICS	MAJOR INTERESTS	SIGNIFICANT NEEDS	USUAL RESPONSES	EFFECTIVE STIMULATION
1. Physical and physiological growth and changes are obvious 2. Some independence from teachers and parents; can work on his own much better and longer 3. By age of 10 has usually reached prepubertal stage 4. Sees self as part of the environment; social growth is automatic 5. Self-motivated and self-assertive to some extent 6. A new consciousness of people and and environment; knowledge has accumulated 7. Free to ask questions about many things, including art 8. Awareness of sex difference develops gradually 9. Beginning dissatisfaction with own accomplishments; seeks improvement; critical faculties develop fast	1. Broader interest in other people, classmates; social concept involves others 2. Slight interest in opposite sex because of new awareness of differences 3. Action: people and animals doing things 4. Imaginative situations in which he takes part or leads 5. Wants to know the "why" of things and events, especially by Grade 6 6. Dramatic events such as fires, storms, parades	1. Opportunity to do and make things 2. Friends, clubs, "gangs" 3. New and more adequate symbols to express larger world he now senses 4. Encouragement to continue search for adequate ways of expressing what he senses and sees 5. Experimentation with materials of art to find out, to arrive at answers 6. To express early sense of realism in textures, forms, direction of line	1. Enjoys doing things in organized but not limiting way; design becomes meaningful 2. Eager to participate in group experiences 3. Enjoys and expresses new awareness of self in relation to subjective use of color, line, form in his art work 4. Enthusiastic and co-operative because more able to accomplish 5. Accepts responsibility for all types of projects	1. Repeated, though guided, experimentation with a wide array of material 2. Flexible program for individuals and groups to retain and advance interest 3. Posed model, self-portrait, portrait of favorite classmates 4. Short trips to see things in action: a house being built, traffic at a corner, a farm, an industry 5. Memory drawing, painting, and modeling of things he has seen or participated in

Table 6.4   (*Continued*)

CHIEF CHARACTERISTICS	MAJOR INTERESTS	SIGNIFICANT NEEDS	USUAL RESPONSES	EFFECTIVE STIMULATION
10. General awareness suggests details, general character, and action in people, animals, objects 11. In art and other creative fields child sees more, senses more, and relates himself to the world 12. Imaginative and likes to express himself imaginatively 13. Sensitivity to color, line, form, and other elements is manifest in work and in social contacts 14. Because of wide range in endowment, children's creative achievements vary greatly 15. Older child tends to be neater in appearance; likes to be attractive 16. Observance increases		7. To develop own techniques to express feeling, mood and appearance: dark and light, distance, perspective, details 8. Broadened experiences in personal and group relations and in terms of new knowledges and techniques	6. Proud of self and school 7. Self-directing, self-confident, self-organizing 8. Capable of sustained application to work 9. Feels own inadequacy, but as a problem to be met	6. Committee organization of class for leadership development and for intelligent following 7. Rewards of a non-material nature, such as praise when due; recognition for accomplishments 8. Self-evaluation of work 9. Discussion techniques 10. Challenging standards

Adapted from I. L. deFrancesco, *Art Education: Its Means and Ends*, New York, Harper & Row, 1958, pp. 260–261.

Table 6.5   CHARACTERISTICS, INTERESTS, NEEDS, AND RESPONSES OF THE CHILD IN GRADES 7, 8, AND 9

CHIEF CHARACTERISTICS	MAJOR INTERESTS	SIGNIFICANT NEEDS	USUAL RESPONSES	EFFECTIVE STIMULATION
1. Very enthusiastic 2. Feels "frustrated" 3. Resentful of authority 4. Zest for "reform" 5. Adventurous 6. Physical changes rapid 7. Energetic, even pugnacious 8. Lacks self-confidence 9. Self-assertive 10. Tendency toward realism 11. Interested in opposite sex 12. Critical awareness high 13. Strong desire to "belong" 14. Attention span wavers 15. Seeks approval of group	*Himself* Explores own capacities Discovers own personality Discovers own special talents Makes most of own appearance Aware of physical self *Contemporaries* Their needs and desires Their social life Making friends Planning together Working together Playing together Participating in group activity (clubs, gangs, parties) *His family* Relation to siblings Share in family work Proper place in social life of family	1. Self-confidence 2. Heterosexual adjustment 3. Coordination and control: mental, physical, emotional 4. Independence of action 5. Recognition by own group 6. Adult treatment 7. Responsibility 8. Sense of belonging: family, club, church 9. Social acceptance 10. Guidance in choice of vocation, curriculum, personal action	1. Cooperation 2. Eagerness to plan 3. Acceptance of leadership within group 4. Flexibility to adjust to role in group 5. Aims to please 6. Interest in vocations 7. Acceptance of responsibility	1. Exploratory experiences 2. Chance to plan own program and activities with guidance 3. Provision of opportunity for strong aptitudes 4. Discussion groups 5. Confidential and personal conferences 6. Opportunity to meet opposite sex socially 7. Self-evaluation 8. Setting up personal goals 9. School journeys, camping, short trips 10. School campaigns, group and community projects

Table 6.5 (Continued)

CHIEF CHARACTERISTICS	MAJOR INTERESTS	SIGNIFICANT NEEDS	USUAL RESPONSES	EFFECTIVE STIMULATION
16. Argumentative 17. Wavering creative powers, attitudes, interests 18. Desire to "grow up" 19. Idealistic	Realizes parental authority Give and take at home *Vocations* Admires some adults Thinks of home, marriage, job Studies requirements in terms of own ability			11. Use of varied expression and media 12. Praise and encouragement

Adapted from I. L. deFrancesco, *Art Education: Its Means and Ends*, New York, Harper & Row, 1958, p. 304.

Table 6.6 SUMMARY OF PROGRESSION OF ARTISTIC DEVELOPMENT FROM KINDERGARTEN THROUGH GRADE 6

	GRADE LEVEL						
	K	1	2	3	4	5	6
DEVELOPMENT OF SYMBOLS							
Scribbling or manipulating materials in uncontrolled, later in controlled fashion. Scribbles and forms represent what and how child *feels*, to some degree what he *knows*, and how things *appear* to him. He is searching for adequate symbols and forms.	X	X	X				
Symbols for house, tree, people appear early: circle for head, lines for arms and legs. Similarity symbols used for same objects by all children. Same symbol used for several objects; e.g., circle for head, sun, wheel. Facial parts similar for people and animals.	X	X					
Logical, rather than visual appearance is common.	X	X	X	X			
Gradual change of symbol by addition of parts.	X	X	X				
Development of personalized symbol for objects.	X	X	X				
Symbols characterized by geometric appearance.					X	X	.
Geometric symbols insufficient; new symbols show interest in parts of body, joints, folds. Inception of realistic awareness.					X	X	X

Table 6.6 (Continued)

	GRADE LEVEL						
	K	1	2	3	4	5	6
Awareness and knowledge of self and others spur quest for more adequate representation. Analytical realism is evident. Attention to creative type is important.						X	X
MANIPULATION AND CONTROL							
Very important for young child. They represent play and pleasure. Encourage gain in control and learning what materials will or will not do. Color, line, form, texture are used at first without meaning. With older child they become adventure and experiment.	X	X	X	X	X	X	X
Controlled arrangement of line, form, color, texture should occur by Grade 1. Pattern or "design" feeling should be manifest by Grade 1 and grow with each grade.		X	X	X	X	X	X
Imagination suggests that designs can have meaning: my dream, a parade.			X	X	X	X	X
Organized arrangements of line, form, color, textures result in "designs." Experimentation					X	X	X

Adapted from I. L. deFrancesco, *Art Education: Its Means and Ends*, New York, Harper & Row, 1958, pp. 294–297.

Table 6.6 (Continued)

	K	1	2	3	4	5	6
with several media is desirable. Moods and feelings are interpreted; dance rhythms and music aid in imaginative conceptions.							
By using various materials, such as crayon, water color, chalk, child from Grade 3 upward develops personal mode of expression. This is a necessity by Grades 4 and 5 when control and manipulation are consciously purposeful and interest in subject and product is keener.				X	X	X	
Ability to name and use primary colors and color schemes.	X	X					
Ability to name, mix, and use secondary and intermediate colors.			X	X	X	X	
Ability to handle clay or a substitute to make thumb pieces and objects by adding and taking away clay; later to shape animals, people, objects.	X	X	X	X	X	X	
Ability to use a variety of materials —weaving, block printing, papier-mâché, various color media piermache, various color media —and several simple tools increases with interest and manipulative ability.						X	X

MEANING

	K	1	2	3	4	5	6
Scribbles and forms are created at random without apparent meaning. Child usually tells stories from his scribbles; different stories are told from the same scribble or form. Change in symbol by added details.	X	X					
Naming of symbol usually occurs by end of kindergarten or by Grade 1.	X	X					
Overlapping of forms may occur; when it does, it represents superior perception. Later it is used more frequently by more children.			X	X	X	X	
					X	X	X
Inside-outside appearance of a house, and simultaneous happenings in the same drawing, may be looked for in Grade 1. The extent of what the child sees and draws is indicative of growth from grade to grade.							

Table 6.6 (Continued)

	K	1	2	3	4	5	6
Characteristics and details in animals, people, objects, buildings observed and used more extensively as child develops.				X	X	X	X
Action of people or animals is noticed; position of body is attempted. In Grades 5 and 6 this become more significant: joints, folds, action line.				X	X	X	X
Contrasts of dark and light become common to show form.					X	X	X
Shading appears in the work of some children to gain round or solid appearance. The concept of form or solidity grows steadily through Grade 6.				X	X	X	X
Interpretation of mood and feeling is a reflection of growing personality from Grade 4 upward, and should be encouraged.					X	X	X
Sensitiveness to line, form, color, and texture may be expected from Grade 5 in varying degrees. It increases in significance by Grade 6. Varied materials aid this phase of development.						X	X

GRADUAL CHANGES

	K	1	2	3	4	5	6
Gradual change in relative completeness and characteristics of people, animals, and objects should be expected as children grow in knowledge of environment. To head and legs are added: body, arms, fingers, and a double line for arms and legs. Extent and rapidity of changes are index of growth.	X	X	X	X	X	X	X
Logical approach continues, but symbols for some objects begin to change with greater knowledge of structure and details.		X	X	X	X	X	X
Awareness of picture plane is constantly growing so that parts are often off by the edges of the paper; relation between ground and sky is realized and represented.			X	X	X	X	X
Conscious planning is shown by selection and placement of objects. Perspective in planning indicates greater maturity.				X	X	X	X

Table 6.6 *(Continued)*

	GRADE LEVEL						
	K	1	2	3	4	5	6
Upsurge of interest in representation of characteristics of people, animals, situations. Observation of real things and memory drawings are stimulating.				X	X	X	X
Child realizes he is part of environment. His work shows his relation to space. Earth and sky become separate entities.					X	X	X
Observation becomes keener with each grade. Posed model and actual environment develop observation and skills.					X	X	X
SPACE AND FORM CONCEPTS							
Objects are at first placed on paper at random; in clay objects are arranged without particular order.	X						
By Grade 1 things are related to space by a ground line; sky is a strip of color at the top of paper; by end of Grade 1 a second base line may appear to indicate near and far. So far there is no concept of a vantage point: above, below, or at eye level. Several views are logical to the child. This may continue into Grade 4.	X	X	X	X			
Picture plane may be realized by Grade 2 when, unconsciously, there may be a foreground, middle ground and background in painting. The concept continues to grow.			X	X	X	X	X
Two base lines may appear by Grade 2 as evidence of growth. Placing objects in zones, one above another, suggests objects near and far. They may be of same size; some children begin to place things in front or in back of each other.			X	X	X	X	X
By Grade 3, child may continue to use ground lines, but sky or background is extended to top of drawing. Space division of ground is more varied. Several ground lines may appear. Objects are usually drawn in front view.				X	X	X	X
Vertical objects on horizontal plane are often represented as lying down when several base lines are used.				X	X		

Table 6.6 *(Continued)*

	GRADE LEVEL						
	K	1	2	3	4	5	6
The ground line is transformed into a horizon line; objects are suggested in distance by overlapping. Some children begin to make distant objects smaller. Some disregard the horizon line, but make objects higher and smaller on the picture plane; details in foreground; use of dark and light appears in Grade 4.				X	X	X	X
Perspective may be used by few pupils, but not by all. It is a gradual development from Grade 3 on.				X	X	X	X
Overlapping of planes to suggest distance becomes more general. This may appear in Grade 2 but certainly in Grade 4.					X	X	X
Fifth-grader may persist in drawing objects from several points of view in the same picture. However, he begins to notice that lines on receding planes appear to come together; that eye level rises or lowers as his position changes; that lines slant down if plane is above eye level or up if plane is below eye level.						X	X
Dark and light (shading) to show things near and far, sensitive use of color for conscious emotional effect, and development of "individual" technique and sense of form culminate by Grade 6.						X	X
PROPORTIONS							
This concept is foreign to young child; *importance* determines size. Exaggeration of head, hands, feet, or other parts of drawing indicates emotional importance. Omission of parts or details means lack of importance for child.	X	X	X				
Closer relations to reality, detail, and color develop by end of Grade 1 and increase in a normal way.		X	X	X	X	X	X
Proportion and action are noticed by few fourth-graders, become important in Grade 5, and continue to interest older children.					X	X	X

Table 6.7   CHARACTERISTICS, INTERESTS, NEEDS, AND RESPONSES OF THE ADOLESCENT IN GRADES 10, 11, AND 12

CHIEF CHARACTERISTICS	MAJOR INTERESTS	SIGNIFICANT NEEDS	USUAL RESPONSES	EFFECTIVE STIMULATION
1. Conscious control 2. Physical buoyancy and energy 3. Analytical attitude toward life and art 4. Critical judgment high and growing 5. Emotional stability of marked degree 6. Consciousness of own abilities, interests, and limitations 7. Perception has developed almost to full capacity 8. Resourcefulness 9. Individuality 10. Creative development high	1. Himself as adult 2. Adults and their society 3. Opposite sex 4. Processes and techniques 5. Emotional security 6. Vocations 7. Life and its relations 8. Logical planning and execution	1. Emotional security 2. Adult acceptance 3. Responsibility 4. Confidence of adults (teachers, parents) 5. Attraction of opposite sex 6. Challenging situations 7. Wholesome attitude toward self and own work 8. Experimentation 9. Freedom to act, to decide	1. Highly objective or subjective art response according to type (visual or emotional) 2. Cooperative 3. Accepts challenges 4. Self-assured 5. Independent 6. Adjusts to situation 7. Idealistic toward life	1. Self-motivation 2. Art vocations 3. Community and school as a "workshop" 4. Life situations as subject matter 5. Aesthetic experience

Adapted from I. L. deFrancesco, *Art Education: Its Means and Ends,* New York, Harper & Row, 1958, p. 359.

Chapter 7
TEACHING ART
TO EXCEPTIONAL CHILDREN

In the preceding chapter we described the sequential emergence of artistic ability and suggested ways for the teacher to encourage this creative visual development at each stage. We pointed out that for practical purposes art is taught to groups of children of the same age-grade level on the basis of what has been found appropriate for the "average" child. In many classes, however, there are exceptional children and in this chapter we shall discuss the responsibility of the classroom teacher toward these pupils.

The term "exceptional children" includes both the gifted and the limited. The gifted child is above average either in general intellectual ability or in ability in a special area such as art or science or music or mathematics. The limited child has a handicap: defective sight, speech, or hearing; emotional disturbance; a crippling physical defect; environmental disadvantage; or mental retardation. Except in the last instance, the limited child's handicap does *not* imply less-than-average intelligence. For example, studies with hard-of-

Any teacher should expect individual differences among his students. These drawings give a good idea of the variation that any second-grade teacher is likely to find in the course of a normal teaching assignment in a typical elementary school. The four figure drawings are the work of four children in the same *second-grade class whose ages range from* 7½ *to almost* 8½. **7.1.** *This drawing is characteristic of the work of a 5-year-old child in the late manipulative stage.*
7.2. *This drawing is characteristic of the work of a child in the presymbolic stage.*
7.3. *This drawing is characteristic of the work of a child in the symbolic stage, the stage that is typical at this Grade 2 level.* **7.4.** *This drawing is characteristic of the work of a child in the realistic awareness stage, the stage that is typical in Grades 4–6. As these drawings suggest, in any given grade, the children vary widely in their mental and artistic ability. In the case of these four drawings, the first two show differing degrees of delayed development; the third shows "average" development; the fourth is the work of a gifted child.*

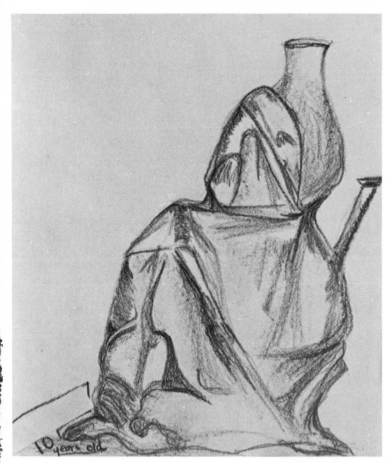

The talented child is easily identified because his creative development proceeds more rapidly than that of the "average" child. **7.5.** This drawing, done by an artistically talented 10-year-old boy, shows keen observation of the folds of the cloth and the effect of light falling on the objects. The still life is a visual representation. Though the boy is at an age when most children are aware of realism, his realism is analytical; he draws with high perception. **7.6.** This oil painting was done by an artistically talented girl not quite $12\frac{1}{2}$ years old. The painting, which is a visual representation, shows evidence of considerable maturity. This maturity in art was made possible for this exceptional child because she was given art opportunities beyond art lessons in the regular classroom.

hearing children show that their intelligence does not differ materially from that of normal children,[1] and studies of gifted children show that superior intelligence is compatible with subnormal vision.[2]

In many public education systems, the very exceptional children—the extremely talented, the severely emotionally disturbed, the totally blind or deaf, the very retarded, the badly crippled—are taught in special classes by specially trained personnel and are therefore not the responsibility of the elementary school classroom teacher. The children who deviate only slightly from the "average" can usually be managed satisfactorily in the ordinary classroom situation, and indeed can gain self-confidence, social assurance, and emotional stability from the experience. The discussion that follows applies to these slightly deviant children.

TEACHING THE TALENTED CHILD

To the gifted and artistically talented child the teacher owes recognition, encouragement, guidance, and freedom. Such a child is easily identified because his creative development, while following the sequence outlined in Chapter 6, proceeds more rapidly than that of the "average" child. His progress should be encouraged, but not forced, by the provision of stimulating materials with which to experiment and discover. He should be free to expand beyond his classmates. One of the great advantages of the creative-evaluative teaching advocated in this book is freedom for the gifted child to advance at his own pace to the height of his ability.

As he grows older, he should be given the opportunity of working with other talented children under the guidance of sympathetic and able art teachers in a special class free from restrictions of the regular school situation. Such "opportunity classes" can meet during or immediately after regular school hours or on Saturdays. Specific arrangements will depend on the size and facilities of the school district and the number of talented children. Nearby museums offer further resources. Art programs for gifted children can often be developed through cooperation of school and museum.[3]

Rose, in reviewing practices that are necessary to enhance the level of perceptual awareness and develop opportunities for aesthetic education, states that the art visuals center is a vital innovation "if aesthetic education is to be available to children in our schools. The use of visuals included in such a center—films, slides, exhibitions—is a way of bringing the museum, nature, knowledgeable speakers, and the benefit of research in art techniques and aesthetics and humanities presentations to the classroom when the 'real' material is inaccessible."[4] She also points out that perceptual awareness is developed through Educational Television Art Programs, the art contributions to humanities programs, using the museum, community, and the out-of-doors as an extension of the classroom.

Figures 7.1–7.4 (left col.)

Although these programs are for the enrichment of learning of all children, it is the gifted and artistically talented who can reap great benefits. These students who will be future artists and teachers will develop a visual vocabulary and be challenged within their capacities to create *ideas* such as the world has ever seen. At the same time all children will benefit by achieving a higher level of perceptual and aesthetic awareness, by developing self-confidence and thus a sense of security, by developing the ability to solve problems, by being culturally enriched and appreciative of their cultural heritage. And these children could in turn eventually benefit society by contributing toward the development of one that is aesthetically oriented rather than materialistic.

Figures 7.5–7.6

TEACHING THE LIMITED CHILD

The classroom teacher has two responsibilities to the limited child: first, identifying him, and, second, helping him make the most of his possibilities.

[1] Rudolph Pintner, "An Adjustment Test with Normal and Hard-of-Hearing Children," *Journal of Genetic Psychology* (1940), 380–381; and Rudolph Pintner and Joseph Lev, "The Intelligence of Hard-of-Hearing School Children," *Journal of Genetic Psychology* (1939), 55:31–48.

[2] Lewis M. Terman and others, *Genetic Studies of Genius, vol. I: Mental and Physical Traits of a Thousand Gifted Children,* Stanford, Calif., Stanford University Press, 1925, p. 26.

[3] Examples of school-museum cooperation are found in Philadelphia and Reading, Pa.; Toledo, Ohio; Providence, R.I.; Richmond, Va.; and Worcester, Mass.

[4] Helen Cynthia Rose, *An Art Visuals Center—A Vital Innovation,* Working Paper, Richmond Public Schools, Richmond, Va., 1968.

A child with a severe limitation is usually identified before he reaches school age and is established in a special situation for treatment and specialized teaching. Occasionally, however, through parental negligence, community indifference, or worsening of a previously mild defect, such a child is first noticed by the classroom teacher. The teacher should immediately seek the advice of the school physician, psychologist, or psychiatrist. No classroom teacher, however well prepared to instruct normal children, is qualified to manage a child with a severe physical, mental, or emotional defect.

But the classroom teacher can manage to help a child with minor limitation and should be prepared to do so. Often the child's abnormality is already known and the teacher is advised how to cope with it by the school physician or psychologist. If the teacher suspects a previously unrecognized limitation, because the child is progressing significantly more slowly than average, he should consult the school medical personnel to obtain professional help for the child and advice on how to deal with him in the classroom.[5]

The teacher's second responsibility is to help the limited child make the most of his possibilities. Every limited child faces the problem of living with his disability and adjusting to a world of normal people. He is emotionally disturbed to the extent that he has not adjusted. He needs to be reassured—to be made more aware of the many ways in which he is like the other children and less aware of the way in which he is different. He needs to live as normal a life as he possibly can. In the area of art this means he should have the same opportunities as normal children for creative art experience. He should have the same experience at the same grade level presented in the same way and in the same classroom situation. Therapy is not the purpose of teaching art to the limited child. A primary goal of

[5] In this connection, it should be emphasized that under no circumstances should the teacher "diagnose" a mental or emotional disorder on the basis of a child's art work; interpreting the pathological implications of a child's drawing can be attempted only by the professional. A child's artistic productions over a period of time may, however, provide useful clues to his problems. Just as the normal child's artistic development parallels his mental, social, and emotional growth, so an abnormal child's art work can reveal his warped psychological development and suggest its cause and possibly its treatment.

providing creative visual art experience for the limited child, as for every child, is to help him achieve security and confidence in his own ability. The teacher should help the child work as normally as possible around his limitation and make the most of his creative potential regardless of his handicap.

The child with impaired sight

The weak-sighted child is unable to see—and therefore unable to draw or paint—details, colors, tones, values, or even entire objects that are clearly visible to normal-sighted children. To some extent this disability can be overcome by developing in him the habit of observing at closer range and encouraging him to draw and paint larger pictures, using stronger colors and more decided contrasts. Any tendency to perceive with tactile-aural senses should be fostered. The child should be encouraged to express himself in three-dimensional media that he can shape by means of touch rather than sight.

The partially sighted child can see even less well than the weak-sighted. Encouraging his tendency to perceive through the tactile and aural senses seems the best way of providing him with a means of creative expression. Through handling objects, he can learn about configuration, relative size, proportion, and variations in texture. He can express himself best in three-dimensional materials and reasonably well by drawing and painting large pictures in boldly contrasting colors.

While most totally blind children are taught in special institutions, some attend regular schools. Such a child can express himself best in three-dimensional and textured materials that he can form by touch. The role of imagery should not be stressed, particularly with a child who has been blind since birth. The child who became blind later in life may be able to remember images and use them in his art work, but this is unpredictable and the issue should not be forced lest the child become discouraged.

Clearly, the visual artistic development of a child with defective sight cannot be compared with the normal, even though his intelligence is not impaired. For such a child, working with art materials is an emotional outlet; his art products express his feelings about the subject, not his interpretation of its appearance. Through art work he may be helped to achieve the inner vision and mental resources that will compensate for lack of sight.

The mentally retarded

The mildly retarded child can be managed in the regular classroom situation. Indeed, guided by a patient and understanding teacher, he can be helped to work successfully with art materials, and this success will aid his social and emotional adjustment.

Studies by Cruickshank[6] and by Robson[7] have shown that the retarded child is considerably below

normal in ability to think abstractly, is close to normal in ability to deal with concrete problems, and is closest to normal in mechanical ability. He can work with actual objects and sometimes with models, but not with maps and plans. He can grasp spatial relations only in connection with concrete objects. An investigation conducted by the author, and his prior and subsequent studies in the area, suggest that the mentally retarded child's development in visual graphic art follows the same sequence as the normal child's, but proceeds more slowly (the rate depending on the degree of retardation) and never reaches adult proficiency.[8] Lowenfeld, studying the relation of creative development and mental growth, noted that the work of retarded children differs from the normal in representation of the human figure and the con-

Figure 7.7

[6] William M. Cruickshank, "Arithmetic Ability of Mentally Retarded Children, LL, Understanding Arithmetic Processes," *Journal of Education Research* (December 1948), 279–288.

[7] G. M. Robson, "Social Factors in Mental Retardation," *British Journal of Psychology* (1931), 133:22.

[8] John R. Sawyer, "The Ability of the Mentally Retarded Child for Graphically Representing Spatial Relationships," (unpublished research paper), Durham, University of New Hampshire, 1953.

7.7. *This is a painting by an 8-year-old in the third grade. The work is characteristic, however, of a child in the late manipulative stage (see Table 6.2). This, therefore, is the work of a retarded child.*

cept of space.[9] This finding is reinforced by those of Schaefer-Simmern[10] and of the author. For example, a study by the author of retarded seventh- and eighth-graders indicated that these children's art products were still based on their feelings about a subject rather than on their perception of its visual appearance. Despite persevering efforts to stimulate them to see space-object relations, their ability to do so progressed only slightly—from (1) representing space-object relations according to the emotional significance attached to the object, to (2) using a base line with objects attached to it, to (3) using space subjectively (folded-over and X-ray pictures, mixed plan and upright views, simultaneous space-time representations), to (4) overlapping pictured objects slightly, to (5) making the sky meet the base line.[11]

This level of creative development is characteristic of an average third-grader. Most retarded children do not progress beyond this stage, and their art lessons must therefore be conducted on the basis of the characteristics, needs, and interests outlined in Tables 6.2 and 6.3 (end of Chapter 6).

Working with a mentally retarded child in a group of normal children requires ingenuity on the part of the teacher. Since the retarded child needs more guidance and his art experiences must deal more with concrete objects, the teacher should set up a teaching-learning situation flexible enough to accommodate both the normal children and the retarded pupil. Stimulating questions asked the retarded child should present a simple comparison about which he can think within his own frame of reference. Initially he can best be stimulated by questions about himself and the parts of his body; these are within his comprehension. Questions about spatial relations are not, and should be avoided until the child indicates his beginning awareness of space-object relations by using a base line in his drawings. He can then be guided toward further understanding of time-space-object relations by questions about activities performed by "us" (he and his group) in a certain "place" (his environment), about time sequences, such as going to buy candy, or about the layout of a simple familiar building. When the child's pictures progress to the point where objects overlap and the sky meets the base line, he can be encouraged to greater awareness of himself in relation to his environment and to other people by working with the other children on a cooperative mural. He should be made to understand that the group working together was needed to do the drawing, that he could not have done the work alone, and to feel that he wanted the group to work with him. At the same time, group leaders provide the retarded child with examples to see and cause him to feel more secure as he tries what others have demonstrated within the group activity. In this way he is not singled out.

In teaching the retarded child, repetition is important. A new learning situation should be linked with old experiences so that repetition can reinforce learning. Generally a few art experiences pursued in depth achieve better results than many superficial ones.

The art materials suitable for the retarded child are the ones appropriate to the normal preschool child—clay, large heavy black pencils, large crayons, thick chalk, thick-bristled brushes, large pieces of paper, quick-drying tempera paints. When the child has acquired some sense of three-dimensional form, he can experiment with paper cutting, box modeling, papier-mâché modeling, and simple sculpture. Working with craft materials usually requires a better concept of spatial relations than the retarded child can achieve. Even if the child can be taught to do it, such craft work tends to degenerate into a monotonous pattern that is meaningless in terms of the child's creative development.

The mentally retarded child can achieve success in art and satisfaction for himself, but neither he nor his work should be placed in a situation that emphasizes the differences from the normal. This does not mean that the retarded child's work should be excluded from class exhibits. It does mean that in such exhibits the work of

[9] Viktor Lowenfeld, *Creative and Mental Growth*, 3rd ed., New York, Macmillan, 1957.

[10] Henry Schaefer-Simmern, *The Unfolding of Artistic Activity*, Berkeley, University of California Press, 1948.

[11] Sawyer, op. cit.

individual children should not be identified, and the retarded child's products should not be placed next to those of the best artist in the class.

The results of a study of art activities show that the following characteristics for art teaching were successful for mentally handicapped children.

At the primary level:

1. The activity should be structured. Have the children start with simple shapes.
2. The product should have "display" character.
3. There should be opportunity, during the work period, for "discovering something new."
4. The process of molding the product should involve operations normally done in the home, such as cutting, tieing, assembling, sewing, ironing.
5. The product should be such that, in its making, the student can see and measure its progress toward completion, day by day (such as weaving a rug, shaping a bowl, making a basket, etc.).
6. The product should be larger than the child's hand.
7. The finished product should have three dimensions rather than be on a flat surface (such as an object that has depth, as well as height and width).

At the intermediate level, these additional considerations are added:

8. The tools used to shape a product should preferably be manual arts tools (such as hammer, screwdriver, etc.).
9. The material should be one which offers active resistance (such as wood, clay, copper).
10. The material used should be one that results in a product the student feels is valuable in itself (such as copper, glass, leather, glazed clay).[12]

The child with impaired speech or hearing

Teaching art to a child who is deaf or who cannot speak intelligibly involves initially a problem of communication. Since most such children are of normal intelligence and have normal manipulative ability, their

[12] Esther Mills, Richard Wiggin, Jean Hebeler, *A Comparison of Especially Designed Art Activities as Used with Intellectually Handicapped Children and Youth*, A Pilot Study, Office of Education, U.S. Dept. of HEW, University of Maryland in cooperation with Arlington County Public Schools, between June 1960 and September 1961.

creative development can be expected to progress normally. Once a method of communication is established between teacher and pupil, the child's art expression can be guided along the lines suggested in Chapter 5 for the "average" child. Creative artistic expression may have even greater value for such a child than for his normal classmates. It is an area in which he can do well, an area in which his deficient speech or hearing is not a serious liability, an area from which he can derive the emotional satisfaction and self-confidence that accompany success. Moreover, art experience aids in the release of serious emotional conflicts that arise because he appears so normal to everyone and, yet, his inability to communicate causes a serious conflict within himself.

The crippled child

Every child with a crippling bodily defect faces the problem of adjusting to his environment and to other people's reactions to his disability. The emotional difficulty is usually more severe for a child who has become crippled than for one who was born so, because he must learn also to accept his new body image—the reality of his unfamiliar condition. The more serious the handicap, the greater the psychological problems.

For purposes of art work, the handicap is greater if the upper, rather than the lower, part of the body is affected. If medical findings suggest that the function of the crippled part may improve, art work that activates this part may be useful. But if the crippling is permanent, the limitation should be accepted and art work planned around it. Since the disabled child's intelligence is not impaired, his creative development can be expected to proceed normally.

The teacher should first make a list for his own use of the actions the handicapped child cannot perform and then conduct the art lessons appropriate to the group's age and level of creative development, using activities that are possible for the crippled child. If certain activities seem essential for the rest of the class, but are not possible for the crippled child, the teacher can guide the child individually to achieve the same experience with his available abilities.

In general, the crippled child seems to work well and happily in a regular classroom situation. The interaction with normal children seems to be stimulating rather than frustrating, and the day-to-day relations with them is good experience in adjusting to life in a world of people more active than he.

The environmentally disadvantaged child

Much attention has been given in recent years to the problems of the disadvantaged child. The term "environmental" has been chosen for this discussion because it delimits an area of exceptional children whose problems stem from circumstances apart from their own physical bodies: problems of their culture, their location, their parental relationships, perceptual problems, language barriers, and urban-rural factors.

All children learn through their sense and perceptual capacities, and experience with these plays a vital role in the total development of children. There is a relationship between the deprivation of stimulating environment and the lack of development of the sensory, perceptual, and, in turn, cognitive functions of children.[13] It seems that art in the visual sensory area is an ideal area of learning experience through which many problems of deprivation can be approached. Art has no barriers of communication. The widespread and accepted use of visual media, educational movies, slides, and television have shown how many deprived children can experience and extend their lot to one that is more typical.

The Hartford, Connecticut, studies have shown that:

1. Disadvantaged children of all types are certainly expressive. They love to be involved with colors, forms, and working with materials, especially when the experience is both real and challenging. An effective compensatory education must begin with multisensory and motor experience rather than only linguistic involvement.

2. Urban children of all types are socially oriented. When this orientation is recognized with honest praise and encouragement, the child's self-image is reinforced. Simply by using his name, the child establishes his identity and a new self-respect (image).

3. In many ways, despite being deprived of cultural experiences, the deprived child is more wise to the world than children in more affluent neighborhoods. Early in life the deprived child has had to fend for himself and has had little experience with love, warmth, and attention. In this negative background it is obvious that acceptance, respect, and warmth will mature latent qualities within the child. The means should evolve through a recognition of the environmental circumstances, understanding of them, and acceptance of them in the form of action.[14]

In addition, there is evidence to support the idea that if the teacher understands the problems of the disadvantaged, he can apply this knowledge to his teaching in ways that will enable him to contribute to *effective* art education for such environmentally disadvantaged children.[15]

These findings, then, seem to indicate (1) that the program developed for deprived children should give children opportunities to be exposed to enriching elements of living for purposes of visual expression and opportunities to be involved with ideas, materials, and visual forms; (2) that children should be approached positively in terms of any success they achieve in the visual media; (3) that their latent qualities be brought out through teachers who understand the problems of the disadvantaged and have the knowledge, competence, and materials to apply their understanding with environmentally disadvantaged children.

[14] Robert J. Nearine, "Hope in Our Time. Some Exploration into Compensatory Education," *Art Education*, Journal of the National Art Education Association (May 1969), 22, No. 5:5–6.

[15] Ronald H. Silverman, Ralph Hoepfner, Moana Hendricks, "Developing and Evaluating Art Curricula for Disadvantaged Youth," *Studies in Art Education*, NAEA, (Fall 1969), 11, No. 1:20–33; Doris Barclay, "A Pilot Study of Art Education for the Economically and Socially Deprived Child," Final Report, December, 1966 (U.S. Office of Education, Project No. 5-8294); unpublished research.

[13] Ronald H. Silverman, "Watts: The Disadvantaged and Art Education," *Art Education*, Journal of the National Art Education Association (March 1966), 19, No. 3:17–20.

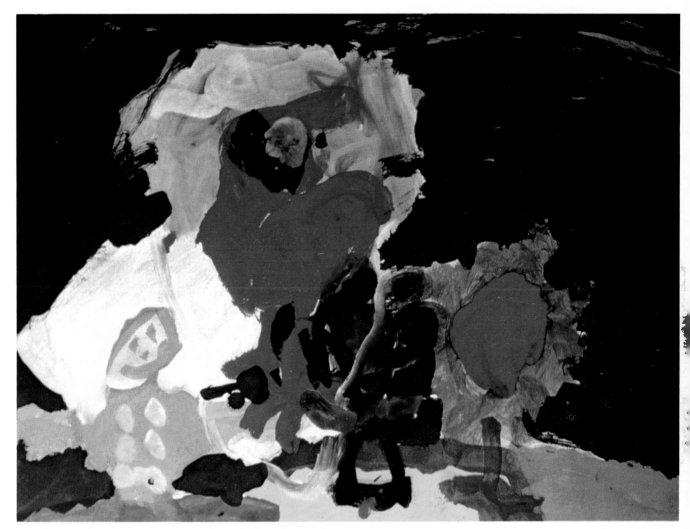

VI. *The young child in the presymbolic stage paints with
enough control to make his forms represent what he is thinking
about at that particular moment. His forms usually are not
clear-cut as real figures or objects. Rather, they are symbol forms
which he invents and may change readily. The child is still
interested in color for its appeal more than as the particular
color of something. He is right on top of the world, making
color forms that do what he wants them to do.*

VII. This picture was done by a classmate of Douglas and Laura, the second-graders whose pictures are shown in Figures 4.6–4.9. Betsy, also in the presymbolic stage, used chalk and yarn to form a line symbol that represents the whirling water in the swimming pool in the yard of her house.

VIII. One child explored the nature of materials and color relationships for some time. Ultimately, after many trials, the child designed and wove this piece. The work shows that the child has achieved quite good control of the yarn and that he can make independent judgments about color combinations and try new effects.

IX. *A child 3 to 5 years old is happy when he is given a chance to create a riot of color on a large sheet of paper with paint (finger paint or tempera) that allows him to work quickly. He usually limits his choice of colors to one or two.*

X. *In the late manipulative stage, a young child often paints several objects that he can identify by name because he is emotionally attached to them. The objects fill the paper; the colors are intense and primitive. The work is not composed, and the child ignores perspective, except in an emotional sense.*

XI. *In the symbolic stage, the child uses bent lines to suggest movement of the body and limbs of the figure. "Reaching for a Flower" was done in poster paints.*

XII. *A third-grader paints the bowl and the flowers in brilliant, gay colors and makes them as tall as she herself is. Children often represent objects according to the importance they attach to them.*

Two third-graders use dark blue to express their emotional impression of the cool, clear, deep water. They also use gay colors to convey the emotion felt during a happy event in each child's life. **XIII.** The vigorously stroking arms and kicking legs, along with the brightly colored swim suit, show this girl's feelings about swimming. **XIV.** Catching a fish is the most enjoyable part of fishing, so this boy paints himself doing just that.

XV. *A child in the stage of realistic awareness shows detailed characteristics of insects and plants in this interesting view of the life of the ant.*

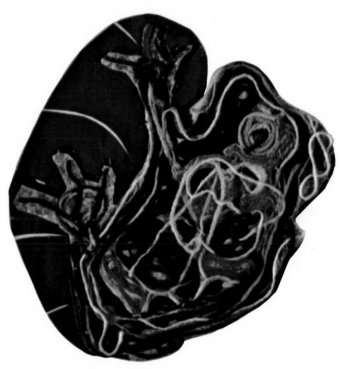

XVI, XVII. *Designing gave two fifth-grade children a form of expression paralleling their increased sensitivity to visual patterns in their environment. Their teacher provided the class with suitable materials and was careful not to propound "principles" and "elements" of design. Both these children chose yarn and felt as their materials, but the results are strikingly individual.*

XVIII. *A group of elementary children made this wall mosaic—an awkward but realistic portrayal of a soldier and his horse and chariot. This is a visual representation.*

A special technique
for teaching the limited child

Usually the kind of creative-evaluative teaching described in this book, carried out by a patient and understanding teacher, is as successful with the limited child as with his normal classmates. But sometimes because of emotional problems resulting from his disability, the limited child finds it difficult to participate in the art experience. In dealing with such a child, the teacher must often rely on intuitive sensitivity to the child's need. The teacher must not only know the physical nature of the child's handicap, but must try to understand empathically how the child himself looks upon his disability and how detached from his environment he feels because of his defect. The teacher must empathize with the child and persuade him into involvement with the art materials. The technique outlined below is useful in this situation. However, it should be used only when no other teaching approach has been successful and only by a teacher with enough patience to see it through the completion—a process requiring weeks and even months.

1. The teacher learns about the child's background through a case study.
2. The teacher observes the child to learn his reaction to his handicap or his environment as it relates to a particular art experience.
3. The teacher gains the child's confidence through empathetic understanding of his situation.
4. The teacher manipulates the art material for the child so that he can become used to it, but keeps the work unformed. Through questions about the meaning of simple, unrelated lines or forms, the teacher encourages the child to take over the work as soon as he relates to it.
5. The teacher relates the child to the making of the art product by relating stimulating questions to the child's thoughts about himself and by making sure the experience is within his ability to achieve.
6. The child gains confidence in doing his own art work in the following sequence: (a) he begins to be involved in the art experience; (b) he repeats similar symbols; (c) he tries a variety of lines, shapes, and forms; (d) he begins to use the materials to express his own ideas freely.
7. The child becomes attached to the teacher in a relation that is similar to a younger child's attachment to his mother. This stage indicates that the child has confidence in the teacher.
8. The child willingly takes over the art material and begins to work freely on his own.
9. The teacher dissolves the attachment of the child to himself in the art experience by gradually receding from the situation.

SUMMARY

The term "exceptional children" includes both the gifted and limited. The classroom teacher has a special responsibility to each.

The gifted child is above average either in general intellectual ability or in ability in a special area, such as art. To the artistically talented child, the teacher owes recognition, encouragement, guidance, and freedom. Creative-evaluative teaching allows him to advance at his own pace to the height of his ability. As he grows older, arrangements for special art education should be provided.

The limited child has a handicap: defective sight or hearing, emotional disturbance, a crippling physical defect, mental retardation. Except in the last instance, his intelligence is not impaired. The teacher has the responsibility of identifying the limited child and then helping him to make the most of his creative potential regardless of his handicap. The art experience is the same for the limited as for the normal child; the teacher should guide the limited child to achieve the experience by helping him to work around his limitation. A goal of art education for the limited, as for the normal, child is achievement of security and self-confidence.

The art needs of the child with deficient sight or hearing, mental retardation, or a physical defect are briefly discussed, and a special teaching technique is described that may help the emotionally disturbed child toward a creative visual art experience.

AIDS TO UNDERSTANDING

For discussion

1. What is the difference between normal and exceptional children?
2. If an artistically gifted child were among thirty children in a classroom, how would you as the teacher become aware of his presence?
3. What aspects of a creative-evaluative strategy of teaching art enhance the gifted child's interest in art?
4. How does a creative-evaluative approach to teaching limited children differ from a therapeutic approach?
5. What is the relationship of emotional disturbance to exceptional children?
6. Is a person who has become totally blind more limited than a person who has always been totally blind?
7. How is a partially blind child's encounter with art different from that of a totally blind child?
8. Why is the problem of the deaf child of greater emotional significance than that of other limited children in an art lesson?
9. What are the advantages of a creative-evaluative teaching strategy in art for the mentally limited child?
10. What is the difference between an environmentally disadvantaged child and a limited child?
11. How do you account for the fact that art is an ideal area of learning experience for the environmentally disadvantaged child?

For involvement

1. Collect a set of drawings of a class of elementary children. Arrange them in order from most artistically developed to least artistically developed according to the criteria established in Chapter 6. What is the creative-visual developmental range of the class? Do any children qualify as artistically gifted? On what basis did you determine this?
2. While blindfolded, create some organic form that is very familiar to you. When you feel satisfied with the product, stop working and place the clay form in an enclosed area so that you cannot see it (cupboard, opaque plastic bag, shopping bag, etc.). Do the following:

   a. Recall and write in great detail the actual thoughts and feelings you had while working.
   b. Using the same amount of clay and without being blindfolded, create the same form while working the same length of time. Write your thoughts and feelings during this experience.
   c. Now compare the two products side by side in regard to the following: size, shape, realistic-abstract, texture, and proportion. In what circumstance did you feel most adequate? Did you feel limited?

3. Use this same technique to simulate the following conditions: partially blind—gauze over a narrow slit in a blindfold; physically impaired—wide cloth tied to wrists while hands are held pawlike at shoulder height with the tie passing from wrist to wrist and on back of the neck, then tape the thumb and little finger together; deaf—use ear plugs and ear muffs over ears; and retarded—bandage the writing hand. (It is only possible to simulate the physical awkwardness that some retarded children experience.)
4. Make a list of the actions you could not perform if you were crippled, blind, deaf, retarded, or emotionally disturbed.
5. Apply the technique outlined in this chapter for working with a limited child who finds it difficult to participate in an experience with a person who claims that he "can't draw a straight line."

Chapter 8
EVALUATING CHILDREN'S CREATIVE VISUAL DEVELOPMENT

A child's creative visual development must be evaluated in the context of his total psychological and physical growth and in the context of the entire art program of the elementary school. Evaluation has two aspects: appraisal of the pupil's development in the visual arts, and appraisal of the teacher's (and the art program's) effectiveness. Evaluating the child's development involves (1) comparing his work with that of his classmates, with that of the "average" child (in terms of developmental growth scales), and with his own past achievements of goals for the art program; and (2) assessing his needs as a basis for planning his future art education. Evaluation of the teacher's effectiveness grows out of the teacher's appraisal of the child, through which he becomes aware of the strengths and weaknesses of his own teaching procedure.

Creative-evaluative teaching is thus a circular process: the teacher stimulates and guides the child to a creative visual art experience, and through his appraisal of the modification of the child's total growth in all of the qualities of an art experience evaluates the effectiveness of his teaching.

In this chapter we shall discuss (1) the general objectives of a program to evaluate children's creative visual development, (2) the importance of evaluating the child's total development, (3) techniques for evaluating the pupil's creative visual development, and (4) techniques for evaluating the art lesson.

OBJECTIVES OF THE EVALUATION PROGRAM

A program for evaluating children's creative visual development has basic objectives which are as follows:

Figures 8.1–8.2

1. To judge the child's art work in terms of criteria appropriate to his age-grade level. The curriculum guide should state clearly the usual characteristics of artistic behavior and qualities of art work at each age-grade level throughout the elementary school so that everyone responsible for evaluating the child has some common basis for the assessment.

2. To judge the child's art work on the basis of appraisal by more than one teacher. The child's artistic development should be appraised cooperatively by both the classroom and the special art teachers, not by one instructor only. The pooling of observations concerning behavior and ability produces a truer picture of the child's growth.

3. To improve teaching by encouraging teachers to appraise their own performance. The teacher should ask himself to what degree he is improving the learning situation, to what degree he is successful in guiding his pupils, and in what areas he has difficulty.

4. To guide the pupil toward self-appraisal. The child should be guided to assess his own artistic progress by comparing his present with his earlier art work and by comparing his work with that of his peers.

5. To develop a continuous program of evaluation throughout the elementary school. The evaluation guide should state clearly, for each age-grade level throughout the elementary school, what appraisal techniques should be used and how often.

6. To relate the child's creative visual develop-

ment to his total growth. A child's creative development should not be evaluated alone; it must be judged in the context of his whole physical, mental, social, and emotional growth.

7. To organize the learning environment in terms of the child's needs. The objectives of the art program should be well-related to the pertinent requirements that are basic to fundamental needs of life, and to particular needs as they relate to the art environment of the children of a specific community. Children need to have protection, physical development, satisfaction, social development. These are gained in art through his visual creation of ideas for homes, clothing, recreation, social involvement, and physical outlets in creative areas such as constructing and building.

8. To judge the child's creative visual development by means of valid techniques and on the basis of adequate data. Traditional standardized tests are not valid measures of progress in art. Artistic growth should be judged on the basis of developmental scales and comparisons of the child's present and earlier work.

JUDGING CHILDREN'S ART IN TERMS OF BEHAVIORAL GOALS

Elementary school art is a "whole" art experience involving seeing and feeling, producing art, responding to and using art objects, and reflective and evaluative reactions to art. It is structured as a scope and sequence of visual encounters determined by children's level of growth in terms of needs, abilities, and interests, by the qualities of art, and by objectives related to artistic behavior. As a manifestation of these a pupil should demonstrate artistic behavior appropriate to his age-grade level as follows:

(1) have intense involvement in and response to personal visual experiences; (2) perceive and understand visual relationships in

*The child's art work should be judged in terms of criteria appropriate to his age-grade level. Each child is an individual, of course, but do you think these two paintings show the usual characteristics of work by children at these age-grade levels? **8.1.** Age 7, Grade 2: A child produces a symbolic representation of "me" and "my friends" frolicking in the snow. Note that the base lines are stacked up. **8.2.** Age 10, Grade 5: Another child paints a realistic impression of a boxing match. Note that the child is aware of the effects of the floodlights.*

117

the environment; (3) think, feel, and act creatively with visual materials; (4) increase manipulative and organizational skills in art performance appropriate to his abilities; (5) acquire a knowledge of man's visual art heritage; (6) use art knowledges and skills in his personal and community life; (7) make intelligent visual judgments suited to his experience and maturity; and (8) understand the nature of art and the creative process.[1]

This set of criteria established by a committee of the National Art Education Association serves as a basis for evaluating art. Behavioral goals should be consistent with them. Any goal established for a child should be validated in terms of the criteria established in Chapter 9 for judging the objectives for a curriculum. In the same framework, these goals serve as a basis for evaluating and judging child art.

EVALUATING THE CHILD'S TOTAL DEVELOPMENT

The child's total educational development comprises his mental, emotional, social, physical, aesthetic, per-

[1] *Essentials of a Quality School Art Program*, A position statement by the National Art Education Association, John Benz, Chairman, NAEA, Publication, Washington, D.C., 1968.

ceptual, and creative growth. While his growth as a whole proceeds according to a pattern, the components develop at varying rates. For example, at a given age a child may be more physically than socially mature, better mentally than emotionally developed. Determination of the child's total development should be based on periodic appraisals over regular intervals of time within a school year. His degree of maturity in each dimension of growth determines the guidance he needs in the future and what the next step in his art education should be.

The various components of total educational development are discussed below, with emphasis upon how they can be evaluated in terms of the child's behavior in art class.

Mental ability

In art work, the child's mental ability is evidenced by his awareness of differences, changes, details, and unusual aspects of a situation, and by his ability to understand and solve problems inherent in the creative process. The act of creation involves conceptualizing, analyzing the idea, and embodying it in the materials available—in

In certain types of situations a teacher can begin to form judgments about children's social maturity. Are they friendly and cooperative? Do they all contribute to the group enterprise? Do they all accept suggestions easily? 8.3. These fourth-graders are involved in a creative arts experience that revolves around giving a play. The children have written their play; now they are making the scenery; later, they will be actors. 8.4. These boys are absorbed as they make their animals. The teacher held this class in an artist's studio near the school, so the children could work with an artist.

general, it requires a high degree of mental ability. It is a good index of potential.

Mental ability is also evidenced by the child's inclusion of new elements in his art work, indicative of the way he retains, utilizes, and increases his knowledge. For example, a child's mental growth is clearly demonstrated in his invention of symbols for people and things in his environment.

Emotional maturity

Emotional maturity is generally defined as satisfactory adjustment to the environment. Emotional growth is therefore judged in terms of improvement in adjustment to people and situations. In art education, emotional maturity is evidenced by confidence, normal freedom within the environment, conceptualizing ability, flexibility, deepened perception, and obvious enjoyment of an undertaking.

The well-adjusted child shows variety and flexibility in his ideas and his ways of expressing them. He identifies himself with his work. The maladjusted child is retiring, fearful, and unwilling to undertake new experiences. In art work, maladjustment is indicated by stereotyped expression and meaningless repetition of subjects and techniques.

Art activity promotes emotional growth by providing opportunity for achievement of satisfaction in producing an art work and for release of tension. The artist identifies himself with his work and acquires self-confidence and self-respect.

Social adequacy

Social adequacy is a chief aim of all education because it improves the child's ability to cope with the demands and problems of school life and of all life. In the art class a child's social maturity can be judged on the basis of behavior toward the teacher and his classmates.

The following behavior indicates social maturity:

1. Thinking about others; identifying with others
2. Accepting help, suggestions, advice from others
3. Seeking self-improvement through self-criticism and criticism by others
4. Being friendly and cooperative; contributing to group enterprises
5. Accepting views of others

Figures 8.3–8.4

119

8.5. The child approaching age 5 who did this drawing is beginning to acquire muscular control and coordination. He has developed enough control and enough skill to make his scribbling represent what he is thinking about at the moment.

6. Appreciating work of others
7. Sharing ideas, helping, participating
8. Willingly accepting his share of responsibility

Physical development

Figure 8.5

Working with art materials requires muscular control and coordination. In the very young child, this control is lacking, and he manipulates rather than guides his crayon. By the time he is 8 or 9 years old, he has acquired muscular control through practice and is able to work purposefully with art materials. Lack of normal coordination at this age suggests physical disability.

Figure 8.6 (right column)

A child's physical development is also reflected in his art products in terms of his awareness of rhythm, balance, spatial relations, shape, color, texture. Failure to develop these perceptions within three years of time of the "average" age may be the result of a physical (or mental or emotional) defect.

Art activity promotes physical development by encouraging muscular coordination and sensory perception.

Aesthetic judgment

One of the chief goals of art education is the encouragement of the child's aesthetic development—his appreciation of beauty, either natural or man-made. In the art class aesthetic and creative development are closely united. As the child works with art materials—choosing colors, shapes, textures to express his ideas—he makes aesthetic as well as creative judgments. He likes or dislikes certain shapes, certain color combinations, certain spatial arrangements. As he grows older, he bases his aesthetic judgments on his general knowledge, his knowledge of aesthetic principles, his familiarity with great art works, and his intuition (which reflects all the rest of his education).

In the art class, development of a child's aesthetic judgment is evidenced by the following behavior:

1. Spontaneous reaction to colors in a picture, in nature, in his own work
2. Evident pleasure in rhythms of form, line, texture, color
3. Spontaneous sense of organization in drawing, painting, or modeling, and recognition of organization in work of others
4. Sensitivity to and awareness of art form in the environment in general and in art works in particular
5. Ability to analyze moods, feelings, and situations
6. Awareness of many possibilities in use of color, texture, form, line; self-improvement on basis of self-analysis

Evaluation of the child's aesthetic development is based on how often and to what degree he shows some or all of the behavior described.

Perceptual awareness

A child exhibits perceptual awareness when he responds with his senses to differences in his environment. In art this is generally a visual response. He gives attention to particular things which when put together give a general mental impression of an object. For this he invents a shape-color symbol. Growth is shown when he develops a more analytical visual impression of the principal parts of a situation in which the elements of line,

color, and form are less important than the effect of the parts in the whole picture. The child grows in awareness of color from merely enjoying it for itself to the effect on it of different light relationships of the surroundings. With materials that are plastic, like clay, the child *Figure 8.7* progresses from simple kneading of the clay to sensitivity to the different textural qualities of the surfaces. He is more sensitive to the textural qualities of natural forms such as a leaf, a rock, and the force of water. The child senses space as the immediate area surrounding him. This space changes as the child grows and he perceives its changes. For a small child, the space around him is the air; that above him is the sky; and he stands on the ground, the earth. He represents this at a very young age as a band at the top of his paper for sky, the untouched center of his paper is the air, and the ground is a solid band at the bottom or base line of his paper. Later, he *Figure 8.8* views space visually or emotionally. Visually a child sees objects at various distances in perspective and emotionally by his moving in space around him.

Children who are perceptually aware include in their art work body movements, textures of objects, numerous objects they have seen, and are very conscious of their shapes, their colors, and the things surrounding them. In contrast to them are children who lack perceptual awareness. They lack these qualities. Their art work lacks imagery, is hesitant, has very little movement in the figures, and has few representations indicating textural qualities.

8.6. One of the ways children achieve aesthetic judgment is by becoming aware of art form in art works by others. These students have been taken to a community art show.

Each child grows in perceptual awareness. The growth is shown in certain more or less typical stages, but any one child is often partly in one stage, partly in another, as these two children are. **8.7.** A 6-year-old in the presymbolic stage senses the textural qualities of the bird's beak, the nest, and the tree trunk. Her painting also indicates the sun and its light by means of a symbol. **8.8.** An 8-year-old fills in the air around her symbolic picture of her house and carefully includes the details of leaves on the trees. Nevertheless, she is still using a band at the top for the sky and a thick base for the ground in her drawing.

Creative development

Creative development means the adequate and progressive expression of the child's conceptual power through art; it is characterized by fluency, flexibility, sensitivity to problems, ideas, ability to abstract, originality, and the ability to rearrange, by process-product development, and by increasing control over materials and tools affecting form which broadens outlook and deepens insight.

A summary of the progression of creative development is presented in Chapter 6 (Table 6.6). Achievement of all the elements cited constitutes normal growth.

The following behavior in art class indicates creativity:

1. Natural, progressive improvement in handling materials and tools
2. Natural, progressive development of the symbols of representation
3. Freedom in expressing ideas and solving problems
4. Sustained interest in experimentation with ideas, tools, materials, and techniques
5. Sustained independence in use of ideas, tools, materials, and techniques
6. Originality in ideas, organization, combination of materials, and use of tools and techniques
7. Inoffensive lack of inhibition
8. Coherence and adequacy in the current creative experience

Figure 8.9

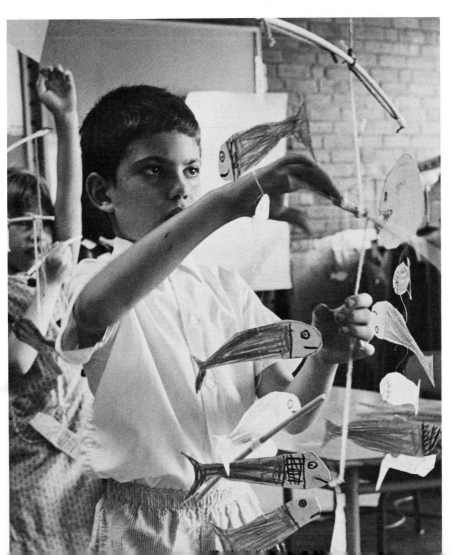

8.9. *One of the criteria of creativity is sustained interest in experimentation with ideas and materials. As this boy completes his mobile of sticks, string, wire, and cardboard fish, his interest is obvious.*

8.10. One of the most meaningful ways to evaluate a child's creative visual development is to guide him to evaluate his own work. Here the teacher has just asked, "Where do you think you should put the next piece of yarn to get the effect you want?" and the boy ponders how well he is achieving his goal.

EVALUATING THE CHILD'S
CREATIVE VISUAL DEVELOPMENT

From his art experiences the child needs to obtain a sense of personal accomplishment in art and a knowledge of how his work compares with that of his peers. Traditionally, schools grade a pupil's art work on the basis of standardized tests. This method has many disadvantages. More meaningful to the child's development are comparing his performance with group performance to determine his position in relation to the "average," comparing his present work with his previous achievements to judge his personal improvement, and guiding him to evaluate his own work as the culminating activity of a particular art experience.

Figure 8.10

Traditional grading

In practice, evaluation is tied to grading—that is, appraising achievement against a norm established by the school district or, in the case of art, on the basis of standardized tests. But tests have not proved valid instruments for measuring art ability or art appreciation or creative visual development. There are at least two reasons for this failure.

First, achievement in art cannot be measured in terms of the quality of the final product. The purpose of teaching visual art is to disclose the qualities of the environment which the senses of sight and touch make available to the individual. Exposure to painting, design, sculpture, and other art works is an experience that may result in creative art expression or in art appreciation. These are forms of behavior.

Second, achievement in art cannot be measured in terms of facts learned. In art (unlike cognitive learning) affective response precedes understanding. The child initially expresses his feelings in his art; he works imaginatively and intuitively. Only later does he develop insight into his work and understand the principles and techniques of production.

In addition to its questionable validity as a measure of achievement in art, grading adversely affects the child's learning. If the marking system is overemphasized, the pupil tends to learn what is required, in the way required, to obtain the grade required for some level of achievement that represents success to him. This is contrary to the goals of creative art education. If the child receives a grade that to him represents failure, the resulting frustration and tension combine to slow his development still further. This certainly is not a goal of education.

Nevertheless, most schools continue to report visual art experience in terms of grades. The reasons are that (1) general education is in practice still oriented toward the acquisition of facts, although in theory it is concerned with growth and development; (2) most parents insist on grades as a convenient gauge of achievement; and (3) most schools of advanced learning insist on grades as evidence of achievement on which to base admissions.

There seems little hope that traditional grading will be abandoned in the near future. The most that can be managed in the area of art is to ensure that evaluation is based on valid measurements, that it is used to instruct the child in his areas of weakness, and that it is recorded in such a way as to give a clear picture of the child's progress throughout his elementary school career.

Comparing individual with group performance

Comparison of individual performance with group performance in art provides information about a child's development in terms of his rank in a group, but it tells little about his individual progress. Below are discussed two methods of comparing individual with group performance: developmental growth scales and classroom discussion.

Developmental growth scales   Although standardized tests have not proved valid measures of progress in art, the recently evolved scales of growth expectancy (see Table 6.6) do provide a basis for comparing an individual child's development with the growth expectancy of a group. When used cautiously, with the realization that creative visual development must be judged in relation to total development, such scales are a valid reference. These scales describe general progress qualitatively and should not be used to prescribe a sequence of art activity directed toward achieving specific objectives. In addition, the teacher using them must have a knowledge of children's development, the psychology of learning, and the symbolism of children's art.

The Lantz Easel Age Scale[2] for children 4 to 8 years old offers a means of comparing the individual child with norms established for 6,000 children. It enables the qualified user to evaluate a child's work by comparing it with pictured examples of children's art in terms of form, detail, meaning, and relatedness. It deals with easel painting media only and depends a great deal on the judgment of the user.

The Lowenfeld Summary of All Stages permits determination of a child's creative development in relation to that of a group of children at the same growth level.[3]

The evaluation chart is general in nature. Only broad criteria are emphasized; therefore, it can be used for all stages of development. The chart is a means of obtaining a profile of the child's creative visual growth by checking quantitative values, little, some, and much. By connecting the responses with a line a profile is

[2] Beatrice Lantz, Easel Age Scale, Los Angeles, California Test Bureau, 1955, pp. 1–22.
[3] Viktor Lowenfeld and W. Lambert Brittain, *Creative and Mental Growth*, 4th ed., New York, Macmillan, 1964, pp. 395–402.

8.11. *Scales of growth expectancy in art should be used with caution, but they are helpful in forming a general idea of a child's stage of achievement. For instance, this picture shows typical work of a child from about 3 to 5. A circle stands for the head, broad horizontal bands for the arms, and one broad vertical band for the legs. Precocious children around this age may use more complete symbols for the human figure.*

Figure 8.11

obtained. The right side of the curve is an indication of superior quality, and the left side the inferior ones. When this chart is compared with the growth expectancy scales, a teacher has a constructive picture of a child's growth in relation to his grade level.

Classroom discussion In the course of classroom lessons, the teacher can compare the individual child with his peers through group discussions with the pupils about their work. Questions, answers, and debate elicit appreciation, criticism, and suggestions for improvement. An atmosphere of critical awareness and shared opinions is soon established. The consensus of the group adds information to the teacher's understanding of the group and adds another dimension to consider in the process of evaluation.

Even more useful to the teacher are tape recordings of these class discussions. An excerpt from a

126

transcript of a recording of a third-grade art class illustrates the place of this type of discussion as an aid to evaluation (the children's responses are in italics).

Last week we decided that we needed to do a better job of making things seem important and in using color so that things would stand out. There are some designs on the bulletin board in groups of two. In the first pair, which design shows up best?
The one on the left.
Why?
The shapes are light on dark paper. In the other design the shapes are just about as dark as the paper, and you can't see them from here.
Look at the next pair. Which would you choose?
The one in which the shapes are darker than the background.
What can you remember from this that will help you while you work today?
We can use the lighter shapes on dark paper or darker shapes on light paper when we want things to stand out.[4]

Such a discussion has the following advantages:

1. The tape recording of the discussion provides information about who responded, to what he responded, and the value and relevance of the response.
2. The tape records the nature of the teaching and permits the teacher to evaluate its effectiveness.
3. No child is conscious of being singled out for questioning, and thus responses are not inhibited.
4. Each child has an opportunity to participate in the lesson, either vocally or just by listening.

Such a record permits the teacher to review the discussion at leisure, away from classroom activities. He can identify each respondent and evaluate the quality of the response more attentively than would be possible in the course of the lesson. To check the reliability of his tape-based evaluation, the classroom teacher can from time to time request the special art teacher to review a tape.

Still more useful as a method of evaluation is a combination of tape-recorded discussion with slides or films of the art work being considered.

[4] Edith M. Henry, *Evaluation of Children's Growth Through Art Experience*, Washington, D.C., National Art Education Association, 1963, p. 14.

Comparing the child's past and present work

Among the tools that may be used to compare a child's present work with his past achievement are (1) sequential tape recordings of the child's responses in art class, (2) checklist record forms combined with informal or formal conferences, (3) anecdotal reports, and (4) a sequential portfolio of the child's art work.

Sequential tape-recorded discussions and visual process records   The tape recordings of class discussions described above can become a means for comparing a child's present and past work if a number of tapes, recorded at specified intervals, are analyzed. From these sequential recordings, the teacher can trace the development of the child's responses in class and form an opinion about his creative visual growth.

Visual process records are obtained through the use of simple self-processing cameras. During intervals in the school year, which are determined by the value in terms of time and money, photographs are taken of the process development of an example of a child's work. Evaluatively, the teacher may gain insight into the developmental patterns through which the child goes in creating his art product.

Record forms combined with conferences   When the teacher fills out a checklist of qualitative items that evidence artistic development and discusses his comments with the child and/or the parents, he adds an instructional element to the evaluation.

One such report form is the Total Educational Growth Record used in the Rickenbach Laboratory School, Kutztown State College (given below). In this form, the qualitative evaluation of the child's progress in art can be compared with his development in other educational areas. For example, "growth consistent with ability" in numbers might be coupled with "unsatisfactory performance" in art, suggesting that the child needs special encouragement in the latter area. The teacher confers with the child's parents between the first and the second reports.

**TOTAL EDUCATIONAL GROWTH RECORD
USED IN THE RICKENBACH LABORATORY
SCHOOL, KUTZTOWN STATE COLLEGE**

Learning activities

(E, exceptional performance; G, growth consistent with ability;
U, unsatisfactory performance.)

LANGUAGE ARTS

(reading, speaking, spelling, writing)	First Report	Second Report
1. Expresses thoughts clearly in speaking		
2. Expresses thoughts clearly in writing		
3. Has grown in reading skills		
4. Understands what he reads		
5. Enjoys independent reading		
6. Gives evidence of thoughtful listening		
7. Writes neatly and legibly		
8. Enjoys participating in dramatics		
9. Is learning to spell words needed in writing		

SOCIAL LIVING

(citizenship, geography, history, health, safety, science)		
1. Shows growth in understanding of problems in the lives of people in local, national, and world areas		
2. Makes use of learnings from social living area		
3. Can locate information independently		
4 Assumes responsibility		
5. Organizes, plans, and evaluates well		

NUMBERS

1. Shows progress in mastery of number skills		
2. Uses knowledge of numbers in school experiences		
3. Shows growth in ability to solve problems		
4. Shows insight and understanding of the number system		
5. Is accurate in work		

MUSIC

	First Report	Second Report
1. Participates in musical activities		
2. Can match tones		
3. Enjoys listening		

ART

1. Is able to use materials well		
2. Shows originality in expressing ideas		
3. Shows growth in understanding himself and the environment		

FOREIGN LANGUAGE

1. Hears well, reproduces the sounds of foreign words accurately		
2. Remembers new words and phrases for later use in sentences		
3. Shows an aptitude for foreign language learning		

PHYSICAL EDUCATION

1. Enjoys a variety of play, skilled games, active group and individual play		
2. Can do some rhythmic interpretation		
3. Is a good sport		
4. Participates naturally and freely		

General development

(1, almost always; 2, usually; 3, sometimes; 4, rarely.)

SOCIAL ATTITUDES

1. Is courteous and considerate of others		
2. Cares for personal and school property		
3. Respects school regulations		
4. Is friendly and cheerful		
5. Accepts criticism or failure as an opportunity to learn; profits by suggestions		

	First Report	Second Report
6. Has self-confidence	_____	_____
7. Exercises self-control	_____	_____
8. Shows a desire to use his knowledge of health and safety	_____	_____
9. Helps promote class activities	_____	_____

WORK HABITS

1. Starts and completes work on time	_____	_____
2. Works well independently	_____	_____
3. Works well in a group	_____	_____
4. Knows how to follow directions	_____	_____
5. Tries to overcome difficulties	_____	_____
6. Works neatly	_____	_____
7. Uses resource materials well	_____	_____

8.12. This is a painting by a first-grader. Assume it is representative of the paintings done over several months by one of your first-graders. How would you be likely to evaluate this child's work on the Grade 1 Art Progress Evaluation Chart on the next page?

Another report form is the Art Progress Evaluation Chart, developed by the author in relation to the Summary of Progression of Artistic Development shown in Table 6.6. It lists, for each grade level, characteristics of art work determined on the basis of growth expectancy scales, and requires the teacher to evaluate on a five-point scale the frequency with which each of the characteristics appears in the child's art products. By employing a five-point scale, the chart encourages the teacher to evaluate objectively rather than to use the safe middle column of a three-point scale. The Art Progress Evaluation Chart is meant to be used at specified intervals through all the elementary school. Collectively, the charts constitute a record of the child's development in the visual arts and permit comparison of his present work with his past achievements. (See the sample below for James W., a first-grader.)

Figure 8.12

The anecdotal report   The anecdotal report is a collection of dated comments about the child's behavior in art class. The comments can be kept in a card file. Over a period of time, they constitute a record of the child's progress and permit evaluation of his present and past work. An example of notation in an anecdotal report is shown below:

Anecdotal Report of
James W.—Grade 1
9/11/70—(Did not attend kindergarten)
9/21/70—Continues to work with uncontrolled scribble
9/25/70—Seems to take to painting at the easel with more solid forms
10/2/70—(etc.)

Sequential portfolio of art work   This is probably the most valuable technique for comparing a child's present and past achievement in art. It consists of actual examples of the child's work, collected as either a class or an individual portfolio. At intervals during the year, each child chooses what he considers his most successful art work and puts it in the portfolio. At the close of the year, both teacher and child compare his later with his earlier work and see the improvement. If a limited number of pictures are saved, the teacher can clip comments to each, and these, passed from teacher to teacher throughout the child's elementary school career, constitute evidence of his progress and prevent the bias of one-teacher evaluations. At some future time, the portfolio can be returned to the child, minus the comments.

ART PROGRESS EVALUATION CHART

| Pupil: James W.   Date: 10/19/70   Grade 1 | | | | | |
| School: Town: State: | | | | | |

Characteristics of art work	Frequency used				
	Never	Scarcely	Somewhat	Great extent	Always
Development of image					
Random scribbling				X	
Symbols for objects			X		
Logical use of form		X			
Symbol has added parts	X				
Symbols look geometric		X			
New symbol shows body parts	X				
Analytical realism is evident	X				

(This chart is a sample to provide an idea for the development of charts of this type for use within school districts.)

If the portfolio can be composed of color photographs or color slides, rather than the actual pictures, the originals can be returned to the child at once. The photograph album or slide tray can travel with the child from grade to grade and, like the portfolio of originals, constitutes evidence of his artistic progress for his parents, his teachers, and himself.

GUIDING THE CHILD'S SELF-EVALUATION

Self-evaluation is a part of the process of growing and learning. The child should have the opportunity to appraise his accomplishments, his weaknesses, the aesthetic and expressive qualities of his work, the satisfaction he has achieved in producing an art work. In the course of self-evaluation, the pupil identifies anew with his creation and relives the art experience.

The teacher should guide the child in comparisons of his earlier with his present work. For example, the teacher might ask: "Why does one drawing look as if it didn't belong together while the other drawing seems to belong together very well?" "What could you do to have the color on this side go with the other side?"

The child should also be able to compare his work with that of his classmates, particularly in Grades 1–3. In Grades 4–6, peer evaluation should be approached cautiously because children are then very sensitive to the opinion of their peers and may be inhibited by it.[5] The direction of group comparison at this age level is most successful when the pupil can present his problems before the class. For example, he may be willing to say, "When I was doing my block print, I had trouble cutting the block in this area, as you can see in my print, and then I discovered that working with the grain helped make my print cleaner. Another time I would do the entire block this way. I got the idea when the teacher suggested that I try this other way of using the tool and compare it with the way I was working."

[5] E. Paul Torrance, *Constructive Behavior: Stress, Personality, and Mental Health,* Belmont, Calif., Wadsworth Publishing, 1965, pp. 340–341.

EVALUATING THE ART LESSON

The teacher should have an opportunity to appraise the effectiveness of his teaching. The Lesson Evaluation Form given here has proved useful in this regard. Answering the questions on the form enables the teacher to determine whether the children had a chance to think creatively, whether any cognitive learning took place, whether the children had an affective experience in the involvement with art, whether they developed or practiced new skills and techniques, how they reacted to the lesson. If the teacher takes time for this sort of evaluation, he will be more alert to the creative visual development and needs of the children in his classroom.

LESSON EVALUATION FORM[6]

Lesson:
Grade:
Date:

Critical Thinking
Did the children have to compare two or more items and make some kind of decision?
     During stimulation _____ While working _____
Were any new concepts learned?
     During stimulation _____ While working _____
Did the children have to observe and make any judgments?
     During stimulation _____ While working _____
Was a concept made more clear through correlation or interrelation of subjects?
     Yes _____ No _____

Information
Was any new vocabulary introduced?
     Yes _____ No _____
Were any new "art" words learned?
     Yes _____ No _____
Did the children discuss any related general information?
     Yes _____ No _____
Were they introduced to any artists?
     Yes _____ No _____

Skill and Techniques
Was a new skill or technique presented?
     Yes _____ No _____

[6] Developed by Sandra Fulmer, Special Art Teacher, Elementary Schools, Boyertown Joint School District, Boyertown, Pa., 1968.

Was an opportunity provided to develop a skill or technique that was familiar but not yet mastered?

Yes _____ No _____

Involvement

Did the children interpret the subject in a way they felt about it rather than how they were told?

Yes _____ No _____

Was there sufficient opportunity to explore all the properties and possibilities of the material used?

Yes _____ No _____

Did they make any discoveries while working with the materials?

Yes _____ No _____

Did the children "talk art" while working?

Yes _____ No _____

Did the children find it necessary to make any observation about their environment?

Yes _____ No _____

Did they have to evaluate their own work?

Yes _____ No _____

Pupil Evaluation

Indicate on the scale how the children reacted to the lesson.

Positive						*Negative*
Involved	1	2	3	4	5	Uninvolved
Resourceful	1	2	3	4	5	Inhibited
Motivated	1	2	3	4	5	Confused
Stimulated	1	2	3	4	5	Disinterested
Creative	1	2	3	4	5	Unimaginative
Self-evaluative	1	2	3	4	5	Indifferent

SUMMARY

Evaluation involves appraisal of (1) the pupil's development in the visual arts, and (2) the teacher's (and the art program's) effectiveness.

Eight objectives of the elementary school program for evaluation of creative visual development are listed:

1. To judge the child's art work in terms of criteria appropriate to his age-grade level
2. To judge the child's art work on the basis of appraisal by more than one teacher
3. To improve teaching by encouraging teachers to appraise their own performance
4. To guide the pupil toward self-appraisal
5. To develop a continuous program of evaluation throughout the elementary school
6. To relate the child's creative visual development to his total growth
7. To organize the learning environment in terms of the child's needs
8. To judge the child's creative visual development by means of valid techniques and on the basis of adequate data

The child's creative visual development should not be evaluated alone; it should be appraised in relation to his mental, emotional, social, physical, and aesthetic growth. His total development should be assessed. The components of total development are discussed in terms of the child's behavior in art class.

The pupil's creative visual development is traditionally evaluated by means of standardized tests and reported as a grade. This method has many disadvantages. More useful techniques of appraising a child's artistic growth are:

1. Comparing his performance with group performance to assess his relative position. This can be done by means of developmental growth scales or through analyzing his responses in a group discussion.
2. Comparing the child's present with his past work to determine his improvement. This can be done by analyzing sequential tape-recorded discussions, checklist record forms filled out at specified intervals, anecdotal reports, or a sequential portfolio of the child's art work.
3. Guiding the child toward self-evaluation. The child is guided by the teacher to compare his present with his earlier work and note the improvement, and to compare his own work with that of his classmates.

The teacher's effectiveness can be analyzed with the help of an evaluation checklist form. The teacher evaluates his instructional procedure as he assesses the child's progress.

AIDS TO UNDERSTANDING

For discussion

1. Suggest how evaluation applied to pupil development is uniquely different from appraisal of teacher effectiveness. What is the relationship between these two aspects of evaluation?

2. How do the objectives for the evaluation of art harmonize with a strategy for creative-evaluative art teaching? Do they harmonize with the process of creating an art work? Do they support directed teaching or teaching providing direction?

3. Discuss in detail the characteristics of creative visual growth you would look for in the total growth pattern of children.

4. Debate the following position: Art begins and ends with a process of evaluation.

5. How do you account for the fact that art, an affective learning response, cannot be evaluated simply in terms of a grade related to the quality of the final product or a collection of learned facts?

6. What are the antagonistic effects of requiring grades for art?

7. What values are there in a program of evaluation from the standpoint of the elementary classroom teacher?

8. What is the difference between *quantitative* grading of art work and *qualitative* evaluation of art work?

9. How can qualitative evaluation of art affect the learning process of children in the classroom?

10. If no evaluation existed in the educational program of the elementary classroom, what would the art program be like? How would it differ from an art program where qualitative evaluation solving) was an integral part of the learnir

For involvement

1. Using as a subject a child from a local elementary school, carry on a regular evaluation of his creative visual growth in relation to other aspects of his physical and educational growth.

2. Analyze a series of crayon drawings or paintings of a child in terms of evidences of characteristic visual growth patterns related to mental ability, emotional maturity, social adequacy, physical development, aesthetic judgment, perceptual awareness, and creative growth (see pages 118–123).

3. Using the growth scale in Chapter 6 of this text (Table 6.6), compare an individual child's development with the growth expectancy of a group you have observed in your training.

4. Carry on a group discussion with a class of pupils about their art works soon after they have completed them. Tape this discussion. (Use the example on ·page 127 as a model for your approach to the discussion). What advantage does the teacher have for more objective evaluation using a tape recorder?

5. Develop an evaluation tool to compare individual children's past and present art work (see page 130).

6. Observe an art lesson in an elementary school and use the Lesson Evaluation Form in this chapter (page 131) in your evaluation of the lesson.

7. List the strengths and weaknesses of the Lesson Evaluation Form used in item 6 and revise it to meet the criteria of your constructive reaction to it.

Part Three
THE ELEMENTARY SCHOOL
ART PROGRAM

Chapter 9
ELEMENTARY SCHOOL ART:
THE PROGRAM FOUNDATION

In art, as in general education, the elementary school program is the foundation for later secondary school learning. The elementary art administrator has the responsibility of organizing learning experiences in cooperation with all the art and classroom teachers to make available to each child a well-integrated education as a basis for further learning. The organized art experience, in terms of the scope and sequence of experiences, is the curriculum. A complete art curriculum describes the scope and sequence of the art program from kindergarten through Grade 12. Each grade provides the foundation of visual learning for the grade immediately following, and as the child progresses through school, the accumulated educational background constitutes his *frame of reference*. Through each new art experience, he expands his frame of reference and achieves creative visual growth in a qualitative manner.

In this chapter we shall first discuss the function of the elementary school art program, what to teach, and

9.1. One of the primary aims of art education is to integrate the child's art learnings with the rest of his life. As these elementary school children appreciate the work of their classmates at the annual school art exhibit, their visual learning is being integrated with their total experiences.

growth, physical, perceptual, aesthetic, and creative components are integrated into a harmonious unity through the qualities of art; (3) to provide the child with behavioral involvement with art within his level of maturity and ability which is modeled after the total dialogue, typical of the artist, between the genesis of idea, processes, and qualities of a work; (4) to provide opportunities in the learning situation for the child to gain understanding about art objects in his culture and to develop ability for independent artistic evaluation within his maturity level. The classroom teacher, in his position of awareness of each aspect of development of the child's being, is able to cooperate with the art teacher in the fulfillment of these aims. These aims are achieved by the child's experience of seeing and sensing visual relationships, of producing his own art work, of the stimulation of works of art, of his sequentially developed total qualitative art program.

What to teach

What to teach and organizing it are curriculum problems. Writers have suggested criteria for selection[1] and the importance of the structure[2] of subject matter. Every curriculum is different because it reflects the unique characteristics of the school program in a particular community. However, certain aspects of the curriculum have common qualities related to the particular area of subject matter. What these qualities are, the emphasis, and fit in the curriculum is a constant question and subject to review. Many studies of curriculum in art education provide insight into the issue.[3]

describe the development and structure of the art curriculum. We shall discuss what the elementary teacher can expect to find in a typical art curriculum guide and present, by way of illustration, two samples of curriculum guides. Finally, we shall make recommendations for teaching art based upon the expected artistic behavior of the child.

FUNCTION OF THE ELEMENTARY SCHOOL ART PROGRAM

Elementary school art is the foundation for the child's subsequent art education and his adult enjoyment of art as an integral part of living. Art has no subject-matter barriers; and therefore it is also a means of uniting all learnings. Primarily, in relation to the discussion in Chapter 1, the aim of art education at the elementary school level is as follows: (1) to integrate the child's art learnings with his total educational foundation; (2) to develop children whose intellectual, emotional, social

Figure 9.1

[1] B. O. Smith, W. O. Stanley, and J. H. Shores, *Fundamentals of Curriculum Development*, rev. ed., World Book, New York, 1957, pp. 278–296.

[2] Jerome Bruner, *The Process of Education*, Cambridge, Mass., Harvard University Press, 1965.

[3] *Seminar on Elementary and Secondary School Education in the Visual Arts*, Howard Conant, Project Director, Cooperative Research Project, No. V–003, Office of Education, U.S. Dept. of HEW, New York, University Printing Office, New York University, 1965; *A Seminar in Art Education for Research and Curriculum Development*, Edward L. Mattil, Project Director, Cooperative Research Project V–002, Office of Education, U.S. Dept. of HEW, University Park, Pennsylvania State University, 1966; *Conference on Curriculum Instructional Development in Art Education: A Project Report*, Alice A. D. Baumgarner, Director, U.S. Office of Education Grant Contract OE(2–6–061772–0804), Washington, D.C., National Art Education Association, 1967.

Nevertheless the problem of curriculum cannot be wrapped up in one neat package with a "this is it" label on it.

Obviously, the art curriculum is the product of continual research by many representative educational and resource personnel whose purpose is to improve it. More recently, studies have observed the milieu and behavior of the artist. These observations of the role of the artist, the producer, and the role of the user, the consumer, provide insight into the qualities common to the art subject matter and the art experience which should be a part of every curriculum.[4] We shall consider these qualities—first, the general qualities of the subject matter of art, and then the specific qualities.

GENERAL QUALITIES OF ART General qualities of the subject matter of art are (1) awareness of the values of the art process and product with regard to the artist's response to his environment; (2) awareness of his rapport with art in society; (3) awareness of the object created, its material, style, use, structure, and meaning within a personal, social, historic, or symbolic context; (4) awareness that the individual and society should benefit from or be affected by the production and consumption of art work; (5) awareness of the relationship of the artist and the consumer of art in contemporary culture and past heritage.

SPECIFIC QUALITIES OF ART Translated for the understanding of children and in terms for teaching them, the specific qualities of the subject matter of art are structured in the form of goals to be achieved in six categories: feeling and responding, knowing about, manipulation of, understanding culture and heritage, social context, and symbolic relationships.

Feeling and responding by:
1. Sensing and having confidence in ideas for visual works (see Appendix I)

---

[4] *Aesthetic Education Program: Report of the Planning Phase,* Manuel Barkan, Director, and Laura H. Chapman, Research Associate, A Project of Central Mid-Western Regional Education Laboratory, Office of Education, U.S. Dept. of HEW, August 31, 1967.

2. Open willingness to try many kinds of art forms (see Appendix II)
3. Feeling for beautiful arrangements of space (see Appendix V)
4. Confidence in doing art work (creative-evaluative approach)
5. Ability to evaluate one's own art and art in the needs of daily life (concept of creative-evaluative approach)

9.2. *A goal of art education is making children sensitive to the design qualities of man-made and natural objects. The seventh-grader who created this still life shows that he has achieved this goal. (He is in the stage of perceptual realism.)*

6. Desire to master skills with materials (see Appendix IV)

Figure 9.2 7. Sensitivity to the design qualities of man-made and natural objects (resource teaching aids, Chapter 11)

8. Spirit-filled expression in making and responding to art work (creative-evaluative teaching)

9. Discriminating good qualities of art and weak qualities of art (see appendixes)

Knowing about:

1. Aesthetic application of line, color, form, and texture to art work and living (see Appendixes III and V)
2. Understanding the arrangement of elements in space
3. Exposure to art of the past as it relates to the work of the children and their understanding
4. Showing good taste in the selection of visual forms and ability to tell why the selection was made
5. Progressively increasing ability and skill with an increasing number of art processes (see Appendixes III and IV)
6. Investigation and evaluation of sensory, real, and literary resources

Manipulation of:

1. Hands and eyes to work together
2. Tools and materials adjusted in sequence to the physical and emotional maturity level of the child (see Appendixes III and IV)
3. Basic materials such as clay, paint, crayons, cardboard, etc., with progressively expanding ability and skill in the control of tools and handling of materials (see Appendixes III, IV, and VI and recommendations in this chapter)

Understanding culture and heritage:

1. Visiting historical sites, art museums, and engaging in other cultural activities
2. Participating in special activities in the school, community, recreation programs, and church
3. Exposure to the resources of artists and craftsmen within the community area

Social context:

1. Working with groups in the production of community art in the classroom and in school and community activities
2. Exposure to art in contemporary culture in the community area
3. Realization of the effect of art on the children's dress, homes, on public buildings, and the plan of the community

Symbolic relationships:

1. To express his thinking and feelings in lines, shapes, colors, and textures as nonverbal communication
2. To talk about forms of symbolic nature in their own art work and in the works of artists (reproductions or colored slides of work: Miró, Picasso, Kline, Arp, etc.)
3. Relating to the form, styles, and techniques of art: realistic, impressionistic, expressionistic, abstract, or nonobjective, etc.
4. Seeing shapes in the natural environment

DEVELOPMENT AND ORGANIZATION OF THE ART CURRICULUM

The art curriculum is planned through the cooperative efforts of the art administrator, art teachers, and classroom teachers. Obviously, therefore, classroom teachers should understand how a curriculum is developed and organized. The "what to teach" of the curriculum is planned in terms of the *scope* and *sequence* of art experience as they relate to each other and as they relate to one of these primary aspects: needs, artistic behavior, or subject matter. The scope represents the overall goals for the art program. Whichever of the three aspects of the curriculum is chosen as the scope or goal, the other two become vital subgoals. Thus, if the scope or basis of organization centers on needs for art, then artistic behavior and subject matter are subgoals; on the other hand, if artistic behavior is the organizing center, then needs and subject matter are subgoals; and so forth. The sequence is based on the progression of children's artistic developmental stages. In other words, the individual units of the curriculum attempt to relate the objectives of art education to the ability of the child at each grade or maturation level.

Whether stated in terms of needs, artistic behavior, or subject matter, qualities of the artist's and art consumer's experience become the organizing center for the goals of art education—the scope of the curriculum. Each goal in the scope of the curriculum is developed in a progressive sequence from kindergarten to Grade 12. It is imperative that the elementary teacher understand this relationship of scope to sequence in the art curriculum, so that he is able to recognize his role in the planning process of the elementary school art program. This is the process of organizing "what to teach."

The areas of art experience, goals, in the scope of the art curriculum are interpreted in terms of the general objectives for each unit of experience in the sequence. These are stated in a manner compatible with the teaching approach (see Chapter 3, Table 3.1), as follows: (1) subject matter of art (academic approach); (2) behavioral art activity (activity approach); (3) need of art in life (experience approach)—that is, essential art qualities needed in life.

There is a distinct difference between organizing a curriculum and actually teaching art. Curriculum is a problem of the mechanics, schematic processing, and organization of *what* is to be learned; this is the overall responsibility of the art specialist. Teaching art is the creative-evaluative, affective-to-cognitive process. It is the science of *how* qualities of art (content and form) are learned; this is the vital responsibility of any teacher who is in contact with children in the elementary school classroom.

Whichever approach is used in developing a curriculum, all of the art *content* described earlier is essential; it is the *viewpoint* taken by the planners that makes one art curriculum different from another. Each art curriculum should have its own particular character; it should reflect both the thinking of those who designed it and the community for which they designed it. It is always essential, however, that the goals for the art program satisfy valid criteria for the curriculum. Smith, Stanley, and Shores recommend the following criteria: the objectives should "(1) be conceived in terms of the

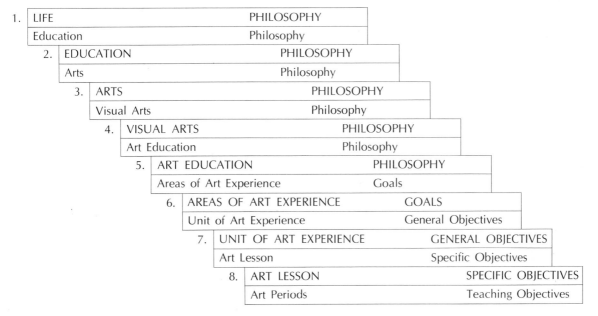

1.	LIFE	PHILOSOPHY
	Education	Philosophy
2.	EDUCATION	PHILOSOPHY
	Arts	Philosophy
3.	ARTS	PHILOSOPHY
	Visual Arts	Philosophy
4.	VISUAL ARTS	PHILOSOPHY
	Art Education	Philosophy
5.	ART EDUCATION	PHILOSOPHY
	Areas of Art Experience	Goals
6.	AREAS OF ART EXPERIENCE	GOALS
	Unit of Art Experience	General Objectives
7.	UNIT OF ART EXPERIENCE	GENERAL OBJECTIVES
	Art Lesson	Specific Objectives
8.	ART LESSON	SPECIFIC OBJECTIVES
	Art Periods	Teaching Objectives

9.3. *This diagram shows the stepwise development of the goals and objectives of the art curriculum from philosophical statements of life to specific art objectives.*

demands of the social circumstances; (2) lead toward the fulfillment of basic human needs; (3) be consistent with democratic ideals; (4) be consistent or noncontradictory in their relationships with one another; (5) be capable of reduction to behavioristic terms."[5] These criteria are basic to the thinking of most educators who are engaged in curriculum development.

Scope of art experience

Figure 9.3

Planning the scope of the art curriculum in terms of goals involves developing, in stepwise manner, increasingly specific goals and objectives from general philosophical statements about life, education, and the arts. This process is shown in the diagram. Thus, the most general determinant of the scope of the art curriculum is the philosophy of the people of the community about their life needs, education, the arts, and the content of visual art (Steps 1–4). On the basis of this philosophy, increasingly specific goals are developed for art education, areas of art experience (the scope), units of art, art lessons, and art periods (Steps 5–8).

In practice, the curriculum planners are concerned generally with the areas of art experience, the goals that represent the scope of the curriculum. The realm of the involvement of the community with art in relation to a contemporary art philosophy is the background against which they must work in terms of a generally accepted set of principles for art education. The planning of art lessons and the art periods is the responsibility of the special art and classroom teachers.

The areas and units of art experience are stated in a manner consistent with the educational philosophy of the school district. For the purposes of this book, the *areas of art experience* (Step 6) are expressed as needs of life, individual and social—need for visual communication, need for art in industry, need for art in personal living, need for art in society, need for art in commerce (see also Table 9.1). In this context, it is accepted that behavioral goals and subject-matter goals are subgoals. These subgoals, the *units of art experience* developed

for each area, are phrased as general objectives (Step 7). For example, from the area of art experience "need for art in personal living" is developed the objective "to understand the content of art in the personal life of the individual"; from "need for art in industry" is developed the objective "to understand the effect of visual art in the industrial enterprises of man and society." *Art lessons* (Step 8) are phrased as specific objectives intended to lead toward understanding of the general objectives of the unit.

Sequence of art experience

The sequence of art experience is planned on the basis of what is known about children's norms of artistic development (see Chapter 5) in relation to the scope of the areas of art experience. The sequence is coordinated with the mental, physical, emotional, discriminative, social, and aesthetic ability levels of the child in connection with the qualitative values essential to affective and cognitive visual learnings in art.

Art educators are divided into two diametrically opposed groups in their view of readiness in elementary school art. One group sees readiness as having children make "works of art with a *variety* of materials and processes."[6] The other group focuses on *depth* of experience through a cyclical repetition of similar experiences in which the use of basic materials is increasingly more challenging, and the child's frame of reference in art content and form expands as he sequentially progresses in each grade.[7] It is a spiral-like process. In fact, this is what Bruner refers to as the "spiral curriculum."[8] In the process, the concern is with the structure of content in terms of the child's maturation. It is an essential aspect of the sequence of the curriculum.

[5] Smith, Stanley, and Shores, op. cit., pp. 252–270.

[6] *The Essentials of a Quality School Art Program, A Position Statement of the National Art Education Association,* John Benz, Chairman, NAEA, Washington, D.C., 1968.

[7] Edward L. Mattil, Kenneth R. Beittel, and Robert C. Burkhart, "The Effect of Depth versus a Breadth Method of Art Instruction at the Ninth Grade Level," *Studies in Art Education,* Charles M. Dorn, ed., Washington, D.C., National Art Education Association, 1961; E. Paul Torrance, *Guiding Creative Talent,* Englewood Cliffs, N.J., Prentice-Hall, 1962, chap. 5.

[8] Bruner, op. cit., pp. 13, 52-54.

Table 9.1   RELATION OF SCOPE AND SEQUENCE OF ART EXPERIENCE IN THE ART CURRICULUM

GRADE LEVEL	AREAS OF ART EXPERIENCE (GENERAL GOALS FOR THE ART PROGRAM)				
	NEED FOR VISUAL COMMUNICATION	NEED FOR ART IN INDUSTRY	NEED FOR ART IN PERSONAL LIVING	NEED FOR ART IN SOCIETY	NEED FOR ART IN COMMERCE
12	– – –				
11			Each box horizontally articulated represents a unit of the scope		
10			of art experience for the grade level		
9			SECONDARY ART PROGRAM		
8					
7					
6					
5					
4					
3			ELEMENTARY ART PROGRAM		
2					
1	Units – →				
K	– – –				

Sequence of Experiences (vertical, left axis)

←————————————— Scope of Experience —————————————→

In structuring a curriculum of elementary school art, the prime concern is with adjusting the areas of art experience to the developmental growth of the learner. This is a process of joining together in a sequence the art content of experience to provide continuity of learning from the kindergarten to the sixth grade.

Relation of scope and sequence

The relation of scope and sequence in the art curriculum is shown in Table 9.1. The progressively organized content of art from kindergarten through Grade 12 relates to the goals for the art program and is stated as areas of art experience—the scope. The learning experiences in the sequence are organized as units and are coordinated through each grade level with the scope of the areas of art experience within each grade. The units of the curriculum coordinate with the sequence: they join in a logical progressive order from low- to high-grade level to constitute the *vertical articulation* of the curriculum; they coordinate with the scope: they join within a single grade level, providing experience in all areas of art experience to constitute the *horizontal articulation* of the curriculum.

This twofold articulation of the scope and sequence of the art curriculum makes it possible to adapt the curriculum to the immediate needs and interests of the students, differing behavioral artistic activities, and varied aspects of the subject matter of art. Such a curriculum provides a flexible structure for the creative-evaluative teaching of art. Used as a guide, it provides the classroom teacher with a record of what the class has learned and what it needs to learn. Used to plan the art program, it encourages the teacher to adapt the art lessons to each new class and at the same time assures the children of variety, depth, and continuity in their understanding of the qualities that are the basis of a sound frame of reference in art.

CONTENTS OF THE CURRICULUM GUIDE

The curriculum guide is developed by the art administrator in cooperation with all the art and classroom teachers in a school system. It replaces the old fixed course of study. It is generally arranged in loose-leaf format so that when revisions resulting from action research are necessary, pages can be easily replaced. It is intended to be used widely and flexibly, so that its content can continually be improved. It should provide space for notations by teachers, consultants, and administrators, either in the margins or at the end of each section. These notations serve as the basis for further refinements.

In the following discussion we shall briefly describe the material that should be included in the curriculum guide. Tables of contents of two guides are presented near the end of the discussion.

Statement of the philosophy of the art program

The curriculum guide should explain the philosophy of the particular art program. It should be consistent with the directions for teaching art that evolve from theories and research (see Chapter 2).

Description of the characteristics of creative visual growth

The curriculum guide should describe the characteristics of the average child's visual growth and development so that the teacher can identify and deal individually with children who deviate upward or downward from the norms. These may be stated in terms of goals related to needs for art in life, artistic behavior, and art qualities in art work.

Suggestions for art experience

The curriculum guide should suggest art experience that will involve children, individually and in groups, in the solution of art problems typical of those in the experience of artists. Group work involves sharing ideas, experience in democratic living, understanding the freedom and limitations of one's ideas and movements, and achieving social values and goals.

Orientation of the significance of freedom

The curriculum guide should indicate that art education promotes growth in visual expression related to the artistic behavior of the artist. It should suggest the means and ends for accomplishing this aim. It should point out a means for a creative-evaluative strategy of teaching. It should show that freedom of thinking by children within the limitations set by normal restraint results from the manner of teaching, from the classroom atmosphere, availability of materials, and the acceptance of individual ideas for and of art work.

Statement of the function of art education

The curriculum guide should point out the special contributions art can make to the child's creative visual growth and development. The goal of education is the maximum development of each pupil; yet for each level of development certain considerations are more important than others. Therefore, the curriculum guide indicates what aspects of development are best stressed at each level in terms of the scope and sequence of art experience.

Art and social living, culture, and heritage

The curriculum guide should indicate the contribution art can make to life. Pupils must be prepared to assume the responsibilities of leadership and of participating

Two children in the stage of
perceptual realism came up with
very different ideas in response to
a stimulation by their teacher.
XIX. This still life is quite intriguing.
XX. The other child chose to
create an impression of a city.

XXI. *This section of a mural by a third-grade class shows that though the children are aware of the actual appearance of their surroundings, they are continuing to represent the elements symbolically. They do not perceive spatial relations, and the proportions of the objects still have an emotional significance.*

effectively as a group member in school and community activities requiring art contributions. Many art activities require group decisions and group cooperation. The curriculum guide should relate, within the limitations of child understanding and aesthetic growth, knowledge about art in his culture and his heritage.

The substance of art

The curriculum guide should suggest goals in terms of needs, artistic behavior, and the qualities of art. It should point out that the subject matter of art grows out of the child's daily experiences in his environment, his culture, and his production of and response to art works in the manner of the artist.

Balance and diversity of the art program

The curriculum guide should unify the whole art program. It should emphasize the need for differentiation in types of experiences, media, and approaches to qualitative creative problems. Variation and balance of the structure of art subject matter, content and form, sustain interest, broaden concepts, utilize new knowledge, achieve new insights, and develop appreciation for many types of art expression.

Evaluation of art experience

The curriculum guide should state briefly and clearly goals of the curriculum, the objectives of the art experience of each unit and each lesson, and should suggest procedures to determine whether the objectives have been attained. The information presented in Chapter 5, recommendations in this chapter, and the appendixes of this textbook collectively serve this function for evaluation.

Samples of curriculum guides

The contents of two typical art curriculum guides are quoted here to illustrate how these principles are carried out. The first guide was developed for a laboratory school; the second was developed for a large city that has a program of art education that is among the most

contemporary. In each case, the guide was the result of the combined thinking of art administrators, art teachers, and cooperating elementary teachers. The first contents is taken from the *Art Curriculum Guide*, Rickenbach Research Learning Center, Kutztown, Pennsylvania.

1. Statement of the philosophy of the art education program
2. Tabular presentation of the areas of art experience to be covered in each grade and suggested art activities
3. Tabular presentation of the scope and sequence of art experiences related to painting, drawing, graphics, modeling, sculpture, construction, and crafts
4. Outline of the characteristics of creative visual development
5. Bibliography

The Art Department of the Richmond Public Schools, Richmond, Virginia, has developed an attractive 96-page guide, *Art for Richmond's Children*. Its contents, now quoted, shows what a well-planned guide generally includes.

Development of This Guide
Ways To Use This Guide
Introduction
Our Point of View
Points of Emphasis
Junior Primary and Second Grades
Third and Fourth Grades
Fifth and Sixth Grades
Art and TV
Evaluation
Cooperative Planning
The Setting for Art
Art Trips and Tours
Art Supplies in the School
The Time for Art
Art Appreciation, Grades J.P.–6
The Materials Chart, Grades J.P.–6
Recommended Art Books and Magazines
Art Films

Table 9.2 shows the "Art Appreciation and Art History" section for the fourth grade as an example of the kind of information provided for all areas of art for all grade levels in the Richmond guide. Table 9.3, also taken from the guide, lists the general content areas in the guide which permit the elementary teacher to plan art lessons in terms of a qualitative art program. Also

Table 9.2 ART APPRECIATION AND ART HISTORY   GRADE 4

GRADE 4	GENERAL ART UNDERSTANDINGS	ART HISTORY

DISCOVERING ART QUALITIES IN NATURE AND SURROUNDINGS	*CONSIDER*
	Nature as an inspiration and source of ideas and materials for art
	The relationship of African, Eskimo, and other art to nature
	Materials and processes
	    from sand to glass
	    from clay to brick
	    from plant to dye colors
	Learn to see details, and color changes in:
	    sunshine and shadows
	    reflections in water
	    wind, rain, ice
	    local vegetation and animals
	    mountains, trees, buildings, and other surroundings
		SHOW AND TALK ABOUT
		Eskimo art–masks, carvings, toys, costumes, weapons, and pictures
		African art–masks, wood carvings, bronze castings, ornaments, and decorations
		French impressionist paintings showing out-of-doors color effects (broken color)
		Dutch painting showing scenes from their daily life
		English landscape painting showing sky, earth, and water

LEARNING ABOUT OUR WORLD OF ART	*IDENTIFY*
	Colors:
	    primary
	    secondary
	    opposite
	Types of Pictures:
	    portrait landscape
	    still life seascape
	    cartoon illustration
	Lines which have personalities such as bold, angry, calm, and nervous
	Textures to see and to feel such as in drawings and paintings
	Our feelings or emotions and how different colors, lines, shapes, and space affect us
		TALK ABOUT AND SHOW
		Virginia artists of past and present
		    Julian Binford, painter
		    Mann S. Valentine, sculptor
		    Ted Turner, print maker
		    Colonial craftsmen–wood carvers, metalsmiths, glass blowers, weavers, potters
		    Thomas Jefferson, architect
		Architectural styles in Virginia from early houses to modern, costumes, furniture, tools, and utensils
		Drawings and paintings showing qualities of line and color
		    Pablo Picasso–Spanish
		    Vincent Van Gogh–Dutch
		Scandinavian crafts

DEVELOPING AND USING CRITICAL JUDGMENT	*TALK ABOUT*
	Selecting, combining, and arranging as applied to:
	    personal appearance
	    classroom
	    school building
	    homes
	    personal possessions
	    our art work
	The suitability of materials to their use and design
	The meaning of crafts, craftsmanship, skill, and practice
	The techniques and materials in specific art products
		DISCUSS HOW
		People have different ideas about what is beautiful
		People in every time and place like to make and own beautiful things
		Geographical factors influence the design of clothes and homes
		People everywhere value good craftsmanship
		Styles, fashions, and taste changes
		People everywhere like old things and new things
		"Many people" means many ideas

EXPERIENCES	VISUALS	

Take trips to:
    The Virginia Museum of Fine Arts to see landscape
      painting
    The Valentine Museum to see Indian art
    Jamestown to see the glass works
    Williamsburg to see the pottery and the Abby
      Rockefeller Museum
    The Shenandoah Valley and the Skyline Drive in
      the fall
Take a walking trip to observe beautiful colors, textures,
   and shapes around the school building, in other
   buildings, the sky and the sidewalk
Keep a sketch book and notebook of beautiful things
   collected visually
	FILMS:
	
	SLIDES:
	
	EXHIBITS:
	
	BOOKS:
		The Dismal Swamp
		The Seasons
		Watusi
		Trees
		Landscapes
		Seascapes
		Color
		Mountains in Art and Nature
		Eskimo Art
		African Art
		Dutch Painting
		English Landscapes
		World of Faces
		The Man Who Painted the Sun
		The Anatomy of Nature
		African Art
		Eskimos

Collect pictures by impressionists
Invite local artists for demonstration in preparing and
   mixing colors and painting techniques
See drawings and etchings at local museums for kinds of
   lines which the artist has used
Take a trip to Capitol Square, Monument Avenue, and the
   Virginia Museum to observe the sculpture
Collect pictures of early and modern buildings for
   comparison
Take a trip to the Historic Richmond Foundation on
   Church Hill
	FILMS:
	
	BOOKS:
	
	EXHIBITS:
	
	SLIDES:
	
	TV LESSONS:
		Historical Virginia
		Art in Our World
		Discovering Color
		Guatemala, Land of Looms
		Our Expanding Vision #4
		Art Is Everywhere
		Do You See What I See?
		Picasso
		Historical Landmarks of Virginia
		Glass and Pottery, Old and New
		Scandinavian Designs
		Paintings of People by children and adult
		   artists
		Paintings of Landscapes
		See manual for contents

Discuss the arrangement and the color scheme of the
   classroom
Discuss combinations of colors and texture in the
   clothes of the students
Discuss good qualities of the paintings by famous artists
Evaluate orally the art work of students in the class on
   the basis of positive criteria set up by the class
Invite foreign exchange students to discuss art and social
   elements of their countries
	SLIDES:
	
	BOOKS:
	
	TRAVEL
	  POSTERS:
	MAGAZINES:
	EXHIBITS:
		Colonial Williamsburg
		Modern Art Objects
		Picasso for Children
		Farm on Fifth Avenue
		
		By countries
		Of furniture and clothing
		Good Design for Everyday
		Towns and Gowns
		Houses That Fit

Table 9.3 IDEAS FOR ART

ART ACTIVITIES	SOURCES OF IDEAS	
PAINTING	*ART*	*VIEWPOINT*
DRAWING	·Line · Shape	·Airplane view
PRINTS	·Color · Pattern	·Underwater
CARVING AND	·Texture	·Underground
MODELING	·Light and dark	·Perspective in
POSTERS	·Order	streets and buildings
CRAYONS AND	*DESIGNS*	*TIME*
COLORED CHALK	·Motifs from nature	·Long ago · Now
3-D CONSTRUCTION	·Abstract	·When I grow up
APPRECIATION	·Geometric	·Night and day
COSTUMES AND		·Sequences of events
SCENERY	*LIVING THINGS*	
COLLAGE	·Fish · Insects	*ILLUSTRATIONS*
CUT PAPER	·Reptiles · Fowl	·Poems · Myths
PAPIER-MÂCHÉ	·Mammals · etc.	·Stories
FRIEZE	·Trees · Leaves	·Fables
SEWING AND	·Flowers · Fruit	·Facts
EMBROIDERY	*STUDIES*	*MAKE-BELIEVE*
MOSAICS	·Observation and recording	·Fantasies
ARRANGEMENTS	of characteristics and	·Dreams
AND DISPLAYS	details of things	·Wishes
		·Fears
	SEASONS	
	·Fall	*FEELINGS*
	·Winter	·Happy · Sad
	·Spring	·Calm · Angry
	·Summer	·Afraid
		·Lonely
	WEATHER	
	·Storms · Rain	*HEADS*
	·Sun · Fog	·Portraits
	·Snow · Floods	·Masks
	·Earthquakes	·Characters
		·Moods
	EVENTS	
	·Personal	*PEOPLE IN ACTION*
	·Local	·Work
	·National	·Play
	·International	·Motion
		·Gesture
	PLACES	
	·Faraway	*RELATIONSHIPS*
	·Outer space	·Self–family
	·Interiors	·Self–friend
	·City · Country	·Self–pet
	·Seashore · etc.	·Self–toy

listed are a number of sources of ideas. The two lists provide the teacher with a way to correlate the resource information in the guide with immediate learning experiences in the classroom.

Curriculum planning of this nature is the result of a total effort by an art staff with the cooperative aid of elementary teachers and of well-qualified supervisory leadership in terms of the needs of the elementary children and the educational problems the elementary classroom teacher may encounter in the process of teaching.

RECOMMENDATIONS BASED ON BEHAVIORAL CHARACTERISTICS OF CHILDREN PRODUCING ART WORK

The following discussion presents recommendations to guide the teacher in conducting art lessons that coordinate the child's visual learning with his whole education. For a detailed description of the characteristics of children's art at various stages of creative development, the reader should consult Chapter 6.

Kindergarten and Grades 1 and 2

A child has a natural instinct to create. In these early years, his expression of his feelings and thoughts about his surroundings should be as natural as walking and talking. His early art work progresses from merely manipulating a pencil or crayon to expressive scribbling to drawing symbols that he names. Gradually, he should be able to use certain symbols to express certain things, although they bear little relation to the actual appearance of the things they represent and are meaningless to the adult. At this stage most children express themselves through similar symbols.

The child should be able to conceive symbols for elements of his surroundings because he is not yet able to perceive them in an adult sense; thus if one defines art as "nature passed through thought," one can call the child an artist. But he is not an artist in the adult sense. He should be able to develop symbols composed of lines, shapes, and colors and express his feelings about

his surroundings. He should show interest in color because it is red or blue or yellow; in line because it is wide or dark or long; in shape because it is big or square or round. He should be aware of nonobjective ordering of color, line, and shape. This expression should be spontaneous and should not be interfered with by the teacher. The child should never be admonished to "make a picture look as it really looks."

At this stage, the classroom teacher (usually not an artist) is able to encourage the child's natural expression better than a trained artist, who is often inclined to over-teach. In addition, the classroom teacher best knows the child's interests and can thus integrate the art lessons with other aspects of the child's life.

Art lessons in these early grades should not be just play periods. The once-popular nondirected, laissez-faire approach to teaching art is discredited. The child should not merely be allowed to manipulate and try out a wide variety of art materials, gaining only superficial acquaintance with all. Rather, he should be guided to work in greater depth with fewer materials. He should work repeatedly with the basic materials of painting, drawing, and modeling, in progressively more challenging experiences. The child should understand the advantages and limitations of each medium. Taught by the creative-evaluative approach, he is involved in the process of awareness, selection, making, evaluating, and divergent thinking.

SUGGESTIONS FOR GUIDANCE IN TEACHING AN ART LESSON: GRADES K–2

1. Develop experiences in painting, drawing, modeling in clay, using simple craft materials, building, and making paper constructions.
2. Select materials and tools the child can handle easily which are large enough and light enough to suit a child.
3. Select basic materials whose handling you can guide.
4. Select activities that relate to the child's major ideas, interests, needs, behavioral abilities, and that extend the qualities of art.

Figures 9.4–9.6

The child in kindergarten and the first two grades progresses from manipulating crayon or brush to depicting symbols that he names. **9.4.** A 5-year-old in kindergarten explores the use of the brush and tempera paints. Though the child makes no orderly arrangement of background, middle ground, or foreground, she obviously is beginning to notice spatial relations. The painting also shows some imagery. **9.5.** This is another kindergarten child's symbol for a dog. **9.6.** A 6-year-old in first grade draws "My Family" in crayons. His chief interests, which relate to "me" and "my," are reflected in his picture. (Which figure represents the artist himself?)

5. Present the materials by setting up evaluative situations comparing art qualities.

6. Give experiences with basic materials in depth which permit the child to compare results under guidance through questions.

7. Development of an understanding of materials begins at this level.

8. Note that significant needs of the child include:

   a. Guidance of a child-maternal nature
   b. Feeling wanted in a natural loving manner
   c. Freedom within specified limitations
   d. Development of sensitivity and appreciation of his work
   e. Support of his art by older persons—let him talk about it
   f. Supportive and honest encouragement
   g. Clear understanding through orientation of information
   h. Questions with divergent power

9. Develop evaluative discrimination of the art work of the children and the art work of artists. Have works of artists around his environment but not so that it will contrast with the child's art.

Grades 3 and 4

At this stage the child should be able to represent the elements of his environment symbolically, but he should be aware of their actual appearance. He should begin to perceive spatial relations. In his drawings, proportion should have some emotional significance, not visual: important objects are large, less important ones small. He will not be aware of linear perspective, but should place people and objects in his pictures in relation to their importance to him. His pictures should seem flat and two-dimensional. He draws X-ray pictures and folded-over pictures.

    He should begin to use color in relation to objects rather than symbolically. He should sense the blue sky,

Plate XXI

Figure 9.7

151

9.7. This is a water color by a third-grader in the symbolic stage. The sun is prominently included, as it is in most outdoor pictures done at this stage. The proportions are emotional, rather than visual; his house and the sun are important to the child, but the trees are not.

the green grass, his red house. He should begin to paint the sky so that it touches the horizon (at an earlier stage, the sky was a blue band at the top of the picture, the ground a brown or green line at the bottom, and the "air" the clear space between).

There should be some attempt to sense design qualities, but he does not yet consciously compose his pictures. The teacher should encourage him to notice the arrangement of objects and space in his work, but should not instruct him in the formal elements of design. Toward the end of this period the child should portray differences in his environment; therefore, a country scene should look quite different from a community scene. Figures of people and of animals should clearly give some evidence of motion and action, yet within their characteristic stiffness.

*SUGGESTIONS FOR GUIDANCE IN TEACHING
AN ART LESSON: GRADES 3–4*

1. Begin three-dimensional work using cardboard and wood.
2. Use materials similar to those used in previous grades, but expand experiences to an increased variety of materials in the technique areas to include watercolor, illustrating, lettering, making puppets, printing, making paper sculpture, using a Polaroid camera.
3. Use materials that require use of smaller muscles.
4. Use greater amounts of sensory and visual aids so that children can sense art forms in natural and man-made objects: lines, color, and texture with design qualities.
5. Select activities that can continue for longer periods of time or over two working periods.
6. Encourage group participation.
7. Have enough variety in the stimulations and selection of types of materials within a lesson to challenge the range of abilities in the class.
8. Guide the understanding of materials with comparative observations of conditions.
9. Ask questions relating to two or more comparative visual situations to stimulate the child's reflective abilities and thereby evoke ideas.
10. Consider art qualities in nature and surroundings.
11. Begin to have children learn about art in the contemporary world around them using art works and various multimedia.

Grades 5 and 6

During this period, the child's art work should be increasingly realistic. He should be aware of linear perspective, of planes formed by the overlapping of objects, of the effect of distance on the value and intensity of color. He should notice details as well as general characteristics. (Marked use of stereotypes at this age is not a normal characteristic.) He should arrange line, shape, color, and texture in an organized way, and art experience should encourage this natural sensitivity to design.

At this stage, the child should demonstrate a tendency toward a characteristic way of perceiving. He should perceive people, objects, space, and color (and represent them in his art work according to how they look or according to how he feels about them). He should exhibit a tendency to perceive visually or emotionally. This tendency becomes more apparent in Grades 7–8, and the characteristic types are more distinct. The work of the child who perceives visually is linear, detailed, natural in color, and in perspective. The work of the child who perceives emotionally is flat, simple, bright in color, and lacking in perspective. It is important to understand that all children perceive *both* visually and emotionally: the distinction is that some tend more toward the visual and others more toward the emotional type of perception. As a rule-of-thumb, if more than half of a child's pictures are linear, detailed, naturally colored, and in perspective, the child perceives visually. If more than half of the child's pictures reflect the opposite of these characteristics, he perceives emotionally. In addition, many children produce both types of pictures with about the same frequency and thus are not classifiable.

The teacher should encourage each child in his natural way of perceiving. The child who prefers to depict things as he feels about them should not be reprimanded because his work lacks realism. Many children work in both ways. Very few children are either all-visual or all-emotional in their approach, though some are; but there is usually a tendency to work more in one way than another.

Plate XXII

Figure 9.8

Figure 9.9

*SUGGESTIONS FOR GUIDANCE IN TEACHING
AN ART LESSON: GRADES 5–6*

1. Expand the opportunity of the children to be challenged by ideas and concepts about art by exposing them to art, artists, and art values of their contemporary culture and past heritage.
2. Expand the opportunity to use tools and materials that increase the child's frame of reference and are extensions of his past experience.

In Grades 5 and 6, most children show a tendency to perceive visually or emotionally. These two paintings exhibit visual characteristics. **9.8.** A 10-year-old in the stage of realistic awareness paints a horse race. The relative positions of the horses are indicated by hiding parts of some of the horses; also, nothing in the picture is anchored to a base line. **9.9.** An 11-year-old in sixth grade represents a kneeling figure in a spontaneous and visual manner. The work shows signs of genuine talent, since it has characteristics of the late stage of analytical realism usually found in somewhat older children.

3. Use a greater variety of tools and materials.

4. Increase the child's experiences with three-dimensional constructive and craft activities.

Figure 9.10

5. Select activities that involve group work.

6. Through solving problems, and by expanding his experience with materials similar to those used in prior grades, guide the child's understanding and help him develop his personal approaches to and skill with various materials; provide repeated and guided experimentation with a wide array of material.

7. Provide a flexible program for individuals and groups to allow interests to expand.

8. Encourage self-evaluation of work.

9. Engage the child in discriminating and evaluating art qualities in his own work and in the work of artists.

10. Encourage the child to develop his own techniques to express feeling, mood, appearance, dark and light, distance, perspective, and details.

11. Encourage interpretation of ideas, and moods and feelings in terms of symbolic, social, and subject-matter contexts.

12. Use sound, light, rhythms, visual organic natural objects, and music to aid in developing imaginative concepts and encouraging the child's creativity.

13. Use a great variety of materials to aid this imaginative phase of artistic development.

14. Deal with perspective with individual students as they develop an awareness of it. Teaching should be natural and not imposed.

15. Encourage the child's characteristic way of perceiving.

16. Expand the child's sensitivity to nature and art works.

17. Begin to involve students in art of their contemporary culture, symbolic context, and historical content.

18. Intensive development of art in the expanded world of understanding through sensory, audiovisual, and multimedia aids. Use photographic and phonographic media in dual relationships.

RELATION TO FUTURE ART EXPERIENCE

The logical progressive expansion of elementary school art experience from the in-depth involvement of the early grades to acquaintance with a wide variety of materials and techniques in the later grades provides a foundation for further art experience in secondary school. The student has learned to relate his ideas to a visual means of communication and to select materials and formulate them, in relation to his own ideas, into a satisfying and qualitative art work. The key word here is "qualitative." Because the child has achieved qualities of art in his personal work and satisfaction through his art work, he should have confidence in his own visual creative ability.

Adolescence may be a time of crisis in a student's creative visual development,[9] as in all areas of his life, if the teacher makes him acutely aware of adult standards and painfully conscious of his own temporary inadequacy. At this time, a child either continues interest in art or stops being interested on grounds that he is not talented. If the program of instruction has structure and qualities of art in the content, the child will achieve personal satisfaction from elementary school art. He will be more likely to continue to develop creatively in adolescence than the child who has early been frustrated by his inability to produce an art work that meets his teacher's criterion of excellence for an adult. Creative-evaluative teaching of art in the elementary school encourages the child realistically to enjoy art as a satisfying personal experience, uninhibited by comparisons of his work with standards too mature for his level of ability. A child thus taught will continue his interest in art throughout his school career and transfer this interest to his life as a producer or consumer of art.

SUMMARY

The art program in the elementary school is the foundation for future art education. Learning experiences in art are organized to provide an integrated program from kindergarten through Grade 12. This organization is the art curriculum. The curriculum is developed by the art administrator in terms of the scope and sequence of art experience to be achieved. The scope reflects the goals of art education; the sequence is based on the progression of children's creative development. The individual units of the curriculum coordinate the educational objectives with the child's ability at each grade level. Each grade provides the foundation of learning for the grade immediately following, and as the child progresses through school, the accumulated educational background constitutes his frame of reference.

The curriculum guide, cooperatively prepared by the art administrator, the special art teachers, and the classroom teachers, presents suggestions for art experience suitable for each grade level.

A group of recommendations for the elementary teacher for teaching art based on behavioral expectancies of children producing art is provided for the purpose of recognizing achievement of the curriculum goals.

9.10. One of the suggestions for guidance in teaching Grades 5–6 is to select activities that involve group work. This teacher is guiding her students as they start in on a mosaic made of cut paper. The children are absorbed in their joint project. Even better, they obviously are communicating with each other—they are thinking together and are not totally dependent on the teacher.

AIDS TO UNDERSTANDING

For discussion

1. Why, in art, as in general education, is the elementary school program the foundation for all future learning?

2. What is the advantage of in-depth teaching of a few basic materials in the early grades over breadth teaching, which employs a wide sampling of materials in the development of child understanding of techniques?

3. What is the difference between a scope and a sequence of art experience in the curriculum?

4. What are the components of a well-developed curriculum guide for a school art program?

For involvement

Analyze the scope and sequence of an art curriculum guide of a school system and write a constructive critique of the art program.

Chapter 10
DEVELOPING THE UNITS OF ART EXPERIENCE

In Chapter 9 we described the development of the art curriculum in terms of the scope and sequence of art experience and pointed out that the individual units of the curriculum attempt to coordinate scope with sequence, that is, to adjust the educational objectives to the child's ability at each grade level. In this chapter, we shall discuss the individual teaching units.

There are two types of units: the resource unit and the teaching unit. The resource unit is a comprehensive collection of suggested learning and teaching activities, procedures, materials, and aids, designed to help teachers in developing their own teaching units. It is broad in nature and is adaptable to many teaching situations. It is usually planned by the special art teacher to assist the classroom teacher. However, we are concerned here only with the teaching unit. The teaching unit is a systematic plan built around a central idea and intended for a particular teaching situation. It is planned by the classroom teacher with the aid of a resource unit developed by the art teacher and represents an attempt to integrate art experience with the total learning experience. In many large school systems this is the function of the curriculum guide.

A teaching unit may be subject-matter-centered, behavioral activity-centered, or experience-centered.[1] A subject-centered unit is built around a central subject-matter area to teach specific, predetermined information about a particular subject. This type of unit is not often used at the elementary level, nor is it particularly conducive to creative learning. A behavioral activity-centered unit is built around typical activities of life related to art, designed to help the child acquire visual learnings that will be useful to him in his own everyday life. An experience-centered unit is built around the needs of the individual and of society. The teacher structures experiences around problems that interest the learner, and by questioning stimulates him to elicit ideas about the problems. The pursuit of solutions to the problems results in achieving a goal set by the learner for himself. The total experience engages the pupil to the acquisition of learning inherent in the original structure of the experience. This is creative-evaluative teaching.

Organizing art experiences into units has several advantages. First, it minimizes segmental teaching. Second, it focuses on the learner; it relates learning to the individual child and allows the teacher to adapt instructional processes to the level of ability of each class member. Third, when organized as an experience-centered unit, it takes account of the basic principles of learning and concentrates on the solution of problems that are real and interesting to the pupil.

The unit is planned for the teacher's use. It should never be given to the student, though it may be discussed with parents if this seems useful in a particular situation.

[1] William H. Burton, *The Guidance of Learning Activities*, New York, Appleton-Century-Crofts, 1944, pp. 244–309; B. Othanel Smith, William O. Stanley, and J. Harlan Shores, *Fundamentals of Curriculum Development*, New York, Harcourt, Brace & World, 1950, pp. 554–580; G. Wesley Sowards and Mary-Margaret Scobey, *The Changing Curriculum and the Elementary Teacher*, Belmont, Calif., Wadsworth Publishing, 1961, pp. 490–503.

Three sample teaching units are presented below. The first is behavioral activity-centered; the second and third experience-centered.

The behavioral activity-centered unit relates to the total learning process in a first-grade class and illustrates the correlation of general learning with art experience (the latter is printed in italics). Such a correlated program must be planned so that the general learning occurs *before* the art activity and can thus stimulate the pupils' ideas for creative expression.

The experience-centered units are presented specifically in terms of art experience for fourth- and sixth-grade classes. In actual school situations, the art experience unit would be part of a general educational unit. The reader is urged to prepare a general educational unit for a fourth- or a sixth-grade class that will lead to an art experience unit similar to this, and then to plan the art experience unit.

BEHAVIORAL ACTIVITY-CENTERED UNIT[2]

Springtime on the Farm—Grade 1

I. Preface

This unit covers the three phases of spring growth. The first part introduces the sources, needs, growth, parts, and kinds of spring plants; it emphasizes each of these areas for the seed and bulb plants, and the spring-blossoming plants and the fruit they bear. The second part of the unit covers the appearance, importance, and needs of the farm animals; it emphasizes the products from these farm animals and how they are made and distributed. The third part covers the growing of grain and vegetables and the farm itself.

II. Objectives of the unit

A. Knowledge and understanding objectives

1. To understand the importance of crop- and animal-raising to our modern world
2. To learn the importance of the seed and bulb in the plant cycle
3. To be aware of the appearance of the various types of plants and animals
4. To realize the needs of plants and animals and how each relates to needs of the other and to the needs of human beings

[2] Courtesy of Anna Lee Boyer, first-grade teacher, Tyson-Schoener Elementary School, Reading School District, Reading, Pa. (unpublished).

5. To understand the production of farm products like wheat and butter
6. To understand how farm methods have changed through the years
7. To understand the blossoming of fruit trees and the formation of the fruit
8. To learn about the many buildings of the farm and the uses of these buildings

B. Behavior and attitude objectives
1. To help the children develop a sense of cooperation and an attitude of good citizenship
2. To realize the importance of agriculture to our self-preservation
3. To help the children work individually in the school projects

C. Skill objectives
1. To use the unit to teach the language arts skills, both oral and written
2. To develop oral and written vocabulary
3. To teach the arithmetic skills in measuring specific quantities

III. Content of the unit
A. The spring plant and tree
1. Source of the spring plant
a. The bulb
(1) Appearance of the bulb
(a) Rough brown outer shell
(b) Light pulpy inside
(2) Contents of the bulb
(a) Small plant
(b) Food for the growing plant
(3) Kinds of bulbs
(a) Onion
(b) Tulip
(c) Begonia
(d) Hyacinth
(e) Lily
(4) Etc.

[NOTE: Details of the unit have been omitted from this point on, as the section on bulbs serves as an example of what was done by the teacher for all similar headings.]

b. The seed
(1) Appearance of the seed
(2) Contents of the seed
(3) Kinds of seeds
(4) How seeds grow
(5) Use of the seed as food
c. Plants and flowers
(1) Kinds of plants and flowers

(2) Parts of the plant
(3) Needs of the plant
d. Fruit trees
(1) Kinds of fruit trees
(2) Appearance of the tree
(3) Needs of the tree
(4) Formation of the fruit

B. Farm animals
1. Kinds of animals and poultry
2. The cow
a. Appearance of the cow
b. Care of the cow
c. Anatomy of the cow
d. Breeds of cows
e. The dairy farm
f. The dairy
(1) Make butter
(2) Make cheese
(3) Pasteurize milk
g. Products of the cow
3. The pig
a. Appearance of the pig
b. Breeds of pigs
c. Food of the pig
d. Products of the pig
4. The sheep
a. Appearance of the sheep
b. Care of the sheep
c. Breeds of sheep
d. Products of the sheep
5. The goat
a. Appearance of the goat
b. Breeds of goats
c. Products of the goat
6. The horse
a. Appearance of the horse
b. Care of the horse
c. Breeds of horses
d. Use of the horse
7. The chicken
a. Appearance of the chicken
b. Care of the chicken
c. Anatomy of the chicken
d. Breeds of chickens
e. Hatching of the chicken
f. Products of the chicken
8. The turkey
a. Appearance of the turkey
b. Needs of the turkey
c. Breeds of turkeys
d. Products of the turkey

9. The duck
   a. Appearance of the duck
   b. Needs of the duck
   c. Breeds of ducks
   d. Products of the duck
10. The goose
    a. Appearance of the goose
    b. Characteristics of the goose
    c. Breeds of geese
    d. Products of the goose

C. The farm and its grown products
   1. Farm buildings
      a. Barn
      b. Silo
      c. Outbuildings
      d. Farmhouse
   2. Vegetable-growing on the farm
      a. Types of vegetables
      b. Needs of the vegetable farm
   3. Grain-growing on the farm
      a. Types of grains
      b. Needs of the grain farm
D. Importance of the farm
   1. Furnishes cities with the necessary food products
   2. Uses products produced by the city
E. Vocabulary words to be developed

Sheep	Wool	Stallion
Ewe	Hoof	Colt
Lamb	Horse	Palomino
Ram	Mare	

IV. Motivation
This springtime unit is initiated by a bulletin board and book-corner display. The bulletin board displays pictures of spring flowers and spring plants. Between the pictures are poems about these spring flowers, bulbs, and seeds. Some of the pictures are labeled by the poems. There is also a large felt flower with the parts labeled to interest the children in a study of flowers. There is a sheet of paper covered with a variety of seeds showing their many sizes, shapes, and colors. In the book corner are books telling about the seed, plant, and flower.

V. Activities[3]
A. Classroom activities during the unit
   1. Collect a variety of seeds and place on a chart
   2. *Create a flower form with paper (cutting, folding, pasting, bending), and have children design a new flower*
   3. Plant gladiolus, begonia, and hyacinth bulbs in the classroom

[3] Art activities are printed in italics.

4. Plant bean seeds in a glass jar and watch the growth
5. Have the individual children plant marigold seeds in small containers
6. *Make three-dimensional paper garden of created flower forms*
7. Have whole class write an experience story about the chicken
8. *Design a cover for a booklet about the flowers studied*
9. Have children write a poem for each flower
10. Have children write individual stories about the chicken, cow, and pig
11. Make butter in the classroom and let children eat the butter on crackers and drink the buttermilk
12. Use the "Show and Tell" record and pictures for the pig and cow
13. Show filmstrips
    a. "Red Rooster"
    b. "Fluffy the Chick"
    c. "Fleecy the Lamb"
14. Charts and diagrams
15. Poems
16. Music
    a. "Red Rooster"
B. Culminating activities
   1. Reading the charts collected during the unit
   2. Singing songs about the unit
   3. Writing simple animal-story plays
   4. *Writing and illustrating a sequence movie*
   5. Reciting some of the poems learned
   6. *Development of a wall mural*

VI. Evaluative techniques
Because of the grade level of this unit, no formal test will be given. A complete informal evaluation will be given. This will include a recall of the vocabulary learned, reciting the poetry learned, and singing the songs learned throughout the unit. There will also be a reading of charts to show the growth and extension of reading ability. The mural on the farm will be included as a recall of their learning. The children will also tell simple animal stories and read a sequence narrating a film on the cow. All this will be included in a program given by the children.

EXPERIENCE-CENTERED UNIT[4]

Art Revealed in Nature as an Influence in Our Lives—Grade 4

[4] Courtesy of Kathy Snyder, student of the author at Kutztown State College.

Among the many objectives of the unit on the farm are: to learn about farm animals and to learn about farm buildings. A teacher might use appropriate questions to lead children to understand and discuss points such as these as they look at the pictures. **10.1**. *The needs of human beings, sheep, and plants relate to each other in many ways.* **10.2**. *A barn has many possible uses, but a silo has only one specialized use.*

General objectives of the unit:

Figures 10.3–10.5

Figure 10.6

A. Knowledge Objectives
1. To understand the textural qualities of objects of nature that will influence design of our art products
2. To understand the feeling of motion in the structural elements and surface patterns of natural forms

B. Abilities and Skills
1. Increase ability to be aware of design in nature and to relate it to a created form
2. Increase ability in the use of materials to create patterns which unify the overall appearance of visual forms
3. Increase the ability to develop new ways of transferring design concepts existing in nature to new visual expressions
4. Increase skill with tools and materials that create textural qualities

C. Attitudes
1. To appreciate that nature is a resource for ideas for an art expression
2. To gain confidence in interpreting natural forms in a visual expression
3. To appreciate and accept the visual end product as a whole which comes as a result of meaningful interpretation of nature, the discipline of materials, and the expression of reflective thought

164

There are almost innumerable ways to help children appreciate art revealed in nature. During a unit division planned around textures in nature, a site should be chosen for a field trip that will give the children opportunities to see many types of trees, other plants, and rocks. **10.3** and **10.4.** It is amazing how many different textures there are in the branches of a pine tree and in blades of grass. Some children would immediately be interested in working from either of these plants. **10.5.** These rocks also present many possibilities. The main rock may be very like the one both Kurt and Kristin worked from—with such different results (page 167).

10.6. *During a unit division planned around understanding motion through nature's repetition of patterns, a teacher could take the children to a rocky coast or stream. Do you think these patterns are likely to repeat themselves and yet always be individual?*

Unit divisions

A. To understand the problem of transferring the inherent qualities of texture in nature into an individual interpretation of textural designs (relates to knowledge objective 1)

B. To understand motion through nature's repetition of patterns in an individual expression (relates to knowledge objective 2)

Development of unit division

Major Problem I (Unit Division A) A field trip is planned to a small wooded area. The site was selected because it was equipped with various types of trees, shrubs, rocks, and plants.

As the students were in the process of planning cloth designs, they observed nature forms to achieve different qualities of texture using black india ink and a brush, on white paper.

The students began working as soon as they found a nature form that interested them. Kurt, a fourth-grade boy, decided to work from a rock that he spotted. He carelessly began to apply the ink in unorganized blobs that had little relationship to the apparent textural qualities in the rock. He began to lose interest in his work almost as soon as he began. He looked at his paper that was aimlessly covered with ink and decided to begin again on a clean sheet of paper. Again he applied ink in the same manner and completely disregarded all knowledge of how to use the dry brush in the incorporation of texture. Kurt, unknowingly, wasted the entire class period by merely "playing" with the ink instead of trying to relate the textures of the rock into a textural design of his own.

Kristin, a classmate of Kurt's, was also working with the same rock as Kurt. She concentrated on the ridges and smooth surfaces of the rock and designed an interesting textural design with the use of plain ink and the dry brush. Kristin worked contentedly on the paper to achieve a black-and-white area treatment of the rough and smooth surfaces respectively. She created a good example of individual interpretation of textural designs in nature.

Back in the classroom, Kurt looked at Kristin's finished textural designs and then looked down at his own. He quickly leafed through his many sheets of paper to try and find one example to hand in. Each one looked the same to him—a series of ink spots that had no relationship to texture at all. As he walked up to the teacher's desk to hand in his paper, he nervously wondered if the teacher would like his design and his thoughts then wandered to the question of why he did not try to achieve textural designs.

This is an example of a child who did not view nature as an important part in the interpretation of individual textural designs. Kurt therefore felt insecure about his work, whereas Kristin would most likely feel rather confident in her interpretation of the lesson.

A. Objectives—Specific
   1. To understand the textural qualities in nature that can be interpreted into individual concepts of design
   2. To understand the part that nature plays in life and how one can relate to nature to develop a concept of textural design
   3. To understand that observation of nature influences imagination and feelings and emotions through its textural qualities
   4. To understand that a texture can be developed through awareness of nature, an experimentation with art media

B. Scope and Subject Matter
   1. The understanding of how nature can relate to us from the visual observation of texture
   2. To develop individual interpretation of nature's textural qualities
   3. To understand through various uses of a media that texture can be creatively expressed
   4. To understand that the desire to express oneself through textural designs can be satisfying and rewarding

EXPERIENCE-CENTERED UNIT[5]

*Our Community: Its Plan
and Architecture—Grade 6*

I. General Objectives of the Unit
   A. Knowledge objectives
      1. To understand that the plan of a community is designed to meet the common needs of a group of people living in an area
      2. To understand that the buildings of a community are designed to meet the needs of the people living in the community
      3. To understand that the ideals of the community are expressed through community planning, buildings, parks, murals, and sculpture of civic nature
   B. Ability and skill objectives
      1. To develop ability to resolve aesthetically problems in the area of community planning

[5] Prepared by the author.

2. To develop ability to plan buildings that function in relation to the needs of those who will use them
3. To develop skill in the use of drawing tools and mechanical instruments to convey the idea of public buildings to those who will use them
4. To develop skill in using materials to make actual scale representations for community plans and buildings for the understanding and acceptance of the general public

C. Attitude objectives
1. To appreciate the need for the aesthetic development of the community

2. To appreciate the role of art in developing a community which is attractive and pleasant to live in
3. To appreciate that art is a means of expressing the ideals of a community of people through the community plan, public buildings, parks, murals, and civic sculpture

II. Unit divisions
A. To understand the design problems in achieving a well-planned community that functions in terms of organization, order, and aesthetic value in meeting the needs of the people (relates to knowledge objective 1)

In the course of a unit on the community, a small village is contrasted with a big city. A teacher might show the children pictures like these as he asks why the people in the village seem calm and the people in the city seem hurried.
10.7. *Answering the teacher's questions, children would probably say that this village church gives them a feeling of peace and quiet, that it looks as though it would be there forever (Christopher Wren Church, Sandwich, Massachusetts).* **10.8.** *Children might respond that this city scene makes them think of many people, motion, constant activity. This picture would produce a particularly lively discussion if the teacher asked what it shows of the effects of the automobile on modern life (downtown Detroit).*

B. To understand that the function of a building is the basis of the design form which contributes to the attractiveness of the various areas of the community (relates to knowledge objective 2)

C. To understand that various community art forms tend to express the ideas and ideals of the people of a community (relates to knowledge objective 3)

III. Development of unit divisions

Major Problem 1 (relates to unit division A)

A family lives near a small village in a small group of farm buildings by fertile fields of productive land. Many other farms are in the vicinity. The family has storage facilities for meat, vegetables, fruit, and dairy products raised on the farm and a well-kept house in which to live. In the village, there are buildings to meet their additional needs. They drive to the village church, the blacksmith shop, and the country store. There is a small civic building in which to carry out the community business, near a small wooden school building. Only occasionally are there trips to a larger community to exchange crops and produce for fertilizer, equipment, and a few luxuries. Life here is happy, and people seem calm and satisfied. This village is called Bowers. It seems to get along all by itself.

Twenty miles away is a city of 100,000 people. There are many streets. To go in and out of the city, the people have to use car, subway, train, or elevated railroad.

The people depend on a milkman, breadman, and dry cleaner. A gas or electric company supplies most of the heat and electricity. A small break in the water line, a broken power line, or a small gear broken on a subway car wheel stops the activity of hundreds of people. The people living in this city have given up much of their life to dependence on other people and on industrial, technical, civic, and mechanical facilities. They often seem hurried and rushed, yet they seem to get along well.

How do you account for the fact that the family in the village, who seem to have very little compared with the people in the city, are calm and the people in the city are hurried? Why do you suppose that the people in the city get along well together like the family in the country?

A. Specific objectives of lesson plans (see Chapter 4)
1. To understand that many different kinds and sizes of communities make up our American society
2. To understand the need of planning streets to meet the function of a small village or a city
3. To understand that different community plans are of many types and forms related to their historical development
4. To understand that redesign is necessary today to adjust the plans of cities to the new modes of living of our jet age

B. Scope of subject matter
1. Ribbon, centric, grid, and organic community layouts meet the functions of various types of communities such as villages, towns, and cities
2. A community street plan depends on the activities in the community
   a. Transportation
   b. Zoning areas
   c. Economic welfare
   d. Industrial and commercial access
   e. The health of the people
   f. Social organization
   g. Civic government
3. A community plan considers the natural geography
   a. Streets are laid out in relation to the land contour
   b. Street slopes consider the climatic conditions
   c. Street layouts retain most worthwhile features of nature
   d. Street layouts are designed to serve the function of the community
4. A community plan gives the people who live there a sense of order, adequate locations for civic and public buildings, and settings for monuments and memorials of art
   a. Industrial zone
   b. Commercial zone
   c. Residential zone
   d. Recreational zone
   e. Transportation zone
5. A community is an organization of land, streets, and buildings for its people to live together
   a. It is a social art
   b. It expresses the culture of the people
6. A community that does not meet the needs of our jet age should be redesigned

C. Student experiences
1. If you lived in the little village of Bowers and moved to the big city, you might be confused. What can a big city do in its planning to help a stranger get acquainted?
   a. A pictograph of the city
   b. A model of the city
2. Develop evaluative conditions through divergent questions for other art activities

D. Resource Material for Teaching
Major Problem 2 (relates to unit division B)
A. Specific objectives of lesson plans
B. Scope of subject matter
C. Student experiences
D. Resource material for teaching

SUMMARY

The art unit is the plan by which the teacher coordinates the educational goals with the ability level of the student and correlates the art experiences with the total educational experiences.

There are two types of units: the resource unit and the teaching unit. The resource unit is a general plan, adaptable to many teaching situations; the teaching unit is intended for a specific instructional situation. Only the teaching unit is discussed.

Teaching units may be subject-matter, behavioral activity-, or experienced-centered. The subject-matter-centered unit is rarely used at the elementary school level. Examples are provided of an activity-centered and two experience-centered units.

AIDS TO UNDERSTANDING

For discussion

1. What is the function of the teaching unit as compared to the resource unit?
2. How are subject-matter-centered, behavioral activity-centered, and experience-centered teaching units unique?
3. What would happen to the learning environment in the classroom if unit organization were nonexistent?
4. By what criteria can an elementary teacher test the soundness of his educational objectives for an art unit or an art lesson?
5. Following student analysis of units in the chapter, a number of students should present their critiques for group reaction and response.
6. Present your art unit to your college class and have three preselected students respond to it.
7. What is the fundamental purpose of unit organization?

For involvement

1. Prepare a general educational unit for an elementary class that will lead to an art unit.
2. Plan an art experience unit as a follow-up of the previous suggestion.
3. Analyze one unit in terms of the stimulating effect the presentation may have to motivate thought and ideas of children of the particular grade level.

Chapter 11
THE NURTURING ENVIRONMENT
FOR ART

Figure 11.1

Nurturing each child's optimal growth in the visual arts requires an environment that is not only a classroom but also a visual arts laboratory. Such a classroom-laboratory should provide a flexible, adaptable work space, rich with instructional and resource materials, and equipment pertinent for teaching the visual arts. These features, together with an adjustable schedule, allow the classroom teacher and the art specialist to carry out a creative-evaluative program in an atmosphere stimulating to artistic growth.

In this chapter we shall discuss the kinds of classroom arrangements commonly used in teaching art and the components of a learning atmosphere conducive to creative development.

CLASSROOM ARRANGEMENTS
FOR TEACHING ART

Three types of classroom arrangements for teaching art are common in the elementary school: the self-con-

11.1. *In an atmosphere stimulating to artistic growth, a child can achieve true creative development.*

tained classroom, the special art room,[1] and the combined classroom and art laboratory.

In the self-contained classroom, the elementary school teacher coordinates the entire educational experience of the class, with the art consultant as adviser. His responsibility is to develop an educational atmosphere that will foster the integration of each child's personality. The room is designed as a multipurpose environment for teaching all learning suitable for children of a particular age group. To provide a well-rounded art program, each classroom should be equipped with all the necessary materials and facilities; in practice, large, expensive pieces of equipment are shared by several classrooms—a disadvantage.

When all art is taught in a special art room by an art teacher, the children go to the art room in groups, at fixed times, usually weekly. The art room is well-

equipped with materials and facilities for teaching in depth (usually better equipped than the self-contained classrooms, since it is the only room in the building so supplied and is devoted entirely to art). Art is not taught in the regular classroom (except in nursery school and kindergarten), and there is little interaction between the stimulation in the regular classroom and the stimulation in the special art room. In art class the teacher concentrates on special instruction in art and has little time to relate the art lesson to the interests the child has developed in the regular classroom. Only if the schedule permits can the child work on art between lessons. Cooperative planning related to the immediate interests of the child depends on a conscientious art teacher consulting with an equally conscientious classroom teacher as their schedules permit. Thus, integration of the child's art experience with his total learning is difficult to achieve. This is the least satisfactory of the three arrangements.

[1] Josephine Burley Schultz, ed., *Planning Facilities for Art Instruction*, Washington, D.C., National Art Education Association, 1961.

A combination self-contained classroom and resource laboratory is, in the author's opinion, the best arrangement for teaching art. The stimulation and planning of basic art experience occur in the regular classroom, and in-depth art experience and special instruction take place in the art laboratory, through flexible scheduling, at times agreed upon by the classroom and art teachers. In this cooperative atmosphere, the coordinating function of the classroom teacher and the specialized function of the art teacher are realized in a harmonious and flexible setting. The regular classroom is supplied with general art materials and facilities, and large equipment and special materials are in the art laboratory.[2] In such an environment, the classroom teacher's limited art background places no restrictions on the depth of the child's art experience, and the use of a special art room places no limitations on relating art to the child's immediate needs and interests.

Figure 11.2

[2] Such a setup is in practice in the Stratford Avenue Elementary School, Garden City, N.Y. This school employs a similar physical organization in the library, science, and shop programs.

COMPONENTS OF AN ATMOSPHERE FOR CREATIVE EXPERIENCE

A flexible, adaptable work area

The place where art is taught should be adaptable to many different kinds of learning. It should permit the child to move from one learning environment to another as his activities require, without disturbing others or losing time. Furnishings, floor and wall space, lighting, and audio and visual aids should be readily available and portable. The multiart area should, if possible, be located near the main entrance of the school, accessible to the stage, and on the first floor of the building. It

11.2. In the cooperative atmosphere of the self-contained classroom and resource laboratory, the classroom teacher's limited art background places no restrictions on the depth of the child's art experience. For instance, a 9-year-old girl in the stage of realistic awareness used felt-tip markers to sketch these galloping horses. She has achieved a real feeling of motion over the ground. It is interesting to compare this work with Figure 9.8. The individual differences between the two children who are near the same age and in the same stage show up strikingly in these two versions of similar subjects.

should include, near the school entrance, a museum or art display area.

The work area should be equipped with large flat tables; counter space; wall-area storage space; clay bins; a tool cart with tools for construction; easels; workbenches with vises; kilns; small dark rooms; wet- and dry-storage areas; enamel and silk-screen equipment; and a large open work space.

The clean-up area, including a four-well sink so that several children at a time can wash up, should be free-standing or peninsular in design and easily accessible. The sink should be stain-proof, and the floor covered in a stain-resistant, tough, durable, resilient material.

The size of the art room depends on the general educational program, the art curriculum, the size of classes, and the economic ability of the community. As a general recommendation, the space allocated to art activities should be large enough for 30 students to work simultaneously. Allowing 50 to 75 square feet per child, the total area for special art facilities would be 1,500 to 2,300 square feet (a room measuring 30 by 50 feet or 40 by 50 feet). The National Art Education Association suggests 1,200 square feet as minimum space (a room measuring 30 by 40 feet.)

Rich instructional materials

Art materials The art laboratory should provide materials and equipment for activities that cannot easily be managed in the classroom—for example, dyeing, block printing, painting stage scenery, modeling and sculpture, pottery making, easel painting, metal work, and experiences with film.

Because the elementary school program is intended to establish the child's frame of reference for his subsequent art education, the same basic materials should be available at this level as at the secondary school level. The child's work with these materials will become increasingly sophisticated as he advances through school.

Resource materials The art laboratory should have available such additional teaching materials as books, sensory aids, and exhibition equipment.

BOOKS An extension library of art books and periodicals should be easily available for use by both teacher and child.

EXHIBITS In the art program, an exhibit has two functions: educational and artistic. It is educational because it conveys information visually and stimulates individual thinking. It motivates creative activity on the part of the student who enjoys seeing not only his own work but that of other students and of mature artists. It stimulates experimentation in techniques used by other exhibitors. It provides an opportunity for the child to evaluate his own work in relation to other work. An exhibit serves an artistic function because it is conceived, selected, and arranged to be itself a work of art.

Plate XXIII

RESOURCES OUTSIDE THE CLASSROOM As the child grows and becomes increasingly aware of his surroundings, his interest in people and things outside the immediate classroom environment should be utilized in the art program. For example, art experience can be structured around the persons who supply fundamental needs of life—the postman, policeman, fireman, store clerk, school janitor, doctor, dentist, nurse. A visit to a local store or factory can provide experience that stimulates an art lesson. The child can be encouraged to think about what these people do, how they dress for work, what their tools look like. For older children, the awareness of other cultures gleaned from experiences with magazines, educational motion pictures, books, and television can be utilized to stimulate, for example, an art experience in design based on the cultures of other countries.

Figures 11.3–11.5 (left column)

Local history is a good source of stimulation for art experience. Bookbinder[3] describes a series of pageants

[3] Jack Bookbinder, Visual-Aural Essays developed by Mr. Bookbinder and his art staff as teaching aids in the Philadelphia Public Schools, Philadelphia, Pa.

The art laboratory can provide materials for activities that cannot easily be managed in the classroom, including block printing. *11.3.* A group of children in Grades 4 and 5, working together, decided to use block prints when they designed this wall hanging for their room. The result shows a conscious approach to surface texture and pattern. Note that a rhythmic quality is created by the repetition of the three different block prints. These motifs are balanced in their regular pattern in such a way as to produce a sense of unity in the entire hanging.

XXII. This mural by a fifth-grade class shows that the children perceive the general characteristics and details of objects. They show the objects under the sea according to how they look, and yet there is a sense of the emotional fascination with exploration under the sea that their science classes have given the children.

XXIV. *Is this an art teacher or an elementary classroom teacher? When both are working cooperatively, it is hard to tell.*

XXIII. *An exhibit is conceived, selected, and arranged to be itself a work of art. An area like this one in an elementary school serves a number of vital functions that contribute to the learning experiences in the elementary art program.*

XXV. *A classroom teacher and an art teacher cooperate as the art teacher gives a demonstration lesson. The classroom teacher, left, is the one shown in Plate XXIV.*

11.4. *In this detail of the hanging, showing all three prints, the imagery typical of the stage of realistic awareness is apparent.*

11.5. *Painting stage scenery is another of the activities made possible by the art laboratory. These fourth-graders have designed the scenery for their play, and now they are constructing and painting it. Thus the art laboratory enables them to integrate their visual learning with their total learning experiences. Art has no subject-matter barriers.*

combining visual arts, music, games, historic events, public buildings, and prominent people based on the history of Philadelphia and adaptable to any local community.

Well-organized, purposeful trips to a local art museum, private art collection, art shop, historical society, department store, industrial plant, zoo, or farm constitute other sources of material to stimulate a child's creative expression.

These techniques, long used in other fields of education, are equally valuable in the creative-evaluative teaching of art.

CRITERIA FOR EFFECTIVE USE OF RESOURCE MATERIALS   To be effective, a resource should meet the five criteria listed below.

1. The resource should be timely and purposeful. The purpose—whether to arouse interest, to exemplify, to clarify a point, or to extend knowledge—should be clear to both teacher and pupil.
2. The resource should be within the pupil's ability to understand. It should be suitable to his intellectual, emotional, and creative ability.
3. The resource should be stimulating. It should cause the child to think. The teacher should avoid suggestions, since these may elicit uniform responses.
4. The resource should be of good quality. Accurate color reproductions, well-mounted visual materials, well-made examples of manufactured objects, carefully arranged exhibits, and attractive displays are silent teachers of good taste and good working habits.
5. The resource should evoke artistic and perceptual awareness in creative expression. It should inspire the student and influence his work.

Pertinent equipment and sensory aids

Visual and audio aids should be available, such as motion pictures, slide films, slides, unmounted and mounted photographs, reproductions of works of art, actual art objects, charts describing different art processes, samples of work produced by different art processes, and recorded music. These materials can be obtained from local, state, and federal governmental agencies; from industry; from museums and art galleries. Most schools own audiovisual equipment or can borrow it from nearby teacher-education institutions. School districts can, at very little cost, acquire collections of slides, photographs, or models relating to specific subjects.

Educational television is an effective aid in the art classroom.[4] Unlike the tricky and shoddy "how-to-do-it" presentations of commercial television, educational television has produced programs that show the processes children experience in creating art work and provide creative experiences for acquainting parents with the concepts of heuristic art education. Educational television is a visual learning medium that can serve to stimulate children and to provide a broad cultural experience in the arts. The purpose is to support the general aims of art education, expand perceptual aesthetic experience, broaden understanding of the arts of other cultures, and develop discriminating ability to see when looking, to compare and make choices, and ultimately to expand one's experiences from earlier visual understanding toward insights to new ideas and concepts. It is an ideal means of affective learning through which cognitive realization may occur.

The purpose of teaching is to effect learning. No television is effective unless the classroom teacher orients the children before a program and works with them after the presentation. The teacher remains essential to the development of the educational tone—directed or creative—in the use of educational television. He sets the stage so that the program may be a means of stimulating ideas. He guides children in visual experiences with art materials that follow up the visual program. Finally, his program selection can expand the cultural horizons of children who otherwise would not be able to acquire them.

[4] It has been used in art education programs in Buffalo, Cleveland, Detroit, Hagerstown, Md., New York, Philadelphia, Pittsburgh, Richmond, Va., and San Francisco.

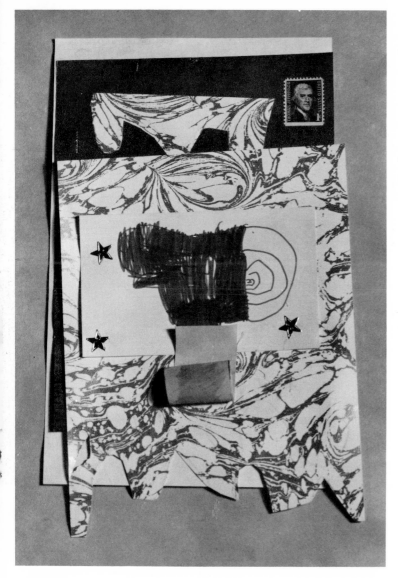

The collage is an exciting medium for children, and it is easy to provide a wide variety of materials for them to choose from. They should also be encouraged to bring in their own materials. As these two examples indicate, children of all ages are stimulated by found materials.
11.6. *A 6-year-old boy in the presymbolic stage created this collage. He apparently conceived the arrangement both as a total composition in itself and as a kind of frame for his own drawing in the center.* ***11.7.*** *A gifted 10-year-old girl in the stage of analytical awareness made this wall mural of materials showing man-created textures. She arranged the collage to emphasize positive shapes (objects) and negative shapes (background) and patterns of light and dark.*

But the greatest sensory aid of all is the child's own immediate surroundings—the materials of nature. He should be stimulated to awareness of the seasonal changes in color in the out-of-doors; of the color and shape of flowers, leaves, twigs, rocks, birds, animals.

SUMMARY

A nurturing environment for learning that provides a flexible work area for art, adequate instructional and resource materials, and an adaptable schedule that coordinates regular classroom and special art activities fosters the creative-evaluative teaching of art.

Three types of classroom arrangements for teaching art are common in the elementary school: the self-contained classroom, the special art room, and the combination classroom and art laboratory. The last,

preferred by the author, permits the integration of in-depth art instruction with regular classroom activities through the cooperation of art and classroom teachers.

Educational aids, selectively used, are valuable additions in an art program. Such resources include educational television, motion pictures, slide films, art reproductions, models, charts, books, and exhibit materials. Field trips, not only to local museums and art galleries, but also to local shops, factories, churches, and historic sites, provide experiences to stimulate creative expression.

Resource materials should be (1) purposeful and timely, (2) within the child's ability to understand, (3) stimulating, (4) of good quality, and (5) capable of evoking artistic and perceptual awareness in creative expression.

AIDS TO UNDERSTANDING

For discussion

1. What conditions of an elementary classroom environment contribute to stimulating creative artistic development in children?

2. Compare three types of classroom arrangements for teaching art in respect to conditions which uniquely make them different.

3. How do the components of an atmosphere for creative experience—flexibility and adaptablity of the work area, richness of instructional material, and pertinent equipment and sensory aids—relate to a creative-evaluative strategy of art teaching?

4. What would be the basic difference between supply requisitions for art materials ordered for elementary art programs of the academic, the behavioral activity, or the experience approaches to teaching?

5. What effect would occur in the classroom environment if all pertinent equipment and sensory aids were eliminated from the teacher's teaching materials? How would teaching art be affected?

6. With the multimedia of resource materials within the classroom, how do you account for the need for educational resources outside the classroom?

7. Imagine how computer retrieval units for visual materials could effect the teaching of art in the elementary classroom.

For involvement

1. Analyze an elementary school situation in regard to the type of environmental conditions which provide for teaching art. What conditions exist that nurture or inhibit creative art teaching?

2. Prepare a floor plan for a classroom complex in an elementary school which, in your best judgment, fulfills the criteria for components of an atmosphere for creative experience.

3. Develop a requisition for art materials for Grades K–6 that is consistent with the principles for creative-evaluative teaching.

4. Using a lesson which you have developed for art in an elementary classroom, analyze your lists of resource materials using the criteria established in this chapter for their effective use. Make any apparent changes that may be needed as a result of your evaluation.

Chapter 12
RELATION OF CLASSROOM
AND SPECIAL ART TEACHERS

Whether art should be taught by the elementary school classroom teacher (who knows the children best) or by a specially trained art teacher (who knows the materials and techniques of art best) has long been a controversial subject.[1] In any case, a recent survey has shown that "the regular classroom teacher was expected to teach art without any help from a specialist in well over half the elementary schools reporting."[2] Compounding the basic pedagogical conflict are the inadequate preparation of many classroom teachers for art education and the scarcity of specially trained art instructors.

Attempts to solve the problem have led to four patterns of art education in the elementary schools: (1) art teaching by an itinerant specialist, (2) art teaching by a resident specialist, (3) art teaching by the classroom

[1] It was discussed as early as 1932. See Sallie B. Tannahill, *Fine Arts for Public School Administrators*, New York, Columbia University Teachers College, 1932, pp. 67–69.
[2] Preface. NAEA Research Monograph, p. 25.

teacher, with the specialist acting as consultant, and (4) cooperative art teaching in which the classroom teacher and the art specialist plan together to give the child in-depth art experiences that are integrated with his total learning experiences.[3]

In this chapter, the advantages and disadvantages of the first three patterns are outlined briefly; the fourth pattern, preferred by the author, is discussed in detail.

ART TEACHING BY AN ITINERANT SPECIALIST

In this plan, which is typical of 10 percent of elementary schools reporting, the art specialist teaches a weekly art lesson in each classroom of each school to which he is assigned. There is no planned relation between the art lesson and the regular classroom experiences; in fact, the classroom teacher is often tempted to use the period allocated to art to catch up with his own work. In any case, the itinerant teacher, at the end of this scheduled 25 to 28 periods a week, has neither time nor energy to coordinate his work with that of the classroom teachers.

In an effort to remedy this lack of coordination, a manual, guide, or course of study is sometimes prepared by an art coordinator for the classroom teacher to use between visits from the itinerant art teacher. Even with this aid, however, such an art program is often stereotyped and lifeless and has little in common with the creative-evaluative teaching of art.

ART TEACHING BY A RESIDENT SPECIALIST

In this plan, a special art teacher is assigned to each school building and is responsible for all art education. The arrangement is more costly than the itinerant teacher plan. The plan has several disadvantages. First, because the art lesson is scheduled for a fixed period of specified duration, motivation and stimulation cannot be developed with the children during the lesson, but must be imposed at the start of the session; this often

interferes with adequate understanding and experiencing on the part of the pupils. Second, since the lesson is usually planned by the art teacher alone, the classroom teacher has little opportunity to correlate general educational experiences with the work done in art class. Third, the art lesson is likely to concentrate on a specific technical area, such as use of color, design, or drawing, because the art teacher wants to ensure a wide variety of experiences on which the child can build a body of knowledge about art.

ART TEACHING WITH THE SPECIALIST AS CONSULTANT

In this plan, the art specialist acts as an adviser to the classroom teacher. The curriculum guide is planned cooperatively by the classroom teachers and the art consultant. While the classroom teacher is responsible for carrying out the program, the specialist is on hand for demonstrations and to help in evaluating children's development and in planning future activities for the children and conferences, workshops, and exhibits for the teachers. Usually the consultant follows a schedule of visits to the various schools and can easily be located if need arises for guidance. While this plan succeeds in relating art to general educational experiences, it is weak because there are usually not enough art consultants to provide all the help needed to enable classroom teachers to carry out an effective art program. Hampered by too much work and too little time, the consultant cannot provide needed in-service training and cannot work individually with classroom teachers. He becomes too far removed from actual teaching.

COOPERATIVE ART TEACHING BY CLASSROOM TEACHER AND SPECIALIST

In this plan, the classroom and special art teachers work together to provide a program of creative-evaluative teaching that integrates the child's art experience with his total learning. The plan utilizes simultaneously the services of two specially prepared professionals: the classroom teacher, who best knows the child's ability,

---

[3] Ibid. Specialists help the classroom teacher teach art in one of the second, third, or fourth ways in about one-fourth of the schools reporting in a survey.

needs, and interests, and the art specialist, who best understands the techniques of art and the process of a child's creative visual development. Together they can guide the child's visual art experience in relation to his total education.

In this arrangement, curriculum planning is a cooperative venture, engaged in by the art specialist and all the classroom teachers, and revised as warranted by actual classroom activities. Art lessons are conducted on a flexible schedule arranged with the classroom teacher; the art specialist generally is present to provide in-depth instruction and always is available should he be needed. In-service training for the classroom teacher working with the art specialist is a daily occurrence rather than an after-hours chore.

Success of the plan depends on adequate staffing and willingness of the two professionals to cooperate. There must be enough special art teachers to provide, in unhurried fashion, the guidance needed by the classroom teachers. Each professional must be willing to work noncompetitively and to devote his special talents to their common goal—nurturing the child's creative development.

Role of the classroom teacher

The classroom teacher's role in cooperative art teaching is to coordinate art lessons with learning activities in other areas to provide an integrated educational experience for the child at a particular grade level.

The classroom teacher is an important person in the elementary school system because he actually teaches most of the art. Small children cannot learn in a departmentalized situation such as is used in secondary school. They need one teacher, a confidant who is always at hand and who understands them individually and personally. In this capacity, the classroom teacher can contribute to the child's art education a personal understanding that the art specialist does not have. The classroom teacher best understands (1) the child's total aspirations; (2) his immediate needs, abilities, skills, and attitudes; (3) his educational progress; (4) his attitudes and appreciations as they emerge in daily education; (5)

the balance and continuity of his total learning; (6) his readiness to learn. In addition, the classroom teacher has the best opportunity to capitalize on situations that promote creative experience and to follow up the experience, the best chance to reinforce the child's motivation and self-confidence, and the best natural occasions to involve and guide the child in long-range planning for his own future learning.

Figures 12.1–12.2

Role of the art specialist

The art specialist's role in cooperative art teaching consists of (1) coordinating the creative visual experiences in all the grades of the elementary school; (2) providing in-service education for the classroom teachers; (3) assuming responsibility for the art program; (4) evaluating the effectiveness of the art teaching.

Coordinating creative visual learning   The art specialist is responsible for coordinating the creative visual experiences in all the grades of the elementary school so that each child will acquire adequate basic knowledge about art. (The classroom teacher integrates art experience with total learning in only a single grade.)

The art specialist best understands the nature of the art experience and the sequence of children's creative visual development; he is familiar with the materials and techniques of art; he is aware of the importance of art in enriching the whole educative process. He formulates the objectives of the art education program, specifies the scope and sequence of experiences to be achieved, suggests materials and experiences to be used in the art lessons, and reinforces the classroom teacher by working with him in the classroom.

Plates XXIV–XXV

Providing in-service training for classroom teachers   As explained earlier, the classroom teacher, because of his close personal relation to each child and his understanding of the child's immediate needs and interests, is the person best able to teach art in a creative-evaluative way that will integrate art experience with total learning. However, to teach art well, the classroom teacher must also have some understanding of the

12.1. *Here the classroom teacher and the special art teacher work together. As they cooperate, they give the children the creative-evaluative teaching that integrates each child's art experience with his total learning. This combination of child specialist and art specialist produces the maximum in art experience for the children in this elementary school classroom.*

12.2. The elementary classroom teacher also shown opposite is carrying out her role of teaching art, so that children may have visual experiences on a regular basis. She is the confidante who is always there. She is the teacher who understands each child individually and personally.

nature of creative visual expression, the objectives of art education, the development of children's creative visual ability, and the techniques and materials used in art work. Not all teachers have received such specialized training in their undergraduate preparation. For them in particular, but also to acquaint all classroom teachers with new methods, activities, and approaches, the art specialist should provide a program of in-service training in art.

Figure 12.3

In the cooperative teaching situation such in-service education is routinely supplied on a day-to-day basis as the art teacher works with the classroom teachers. More formal educational instruments are educational bulletins, individual and group conferences, demonstration teaching, and workshops.

ART EDUCATION BULLETIN The informational bulletin, preferably published on a regular schedule, is an instrument through which the specialist can alert, inform, inspire, or guide the teachers and, in general, promote understanding among them. The bulletin may be brief or extended, depending on the subject and detail of its content. Its cooperative nature should be emphasized by encouraging classroom teachers to contribute notes on outstanding art activities conducted in their classrooms.

INDIVIDUAL AND GROUP CONFERENCES The personal conference is a two-way system. The specialist can advise the classroom teacher, the classroom teacher can help the specialist, and both can establish mutual rapport and gain professional understanding. In the cooperative teaching situation, the importance of mutual respect among the participants cannot be overemphasized.

The group conference is especially valuable when a single art specialist is responsible for 30 or more classroom teachers. Examples of subjects on which group conferences can usefully be held are these:

1. The meaning of art expression of primary-grade children

2. The art expression of intermediate-grade children
3. How to motivate children for creative expression
4. Evaluation of children's growth through art
5. The meaning of a balanced art program in the elementary school
6. Using materials appropriate to the developmental level of elementary school children
7. Emotional development as shown by the art work of children
8. Natural correlation of art with other areas of learning
9. Teaching children to "look and see"

The effectiveness of such meetings can be enhanced by using classroom teachers as discussants, provided they are well informed; by using children's art work as subjects of discussion; by inviting and answering questions from conference participants; by specifically relating the topics discussed to the teacher's classroom situations.

DEMONSTRATION TEACHING When the solution to a problem in art teaching requires a depth of understanding for which the classroom teacher's training has not prepared him, sometimes the most effective way of developing understanding on the part of the classroom teacher is for the art specialist to demonstrate by teaching.

WORKSHOPS The art workshop is designed to give the elementary school teacher experience with stimulating art ideas, with art materials and processes, and with involvement in formulating shapes so that he can more adequately guide his pupils to employ these means to create an art product.

Assuming responsibility for supporting the art program
It is the responsibility of the art specialist to advise the school's chief administrator regarding the financial support necessary for a worthwhile art program. Although basic art education is generally accepted as essential to the total school program, not all school systems are willing to provide adequate funds for supplies and facilities for special art activities. In such

cases, the art specialist should work with the administrator to convince the school board of the value of these extra art activities.

Evaluating the effectiveness of the art teaching   The art specialist is responsible for evaluating the effectiveness of the art teaching. In particular, he is concerned with evaluating the quality of the children's art products and the development of the child's aesthetic appreciation—areas the classroom teacher may find difficult to judge. For further discussion of the evaluation of art teaching, see Chapter 8.

SUMMARY

Opinions differ about whether art should be taught by the elementary school classroom teacher (who knows the children best but is often inadequately prepared in art education) or by a specially trained art instructor (who knows art techniques but is not familiar with the individual children in the class). The conflict has led to the development of four patterns of art education: (1) art teaching by an itinerant specialist, (2) art teaching by a resident specialist, (3) art teaching by the classroom teacher, with the specialist acting as consultant, and (4) cooperative art teaching by both classroom teacher and art specialist. The first two plans offer art education by teachers adequately prepared in art but lack ways and means for adequately relating the child's art lessons to his total learning. The third plan provides for this relation, but places the burden of teaching on the often inadequately prepared classroom teacher. Although the consultant is supposed to supply in-service training, there are usually too few consultants, and consequently too little time, to provide adequate guidance.

The fourth plan, advocated by the author, provides for creative-evaluative teaching through cooperation of classroom and special art teachers. The classroom teacher coordinates the art lessons with learning situations in other areas to provide an integrated educational experience for the child at a particular grade level. The art specialist coordinates the creative visual experiences in all grades of the elementary school so that each child will acquire adequate basic knowledge about art. In addition, the art specialist provides in-service training for the classroom teacher, advises the school administrator about the financial needs of the art program, and evaluates the teaching of art.

12.3. *Here an elementary classroom teacher (left) cooperates with a special art teacher. This classroom teacher is contributing a personal understanding to the children's art education that the specialist cannot give because of her rather brief contacts with a large number of students.*

AIDS TO UNDERSTANDING

For discussion

1. Evaluate each of four patterns of art education in the elementary schools in terms of their effective fostering of the principles of a strategy for creative-evaluative teaching of art.

2. Suggest how the role of the elementary classroom teacher and the role of the art specialist differ in relation to the teaching of art in an elementary classroom.

3. What condition exists nationally in the staffing of art teachers which places the responsibilities for understanding and teaching elementary school art directly on the elementary classroom teacher?

4. What will happen to the total art experience of children in an elementary classroom if, when the art teacher comes, the classroom teacher leaves, or if the classroom teacher teaches all the art lessons?

For involvement

1. Describe in detail two different patterns of art education in elementary schools which you have observed. How do they compare with cooperative art teaching?

2. Write a treatise, a philosophy, an outline, or credo for the elementary classroom teacher which reflects a positive and constructive attitude toward providing children with a creative, integrated, and aesthetic experience in the visual arts.

Part Four
APPENDIXES

Appendix I
RESOURCE GUIDE: SPECIFIC NEEDS AND INTERESTS OF CHILDREN

The following lists provide a specific breakdown of some broad categories of needs and interests of children similar to those presented in Chapter 5. The personal interpretation of children, in their chosen mode and medium, will emerge from a stimulation developed around any of the specific categories of needs and interests. Group work may also result from such stimulation. Whichever the case, it is dependent on the direction an individual or a group is motivated to follow in any of the thematic categories. Any category may be the basis of a unit. It is the teacher's responsibility to guide children toward art experience which provides the widest opportunities for learning, affords the utmost individual possibilities for growth, and permits each child to function at his level of potential.

EVERYDAY NEEDS OF LIFE

1. Getting ready for school
2. Eating breakfast (lunch, dinner)
3. Feeding my cat (dog, etc.)
4. Brushing my teeth
5. Combing my hair
6. Putting on my shoes
7. Putting on my skates
8. Riding my bike
9. Saying my prayers
10. Going to the store

THINGS I SEE

1. On the way to school
2. On the playground
3. On a shopping trip
4. On my way home
5. On the bus
6. From the school window
7. On the farm
8. At the grocery store
9. In church
10. From my yard

ANIMALS I KNOW

1. My dog
2. My cat
3. My pony
4. My rooster
5. My rabbit
6. My brother's horse
7. The squirrel in the park
8. My turtle
9. My duck
10. My sister's pet chicken
11. Animals at the zoo
12. Circus animals

RECREATION THROUGH PLAY

For Younger Children

1. Hopscotch
2. Jumping rope
3. Farmer in the Dell
4. Did You Ever See a Lassie?
5. Stop and start (Red Light)
6. Around the Mulberry Bush
7. Cat-and-Rat
8. Duck-Duck-Goose
9. Bluebird, Bluebird
10. Little Sallie Saucer

For Older Children

1. Baseball
2. Volleyball
3. Badminton
4. Soccer
5. Dodgeball
6. Chinese ball
7. Shuttle relays
8. Three-deep
9. Basketball
10. Touch football

TRIPS TO TAKE

1. To the firehouse
2. To the farm
3. To the big town
4. To the dairy
5. To the bakery
6. To the police station
7. To the post office
8. To the factory
9. To the museum
10. To the woods and fields

SPECIAL EVENTS

1. A fire
2. An accident
3. A wedding
4. A storm
5. The rainbow
6. A sunset
7. A sunrise
8. The first snow
9. A new baby in the family
10. The first trip
11. The circus
12. A space flight

RESPONSIBILITIES AT HOME

1. Raking leaves
2. Carrying in the groceries
3. Bringing in the milk
4. Sweeping my room
5. Feeding my pet
6. Drying the dishes
7. Making beds
8. Working in the garden
9. Putting away toys
10. Setting the table

FRIENDS AND FAMILY

1. My family
2. My older brother
3. My little sister
4. My mother
5. My grandfather
6. My pet
7. My teacher
8. My best friend

THINGS I DO

1. I like to read
2. I like to draw
3. I like to play dolls
4. I like to ride my bicycle
5. I like to visit
6. I like to work with clay
7. I like to walk
8. I like my music lesson
9. I like to sing
10. I like to play house
11. I like to paint
12. I like to meet people

SPECIAL DAYS

1. What holidays mean	6. Special patriotic days
2. The parade will go by	7. Decorating the home
3. My idea for eating	8. Going to services
4. Exchanging gifts	9. Having a program
5. Special religious days	10. Wasn't it exciting

In Chapter 9 a section of a curriculum guide is presented by which these suggestions for need-interest areas can be applied to various elementary grade levels. Appendix II is an example of how needs and interests may be delimited for each grade level as the sequence of the educational program in an elementary school.[1]

[1] The Mary E. Rickenbach Laboratory School, Kutztown State College, Kutztown, Pennsylvania, 1965

Appendix II
NEEDS AND INTERESTS DELIMITED IN GRADE-LEVEL SEQUENCE

K	The home, people, pets, community helpers, nature, seasons, farms, stories, holidays, food, songs, "me," imaginative ideas with divergent possibilities
1	Community helpers, farm, transportation, circus, stories and poems, imaginative ideas with divergent possibilities proceeding toward real experiences
2	New discoveries, farm, sound, communications, transportation, weather, growing things, birds, animals, ourselves, ideas growing from real experience with occasional imaginative stimulation
3	Indians, Pilgrims, special events, reading, the plants, animals, ocean, solar system, electricity, communication, child's own experiences

4	County, state, various lands, travel, transportation, health, eating habits, weather, electricity, stars, growing things, undersea life, literature, climate, man, aquarium, seeds, books, poetry, stories, plays, child's own experiences
5	Industries of the state, American Indians, areas of the state, colonial life, explorers, frontier life, other historical periods, health habits, the earth's surface, child's own meaningful experiences
6	Neighbors in our hemisphere, sports, heroes, music, space, weather, sound, astronomy, fantasy, stories

Note: Consult Appendix III for a list of materials, arranged by grade level, with which to develop these ideas.

Appendix III
SEQUENCE OF EXPERIENCES WITH MODES OF VISUAL ART EXPRESSION

PAINTING   PAINTING
SCOPE AND SEQUENCE OF EXPERIENCE WITH VARIOUS MATERIALS

	WITH THESE MATERIALS	FIND POSSIBLE MEANS OF SHAPING:		WITH THESE MATERIALS	FIND POSSIBLE MEANS OF SHAPING:
K	Easel paint Finger paint Chalk on wet paper Sponge and paint Powder paint Large size paper Large brushes	Experience with color Appreciation of color Experience in handling materials Experience in observation Recognition of colors Care of materials			and watercolor, etc. Awareness of light, dark, medium values Effective arrangement of pictorial elements, placement
1	Powder paint Finger paint Paper Sponges, brushes	Painting in relation to self-image Color identification Experiments with materials Realization of two-dimensional space	4	Paint Watercolor, dry paper Mural and other paper	Awareness of objects as they appear in space and in relation to each other through purposeful observation Mixing of colors Increased awareness of design qualities
2	Powder paint Finger paint Watercolor Manila paper, mural paper Finger painting paper	Use of increased detail related to self Extended experimentation with materials, crumpling paper, spatter, stipple	5	Ink Watercolor Tempera paint Mural and other papers	Use of distance, value, balance, repetition, continuity, emphasis, proportion in pictorial expression
3	Watercolor, wet paper Powder paint Mural paper, Manila paper	Increased awareness of color, line, form Growing understanding of materials Further experimentation with materials, combining crayon	6	Tempera paint Watercolor	Increased awareness of objects as they appear in space as well as means of achieving special effects with materials

Source: Developed by the staff of The Laboratory School, Rickenbach Research and Learning Center, Kutztown State College, Kutztown, Pa.

Note: The purpose of this guide is to make general suggestions for progression. The classroom teacher will adapt, supplement, and anticipate the need for additional tools and related materials.

DRAWING
SCOPE AND SEQUENCE OF EXPERIENCE WITH VARIOUS MATERIALS

DRAWING

	WITH THESE MATERIALS	FIND POSSIBLE MEANS OF SHAPING:		WITH THESE MATERIALS	FIND POSSIBLE MEANS OF SHAPING:
K	Large, thick pencils Crayons Chalk Newsprint Manila paper, 12 by 24 inches	Scribble drawing to develop muscular control with freedom, use of body rhythm Use of imagination; "me" relation to expression	4	Pencil, 2B or 3B Chalk Pen and ink	Expression using contour line Purposeful observation, people in action Development of eye and hand coordination
1	Large pencils Crayons Chalk, wet paper Newsprint Manila paper, 12 by 24 inches and other	Development of skill and freedom in handling materials through experimentation Expression of own feelings, ideas, experiences	5	Pencils, 4B, 2B, and 3B Pastels Pen and ink	Memory drawing Utilization of significant detail and characteristics of the *whole* Expression utilizing people in action Relating drawing skills to other school subjects
2	Large pencils Crayons Felt-tip markers Chalk, dry paper	Use of action lines, broad free strokes Increased ability to plan work Expression of ideas related to friends	6	Pencils, 4B, 2B, and 3B Pastels Conté crayon	Inventive, imaginative drawing Drawing based on purposeful observation, near and far objects, people Experiments in gaining special effects, as sharp and clear, soft and hazy
3	Large pencils Crayons Brush and ink	Quick sketching with sweeping wrist and arm movement, rhythmic stroke Observation of essentials in form Planning effective use of areas Use of textural effects Representation of people in context of familiar activity			

GRAPHICS

SCOPE AND SEQUENCE OF EXPERIENCE WITH VARIOUS MATERIALS

GRAPHICS

	WITH THESE MATERIALS	FIND POSSIBLE MEANS OF SHAPING:		WITH THESE MATERIALS	FIND POSSIBLE MEANS OF SHAPING:
K	Large pieces of erasers Wood blocks Tempera paint Newsprint Manila paper Cloth	Stick printing, developing sensitivity to space, rhythmic expression	4	Unmounted linoleum, 4 by 5 inches Newsprint, Manila paper Cloth Linoleum cutting tools	Preparation and printing a block in a situation where duplicate prints are necessary
1	Vegetables cut suitable for printing Wax crayon Paint Newsprint Manila paper Cloth	Repetitive, rhythmic expression Development of simple motifs	5	Pen and ink Unmounted linoleum, 6 by 9 inches Manila paper and American white paper Cloth	Continuation of block cutting with emphasis on story illustration
2	Wax crayons Ink Stencil paper Newsprint Manila paper Cloth	Use of stencils for making repetitive forms (pupil makes own stencil and practices technique of proper use)	6	Unmounted linoleum Pen and ink American white paper Cloth Articles of clothing, curtains	Development of border or allover designs for application to skirts, handkerchiefs, tablecloths, place mats, etc.
3	Wax crayons India ink Newsprint Manila and American white paper Cloth Water-base stencil paint	Creating a variety of textural effects on paper and cloth by wax resist method			

MODELING

SCOPE AND SEQUENCE OF EXPERIENCE WITH VARIOUS MATERIALS

MODELING

	WITH THESE MATERIALS	FIND POSSIBLE MEANS OF SHAPING:		WITH THESE MATERIALS	FIND POSSIBLE MEANS OF SHAPING:
K	Clay (size of adult fist) Shellac Powder paint	Manipulation of clay Development of simple forms Bisque firing and decoration of piece	4	Clay Rolling pin Modeling tool Small cardboard box Plaster of Paris	Forming a small bowl or tile, making a mold of it, casting the piece Decoration of clay piece by embossing, sgraffito Glazing clay pieces
1	Clay Improvised tools to create textural effects	Formation of bowl by thumb method Decorating with textural effects Bisque firing	5	Clay Light bulb Papier-mâché (strips and mâché) Glazes Salt and flour dough	Modeling puppet head in clay using this on which to form papier-mâché head Pottery building and glazing Construction of relief maps
2	Clay	Formation of figures suggesting action Pottery making by coil method Bisque firing	6	Clay Papier-mâché (strips and mâché) Coil wire	Papier-mâché modeling on wire armature Construction of papier-mâché mask over original clay form Understanding the qualities of sculpture which the blind can perceive
3	Clay Rolling pin Knife	Modeling people and animals by slab method Pottery making by slab method Bisque firing			

SCULPTURE   CONSTRUCTION
SCOPE AND SEQUENCE OF EXPERIENCE WITH VARIOUS MATERIALS

	WITH THESE MATERIALS	FIND POSSIBLE MEANS OF SHAPING:		WITH THESE MATERIALS	FIND POSSIBLE MEANS OF SHAPING:
K	Blocks Clay	Experiences in arranging and building Experiments with "take away" method of using clay	K	Paper, cardboard cartons Scissors, paste Blocks, wood	Constructing with blocks, piling cardboard cartons, painting cartons Folding paper, making original toy from materials at hand
1	Clay, soap	Carving basic forms with a tool	1	Colored paper Small boxes Glue	Free cutting, curling, folding, crushing, combining, glueing and decorating to originate forms
2	Soap, wax Gouge, knife	Carving animal forms with minimal cutting away	2	Paper, scissors, paste	Paper sculpture
3	Plaster of Paris Asbestos	Preparing plaster of Paris block or slab for carving Carving in full round or relief	3	Paper, papier-mâché, towels Scissors, paste Wood and cloth scraps Small boxes	Toy construction
4	Soft wood, knife	Carving figures and heads	4	Paper, papier-mâché Scissors, paste Spools, clothespins Cloth, discs, wheels	Construction of miniature village Construction of movable toy
5 and 6	Wire (chicken netting wire and coil wire) Papier-mâché Branches of trees Scrap metal Paper and cardboard Small logs, branches of trees, tree knots	Wire sculpture Scenery properties Carving objects whose original natural appearance suggests final form	5 and 6	Cardboard carton, cardboard Twigs, grass, ground Cotton, cloth, gauze Paper, wheat paste, scissors Salvage materials, string, yarn Paint, balsa wood	Construction of dioramas, table displays, models Construction of decorative objects Carving and construction of small objects

CRAFTS
SCOPE AND SEQUENCE OF EXPERIENCE WITH VARIOUS MATERIALS

	WITH THESE MATERIALS	FIND POSSIBLE MEANS OF SHAPING:		WITH THESE MATERIALS	FIND POSSIBLE MEANS OF SHAPING:
K	Glove, boxes, paper cups Plates, buttons, spools Towels, string, branches Pipe cleaners, paste	Making puppets (glove type) Construction of party decorations Construction of costume effects	4	Papier-mâché, large sheets of paper Discarded sheeting Crepe paper, metallic and other textured papers	Puppet making Costumes for plays Making useful beanie hat
1	Flat sticks, paper bags Seeds, colored paper Variety of boxes and containers Yarn, string	Making stick puppets Decorating boxes with paper mosaic Hat construction for special events	5	Cardboard, copper foil, papier-mâché, unbleached muslin, felt, oil cloth, jars, shellac, nail kegs, beads, buttons, patches of cloth, cotton roving	Making costumes, book covers, place mats, room decorations, costume jewelry, decorated boxes, collages, repoussé plaques
2	Paper bag (to fit head), oil cloth Large paper bags (to fit body) Construction paper Yarn, cloth strips	Costume making, masks Making favors and ornaments Making puppets	6	Cardboard, copper foil, papier-mâché, yarn, felt, unbleached muslin, leather, plastics, ceramic tile, tin cans, shellac, enamel paint, colored glass, beads Yarns for weaving	Making marionettes, costumes, repoussé, mosaic, corsages, table centerpieces, room decorations, costume jewelry Weaving on 240 Structo loom
3	Stocking, thread, stuffing Cloth, crepe paper Paper bags as above Yarn, cloth strips	Puppet making Costume making Weaving with tongue depressor loom			

202

Appendix IV
RESOURCE GUIDE
TO ART MATERIALS

Each child should have an opportunity to select materials in relation to his ideas about the situation the teacher has structured in the course of creative-evaluative art teaching. He needs to experiment to find out the possibilities inherent in art materials and to reflect upon the many problems involved in the process of using them. Experimenting with art materials involves comparative situations which the child can evaluate and, as a result of the evaluation, select the most appropriate means of using a material in relation to his ideas. This is a part of the whole art experience, and if it is neglected the child's understanding of art techniques is jeopardized.

It is essential, therefore, that the teacher orient the child to the possibilities of using art materials by providing situations, through demonstrations, through allowing him to observe objects, or through the use of visual aids, in which there are set up two or more conditions the child may compare. The conditions should apply to the child's idea. For example, if as a result of a stimulation by the teacher, the child decides to create a pot, a film showing the various possibilities of building clay by coil, slab, or pinch techniques gives him an opportunity to select from among the procedures. If the child has an opportunity to try out each approach in a simple way, he can evaluate his "tries" and decide which approach is most suitable to his idea. In another situation, the teacher can demonstrate working with clay to small groups or to the entire class. In this demonstration, the teacher should bring out, through the children's observation of his working with clay, that the clay may be too wet or too dry or just damp enough to be plastic. He should be careful to ask questions that focus the children's attention on the condition of the clay and the difference it makes in working with the clay. He should avoid telling the children what they obviously are observing. Through this kind of orientation the teacher guides the child in exploring, experimenting, and evaluating the material so that he can select a material which best fits the requirements of his idea of a visual product. A creative approach to the presentation of materials is essential to creative art work for children.

As the child is challenged through this kind of evaluative guidance, the shape of his materials will develop into the shape of his ideas. From this point, the teacher should tackle in a similar creative-evaluative manner the problems of design that arise in the process of the formulation of the visual product. The result will be that the child will create his *own art work* in terms of *his own needs* and interests and in relation to *his own situation*. The product that results will be his. It is important that the elementary school classroom teacher understand that the child's art product is not to be evaluated by adult standards. He must accept the idea that with continued creative-evaluative orientation to art materials, the child's knowledge of materials and techniques will develop as he progresses from experience to experience through each grade level.

This resource guide is presented to give the classroom teacher a basic understanding of the characteristics and limitations of art materials suitable for elementary school art experiences. *Illustrations have been omitted so that the prospective teacher using this text will not be misled into thinking that there is a "right" way to use materials.* In the arts, there are innumerable possibilities within the child's ability for expressing an idea with a suitable material. The following suggestions should not be used to present materials in a step-by-step or directed manner when working with students. They are a guide for the teacher, whose stimulation of an art lesson using slides, large pictures, film, found objects, stories, field trips, immediate experiences, and drama related to the immediate needs and interests of his pupils will cause them to think of ideas for a visual art product. The children should be able to select materials to find many possible means of shaping their ideas as visual art expression that is *their own*.

PAINTING

MATERIALS Finger paint, powder paint, tempera, chalk, watercolor, colored sand, encaustic (wax crayon), acrylic polymer color (hues, gel, gesso, paste), colored ink.

APPLICATORS Brush, sponge, finger, flexible knife, piece of cardboard, toothbrush, sprayer.

SURFACES Paper, cardboard, masonite, canvas, coated paper, wall (plaster, wood, cement, etc.).

Approaches to painting

Dry powder paint Dry tempera or powder paint can be mixed in various consistencies, to suit different applicators, for example, fingers or long-handled, flat-ended brushes of a fairly thick substance. With this medium the child can paint-in solid areas, outline areas of color, or obtain interesting minglings.

Other ways of using dry paint are to sprinkle it on paper that has been moistened with water or to wet a brush, dip it into the dry powder, and then apply the brush directly on to an absorbent paper surface.

Acrylic medium mixed with powder paint can be used to decorate objects as well as to paint pictures. The applicator is dipped into clear acrylic medium and then into the powder paint and applied to the surface of the object to be decorated or to serve as the surface for the painting (*do not use acrylic polymer paint in sprayers*).

Colored chalk   The young child should be offered only a few colors so that he will not be distracted from expressing with and manipulating the chalk. Interesting effects can be obtained with only a few colors by drawing on dampened paper, by using contrasting colors rubbed lightly (shaded), or by using areas of color. As the child grows in experience with chalk, he will discover how to blend one color into another and then paint on the blended areas with brush and ink or with opaque water color.

Finger paint   This is a free-flowing, plastic paint that permits the child to work freely. Glazed paper should be moistened on both sides by dipping it into water or sprinkling the water on the paper. A tablespoonful of finger paint should be placed in the center of the paper and spread evenly over the surface. Using the fingers, sides of the hands, elbows, combs, or pieces of cardboard, the child can move the paint over the surface until an image or design appears. The child can begin with one color and then, as he progresses, add other primary colors. It is useful to keep water nearby to remoisten the surface. Allow the painting to dry on a newsprint surface and press it flat with an iron if it curls.

Finger paint can be made in the classroom by mixing powder paint with liquid starch or wheat paste until a smooth pastelike consistency is obtained. It can be applied as described above. Mixed tempera paint may also be used. Commercially prepared finger paint produces the best results.

Tempera, or poster paint   This paint is opaque water color. The child should have experience with it because it permits him to work quickly while he has fresh ideas. Tempera is relatively easy to control, and overpainting of details is possible because it dries quickly. A paper surface of almost any type, including cardboard, may be used with tempera, or the paint can be applied on dry

paper, on a wetted surface, over wax crayon which resists it, over thick white tempera which has dried, on sandpaper, and on many other surfaces.

Watercolor   Watercolor is most effectively used after a child has had experiences with the approaches previously discussed. The muscular control and manipulative ability need to be developed sufficiently to make the medium appealing rather than frustrating. When this time occurs depends upon the child's development and his previous experience with art materials, and is not particularly related to a specific grade level.

Experiences with washes, minglings, gradations of value, and outlines around large areas of color should be offered. Applying watercolor on dry paper produces a crisp effect, while applying it on wet paper produces unpredictable but unusual effects. As the child learns to use this medium, he will discover that painting with darker colors, or deeper values of the same color, on light washes can be a satisfying experience.

Watercolor may be used as wet color on wet paper or over wax crayon or rubber cement, which resist it. By mixing acrylic colors with water, for thinning, transparent watercolor is achieved. Any surface prepared with an acrylic polymer gesso can be used for watercolor, thereby eliminating the need for special watercolor papers.

Colored sand   Using ordinary white sand, the child can make sand paintings similar to those of the Navaho Indians. The sand can be colored by shaking it in a jar with a few drops of food coloring. Using a container of glue with a nozzle top, the child can apply lines and areas of glue to a surface. He then sprinkles sand over this surface, applying one color at a time. When the glue is set, the excess sand is shaken from the surface. The process is repeated for each color until the picture or design is complete.

Collage, montage, mosaic, and assemblage   The collage experience consists of using pieces of flat materials, textured materials, various kinds of paper, and photographic prints to create a picture that is effective because of the contrasting materials composing it. In a *collage,* the materials are cut in random shapes; in a *montage,* the general shape of each pictured object is retained and used to compose a picture with a particular theme. A *mosaic* may be created with flat paper or with solid materials such as stones, tiles, or seeds. It differs from a collage or a montage in that its component pieces are usually small and slightly varied in size. The pieces are glued to a strong surface that has been sized and are placed so that each one has a space around it. The space is filled with a grout, which hardens. Any material that will dry hard and not crack away may be used as a grout, for example, cement, commercial grout, flour-saltwater mix, tile filler, plaster of Paris.

An *assemblage* sometimes resembles a painting and sometimes is a sculpture. The techique involves working with three-dimensional objects that are glued to a flat surface on or under a canvaslike material. The canvas or other surface is sometimes opened up by slits, holes, or ridges created with other materials, such as folded paper or cardboard. The shape is changed to enhance the object. When the surface is predominantly painted and flat, the assemblage appears as a painting; when predominantly three-dimensional and unpainted, as a sculpture. This experience is a contemporary direction which captures the child's imagination in the late elementary and middle school years. Acrylic polymer medium provides a fine binder for these techniques, as do milk-base glues and various epoxy cements. Epoxy cements should be used with caution, according to the instructions on the commercial packages.

Colored inks Ink may be applied to a dampened surface as a painting medium or directly on a dry surface. When ink is spread over a damp surface, which is allowed to dry, the surface may be drawn upon with pen and ink, crayon, pencil, or other drawing material.

Acrylic polymer colors These colors, as they come from the tube, have a thick consistency that permits their use for painting. Only water is necessary for mixing. When used from the tube, acrylic paint is plastic enough so that the marks of the brush or other applicator are retained in a painting. High impasto (thick paint) affects similar to those achieved with oil paints may be attained. The paint is bright and can be thinned with water to achieve a pleasant glaze (thin layer of color over a dried surface) for exciting effects. Acrylic paint is less expensive and less messy than oil paint. It can be mixed with water, whereas oil paint must be mixed with turpentine, oil, dryer, etc. Acrylic paint can be used on any surface; oil paint can be used only on a sized surface. Acrylic paint dries quickly; oil paint more slowly. For the elementary school child, working with acrylic color is good preparation for oil painting; the latter is used more successfully at the late middle and secondary levels of school.

Encaustic (wax crayons melted) Wax crayons, candles, or paraffin, when melted in muffin tins in a pan of water over a hot plate, provide an effective painting experience for older children. Turpentine is added to the wax to extend it for painting. When wax is used near a hot plate a large flat piece of metal must be placed between the coils of the plate and the containers of wax so that wax will never drip directly on the coils of the hot plate.

Encaustic can be brushed directly onto any surface, such as old cardboard, pieces of masonite, wood cuttings, and large pieces of cardboard box. Later, the surface may be torched with a small alcohol torch to fuse areas of color, scratched and reworked, and finally buffed with a soft cloth.

MURAL PAINTING

MATERIALS Any of the materials mentioned under Painting may be used.

APPLICATORS Any of the applicators mentioned under Painting may be used.

SURFACES Mural paper, masonry, pressed wood, plywood, large industrial packing and box cardboards.

Approaches to mural painting

Any of the approaches to Painting (see above) may be adapted to mural painting; however, the teacher must keep in mind that the surfaces for mural painting are much larger than for easel painting and that for children, mural painting is usually a group effort. Murals are most successful when the materials and applicators used are large and broad enough so that the child can fill in his space on the mural surface quickly enough to avoid discouragement.

Types of mural include painted murals, cut-paper murals, collages, mosaics, montages, assemblages.

Organization of the mural experience Through evaluative discussions, the teacher should guide the children to decide on the mural's location, size, and surface. The teacher should help the children to understand that a mural is a visual message to a community of people. Class discussions should relate to the children's ideas about some community theme and what might best express the ideas. The children should talk about the sizes, colors, and action to be expressed in the work. As the children express their ideas, the teacher might list them on the blackboard for easy recall and reference as the discussion continues. Each child should have some part in the planning and development of the mural. For an older-aged group, each child should make a separate planning drawing, which can be taped in place on the surface. For a group of young children, the drawings should be started directly on the mural surface with materials that can be overpainted or overpasted if the child wishes to make changes as the mural develops. When all the ideas have been assembled, or in the case of small children when the mural is in progress, the class should discuss which parts seem to work together well, which need to be altered or combined to be more effective, and whether anything important has been omitted. At this point, one or two children should lay out the general lines of the mural area in which the particular parts of the mural will be located. When children work directly on the mural surface, periodic evaluations of the work with the class guide the layout stage. In the evaluating process as the mural progresses, the children should look for colors that are too outstanding; inconsistent use of lines, colors, and forms; the emphasis of important areas or objects; the balance of colors, shapes, and forms. The arrangement should be discussed to see if what is needed is there. What might be discarded to make the mural more effective? Is it too jumbled? Does it need to be simplified? Does it all look well together and look like one big unit? The children should feel that they have done as a group what no one child alone could do. The organization of mural painting should vary according to the particular class situation.

SIMULATED STAINED-GLASS WINDOW

MATERIALS Pencil, wax crayon, oil (mineral, cooking), organdy, waxed paper, large cardboard box, white bond paper, shelf paper, glue.

APPLICATORS Soft cloth, cotton, iron, stapler.

SURFACES Brown kraft paper, heavy colored construction paper, organdy, white bond paper.

Approaches for developing a stained-glass window

APPROACH 1 Using thin white bond paper and a pencil, the child should draw an outline of his proposed art work, including the lines that represent the lead of the stained-glass window. The outline is then painted with India ink. The bond paper outline is placed on top of a plain piece of heavy brown paper and the entire surface is evenly coated with oil using cotton wadding. Color is applied with crayons within the India-ink outline and the art bond paper backing is also colored if deeper, richer colors are desired. The finished work is then taped neatly to a windowpane.

APPROACH 2 A piece of organdy is cut to the shape of the stained-glass window—a little larger than the space for the window so that it can be fitted tight when it is put into place. Pieces of construction paper are glued to the organdy, leaving at least 1/8 inch around each piece of paper so that the picture formed will have the desired leaded effect. The organdy around the paper is painted with black tempera and the colored construction paper is oiled lightly. Working is easier if the organdy is stretched tight over a frame.

DRAWING

MATERIALS Crayon, ink, pencil, chalk.

APPLICATORS Brush, pen and pen point, felt pen, crayon (wax and pressed).

SURFACES Paper (newsprint, bond, American white, construction, and Manila), generally 12 by 18 inches to 18 by 24 inches in size.

Approaches using crayons

Large crayons, wax or pressed, permit the manipulative exercise and development of muscular control needed by the child. Crayons are flexible in the sense that the child may use the point, the side, or the end with as much pressure as is required to achieve whatever he wishes to draw. Large flat areas of color can be applied to which details can be added.

CRAYON RUBBINGS OVER FOUND TEXTURES Found textures may be cut and arranged under paper. Broken crayons are peeled and the broad surface used to rub over the paper. As the child observes this happening, he should be encouraged to control the many interesting effects so that they are composed as a design.

CRAYON RESIST The crayon is impressed firmly over the surface of a sheet of American white paper. Some areas of paper are allowed to show through the drawing. Black or colored ink or transparent or opaque watercolor is washed over the surface of the paper and fills in the exposed paper surfaces.

CRAYON TRANSFER A crayon drawing is made by pressing the crayon firmly on the paper surface. The crayon drawing is placed against another paper surface or cloth and pressed with a warm iron until the crayon transfers to the new surface. This procedure may be repeated until the crayon no longer transfers.

CRAYON ETCHING A smooth-finished paper surface is coated with a thick application of wax crayon, either as a controlled drawing or in random areas. The entire surface of the paper which was heavily colored with crayon is coated with black or dark India ink. A contrast enhances the effect. The etching is made by scraping this surface with a sharp instrument (scissors, knife).

CRAYON STENCIL A design is drawn on white drawing paper. Waxed stencil paper is placed over the drawing, and simple forms are cut out of the waxed stencil paper. Spaces should be left between each shape cut out so that the stencil will hold together. The teacher should be sure that children cut the stencils over several layers of newspaper or a piece of cardboard so that desks or tables will not be damaged. The hole cut in the wax paper forms a stencil through which the painting is done. The stenciling process requires that the strokes be made from the stencil to the surface being painted. Textile paint with stencil brushes may be used as well as flat-tipped pens.

CRAYON ON CLOTH The crayon is applied directly onto cloth and sealed by pressing the cloth with a warm iron between two pieces of brown wrapping paper or clear newsprint. The heat is applied until the crayon is made fast to the cloth.

CRAYON ON TEXTURED SURFACE A drawing is made with crayon directly on a textured surface such as sandpaper.

Approaches using chalk

Drawing with chalk is effective when a contrast is realized between the paper surface and the color of the chalk. On this principle, chalk may be applied on colored, black, gray, or white surfaces using straight, curved, wide, thin, short or long strokes. Chalk may be applied in flat areas and overdrawn with lines; it may be rubbed lightly with soft materials to blend colors. A chalk drawing can be protected by applying a fixative spray to the surface. Chalk can also be applied over dampened paper. Like crayons, it can be rubbed over paper under which textured surfaces have been arranged.

Approaches using pencil

A large pencil with a thick lead makes a good drawing tool. Pencil should not be used to make outlines that are then colored with some other material because it prevents effective expression and experimentation with the coloring medium. The child naturally scribbles in early childhood, and often a pencil is the only material he finds at hand in the home. A small pencil with a hard, thin lead is restrictive and inhibiting as an art material. A large black pencil is preferred in the classroom.

Approaches using ink

A felt pen with black ink lends itself to bold, direct expression of ideas in a child's drawing. Drawing with pen and ink should be reserved as an experience for the later elementary and middle school years, after the child has developed a frame of reference for drawing experiences.

GRAPHICS

MATERIALS Stick, potato, carrot, inner-tube piece, string, water soluble ink, finger paint, tempera, linoleum, wood block, modeling clay, and glue, epoxy, or acrylic modeling paste and polymer medium.

APPLICATORS Stencil, stiff brush, brayer, screen, glass, and masonite.

SURFACES Absorbent paper.

Approaches to relief printing

Stick prints In a first experience with print-making, the child can take a small piece of thin wood broken from a larger stick, dip it in color, and then press it on paper or make some rhythmic movement on paper several times. After a few tries, he soon discovers that many materials are suited to printing and creates interesting prints. Carrot-printing and potato-printing are common.

Monoprints Flat, textured materials are arranged on a piece of formica, hard wood, or metal which has first been rolled with a coat of color. A clean sheet of paper is placed on the arrangement and rolled with a clean brayer or rolling pin. When the paper is lifted, it will show interesting results that can be improved upon and diversified with each monoprint. Color can be dripped, flowed, or painted directly on the surface, and effective images will result.

Block prints From the third grade upward, the child is able to cut into linoleum and soft pine to create blocks for printing. By impressing, carving, or modeling clay on a hard surface; by cutting linoleum or wood blocks; by applying materials like inner tubes, glue, and cardboard to a hard flat surface, an area can be created which, when inked with a brayer and printed, produces a print that is the reverse of the surface created.

PREPARING THE BLOCK The child should draw directly on the block, which has been lightly coated with white tempera paint. The parts of the drawing that are black or dark should be left, and all the white areas cut away. With a sharp V-grooved tool, the area to be cut away (i.e., the area that is not to print) should be outlined. Using a small U-shaped gouge and a large flatter gouge for the large areas, the area that is not to print should be cut away. Often the ridges that seem to stick up create very effective textures with areas when printed.

When inner-tube pieces and cardboards are

applied to a surface for printing, they should be glued firmly.

PRINTING THE BLOCK Generally, it is best to have the child cut as many pieces of paper as he thinks he will print. After squeezing a small amount of ink on a glass or formica surface, he should roll the ink out evenly with the brayer, moving the brayer in all directions until the ink seems to be smooth and pulls the brayer slightly. He can then apply the ink to coat the block evenly. The print is made by placing the block in position on the paper, pressing on it, and as the paper sticks to the block, turning it over and rubbing the surface of the paper with the bowl of a spoon until the entire area has been covered. He can lift the corner of the paper until the image of the print appears and check it. If the ink appears even and dark, he should lift the print from the block. The block should be inked each time it is printed for the best effect. If an oil-base ink is used, printing may be done directly on fabric.

DIRECT PRINTING A small child can make a print without cutting the block. The surface of the block is coated with ink as described, and the child can draw on the ink block. The area where the ink is removed will appear as the color of the surface being imprinted. However, like a monoprint, only one print will result from each drawing.

White-line prints This experience is excellent for children in the later elementary grades. In this relief process, a wood (soft pine) block surface is sanded smooth with fine sand paper. The pupil makes a line drawing directly on the wood block and with a single-edged razor blade mounted in a holder cuts out the line as a V-shaped groove. The razor is inserted at an angle on each side of the line to form the groove. A light coating of glycerin may be brushed on the block to aid in the transfer of color; however, this is not necessary. Paper is attached to the edge of the block with tacks or staples so that it will fold over the surface of the drawing. The paper should lift up easily and be folded so that it

will overlie the same spot on the block each time it is lifted and returned for printing. The paper should be absorbent; American white paper is a good choice. The child applies water-base paints to the areas of the block and blots the colors onto the paper before the color sinks into the block. The color is transferred by rubbing the back of the paper lightly with the bowl of a large spoon. The print is developed in color in this way. Colors are blended by reapplication of the different colors.

Approaches to stenciling

MATERIALS Wood or cardboard box frame. Cloth for screens: organdy, crinoline, silk. Brown masking tape. Paint: tempera mixed with liquid starch, acrylic polymer emulsions (2 ounces of color to 1 tablespoon of polymer medium), finger paint mixed to the consistency of thick cream, and powder tempera mixed with wheat paste.

APPLICATORS Squeegee, rubber windshield wiper, straight edge of heavy cardboard.

SURFACES Various types of cloths and papers.

Specific preparations An opening is cut in the lid of a box, at least 1 1/2 inches away from the outside edge of the lid, or a wooden frame is constructed using clear white pine 2 by 2 inches in size. The frame is made so that the inside dimension is at least 3 inches larger than the size needed for the screen print. A temporary frame may be made out of a flat picnic plate. The child can stretch organdy over the opening and fasten it to the outside surfaces of the frame with heavy staples. The screen material must be tight with no wrinkles, before it is taped. He can tape the screen on the top side to form the opening and to seal the corners of the frame from the paint, and should check to be sure no holes are in the taped areas. The taped areas may be sealed with shellac. For a screen that will be used only once, this may be done with acrylic medium.

The surface of the table on which the child is working should be protected with paper. The child can cut pieces of waxed or coated paper to be printed and place them under the screen. The paint is applied across the short edge of the screen and scraped across the opening in the organdy by firmly pressing on the scraper. The design is produced by blocking the screen with wax crayon or a glue fill. The application of these materials needs to be heavy, so that the color will not leak through the screen.

The child should be urged to work along without delay once he starts the screen printing. If the paint dries in the screen, the screen has to be washed before it can be reused. In the case of acrylic paint, a new screen has to be made.

Approaches to intaglio printing
Etching, drypoint, and other metal-plate processes are more suited to the secondary level. Simple drypoint may be adapted to the upper elementary and middle school levels by using sheets of acetate material instead of a metal plate. (See above, *Crayon etching.*)

LETTERING

MATERIALS Crayon, chalk, cut paper, carpenter's pencil, large ''B'' Speedball pen and holder.

SURFACES Large plain newsprint, American white, and construction paper, and railroad, oaktag, and poster boards.

Components of legibility
Legibility is a quality involving the spacing, thickness, and darkness or lightness which make words easy to read. The child can develop a sensitivity to good lettering through comparative situations that the teacher structures in demonstrations. The child is thus stimulated to notice and think about the difference between the poor and good lettering shown in the demonstration aids. With guidance of this kind the child can note in his own work letters and spacing that need to be improved. Measuring out letters with a rule to prescribed sizes will not develop the child's sensitivity to good lettering.

Evaluating thickness Suggestion for an evaluative situation:

ART SHOW
ART SHOW

Judging effective spacing The child should have an opportunity to judge the space relations of letter forms visually. Seeing the spacing of letters in words, of words in phrases, and of sentences in a limited space provides experience in judging the spacing of letters and aids in the development of his sensitivity to legible lettering.

Suggestion for an evaluative situation:

ART SHOW
ART SHOW

Sensing the effect of dark and light values The legibility of letters is affected by their darkness or lightness, or the contrast between letter and paper. Contrast makes a letter easier to see. However, contrast of value, texture, or color within a word, phrase, or sentence causes letters not to unite as they should. Contrast makes individual letters *show up,* but contrast of individual letters within a word makes the word hard to read.

Suggestion for an evaluative situation:

Letter form

A simple block letter, without serifs, is most suitable for the child at the elementary school level. If the child has learned to use a printed letter in the early writing program, this letter form may be made with a piece of crayon or thick chalk. A vertical rather than a script letter is preferred as it is easier for the child to develop with art materials.

Approaches to lettering

Grades 2 and 3 The child should letter as large as possible. He can cut a strip of paper that equals the height of the letter he has decided to make. The strip should be about 24 to 36 inches long. Using scrap pieces of chalk or crayon, the child should be encouraged to make a letter that *bumps* the top and bottom edges of the paper strip. When he has a letter that seems satisfying to him, he should cut it from the strip carefully. The letter may be straightened if necessary with a ruled edge.

The letter, *the child's own design,* may be used as a template from which he can trace and cut out other letters. Cut-out letters can be spaced by eye between horizontal guide lines; thus frustration is avoided—if the spacing does not look well, the child can adjust the letters until they do seem to be spaced well (this is not possible with letters that are drawn). After the spacing is adjusted, the letters can be pasted or traced in the final position.

Grades 4, 5, and 6 At this level it is important to be sure that lettering materials are adaptable and suitable for the size letter to be used in a particular lettering situation. If the child used the side of a short piece of a light crayon, a large flat-ended brush, or a thick flattened lead-graphite pencil, he can letter between two horizontal guide lines in a particular length of space (the letters should not be drawn with a fine-pointed pencil). This approach should be continued until the child has achieved good spacing, thickness, and value in the letters.

As the child's lettering improves, he can make free-brush letters within the guide lines. The spacing of the guide lines should be varied from time to time. Lettering for a purpose is more effective than lettering purely as an exercise. The ruler should be used only to establish guide lines. If the child letters as often as possible in relation to the experiences and events in the classroom and the total school program, his ability will develop rapidly; a simple but effective procedure is to have him letter his name on the backs of all his art papers.

SCULPTURE

MATERIALS Paper, paper bag, wire, plaster of Paris gauze, soap, wood, stone, zonolite mixed with cement, water, liquid soap, newspaper.

TOOLS Carving tool, knife, wood and stone chisels, gouge, scissors, spoon, mixing bowl, improvised carving tools (made from old metal tools), and a hard wood block, 2 by 2 by 12 inches in size, for tapping tools.

SURFACES Three-dimensional molded or natural structures such as cast plaster, zonolite and cement, wood (blocks from mill or small logs), soap, soft stones, and sand core from a foundry. Two-dimensional formed materials such as paper, surgical plaster gauze, cardboard, small wooden sticks, and wire screen.

Approaches to sculpture

In sculpture, material usually is taken away from an original piece of material. However, in the case of wire, paper, and plaster gauze, the process is one of adding materials together, much like molding. With these materials the parts are formed and often when large forms have been developed, other forms are cut away. Commonly, all the processes are termed sculpture.

The teacher should keep in mind that the art materials need to be selected in regard to the age and strength of the child. For example, paper, soap, soft wire, and styrofoam can be manipulated by a small child, but harder materials are a challenge for the older child.

SOAP AND WAX   Soap and wax have the advantage of softness. When fresh and used at room temperature they offer little resistance to the carving tool. The problems are, therefore, similar to those encountered in working with plaster—an experience which would come later. Soap or wax may be carved on one surface, in relief, or in the round; it can be cut with simplified planes or with details and textures. It may be used realistically or abstractly.

PLASTER OF PARIS   This material naturally follows experiences of carving soap and wax. Usually it should not be used below the third grade. Plaster of Paris is mixed with water. Its consistency depends on the purpose. To mix, fill a plastic mixing bowl half full of water. Sift the plaster into the bowl without stirring it. When the plaster has absorbed the water and a little island of plaster remains in the center, wait a few minutes and then stir slowly. The plaster should flow like thick batter. The plaster is poured into soaped or greased molds when it is still like thick batter or thick cream, and is allowed to set after the mold is filled to the desired thickness. Plaster hardens in a few minutes after it is mixed with water, so it should be poured into molds without delay. For relief carving the consistency should be slightly thicker than previously stated. The plaster is poured into a cardboard box top of the size desired and allowed to dry thoroughly before any carving is done. Precautions should be taken to protect the desks or tables when working with plaster. The child can work with the plaster in a cardboard box whose sides are cut down to 4 inches; this will prevent plaster from getting on the floor of the room. *Under no circumstances should plaster, in either liquid or powder state, be put into the plumbing.*

Carving knives, penknives, and improvised tools are necessary to work with this material. The child learns that dry and brittle material requires careful handling; thinking before cutting, solving of problems of form, texture, and volume is a challenging experience. Bone-dry plaster may chip and, therefore, should be dampened with a cloth so that it will cut more easily.

Most often, the natural white plaster is satisfying to the eye. Tones of watercolor may be used to enhance the surface, and the work can be waxed, but this should be done according to the creator's preference.

PAPER   Sculptures may be made from a variety of papers, such as tissue, cellophane, metallic paper, colored construction paper, Bristol board, railroad board, and oaktags. Adhesive materials and binders include paste, rubber cement, masking tape, staples, epoxy cement, vegetable glue, and milk-based glue. Tools are scissors, X-acto knife and blades, and single-edged razor blade.

The child can discover that paper can be curled, stretched, cut, scored, folded, crumbled, torn, and textured by impression. All these attempts to change the paper from its original state involve basically cutting, folding, curling, and tearing. Paper sculpture is a process of adhering or binding together forms shaped by these means.

WOOD   Scraps of wood from the industrial arts department or a local finishing mill may be used in the elementary school for carving. The wood should be soft white pine. Small pieces can be assembled and glued (see under *Assemblage*) or carved. Balsa wood can be used in the early experiences of carving and followed by work with pine.

To finish wood, use coarse sandpaper first and sand with the grain of the wood. Smooth the surface of the wood with medium and then fine sandpaper. When the wood is smooth, apply linseed oil with a brush or cloth until it is soaked in. Wipe away the excess oil and rub vigorously with a soft lintless cloth. After the piece is dry, wax the surface. Wood may be finished with contrasting textures over the surface and waxed with clear butcher's wax. Toys and other wooden objects may be finished with enamel paints in various combinations of color.

ASBESTOS AND CEMENT   Asbestos combined with cement is similar to plaster of Paris, but is harder; its use simulates stone-carving experiences for the child in the late elementary and middle school.

Mix the asbestos (wood sawdust may be used) and cement with water in a large metal container. The hardness of the material can be regulated by varying the proportions of asbestos and cement. If there is a greater amount of asbestos, the material is easier to carve. Generally, the mixture is of equal amounts of each. If cardboard cartons are used for molds, the sides must be taped strongly or wrapped with twine to prevent the heavy wet materials from breaking them down. When the mix is dry, the mold should be removed without delay.

Asbestos can be purchased wherever insulating materials are sold.

SAND CORE This material can be obtained from a foundry: it is used in the same ways as plaster of Paris.

SAND CASTS Moist sand is placed in a cardboard box of appropriate size and at least 1/2 inch thick which has been shellacked. The covering of wet sand should be deep enough so that various materials deposited in the sand will stay in place. The materials are arranged in the sand as in mosaic work, except that the finished surfaces should be in contact with the sand. Plaster is mixed as described earlier and poured into the mold, up to the top. The box should be tapped so that the plaster will settle evenly. When the plaster is hardened, remove the box mold and brush away the sand on the surface of the object. If the piece is to be hung on a wall, a paper clip can be inserted into the plaster before it has become firm.

SLAB SCULPTURE This means of working with wet clay is best for children in the late elementary years and all following grades. Plasticine may also be used, but plasticine products are not permanent and cannot be fired. This discussion applies to clay. The clay is rolled with a rolling pin to a uniform thickness of about 3/4 inch. Two 3/4 inch sticks can be used as guides so that the roller will not compress the clay unevenly. The sections for the slab sculpture are drawn on oaktag and the

oaktag templates are then placed on the slab. Using a pointed knife, the child cuts around the template and completely through the thickness of clay. The excess clay is trimmed away from the template. The pieces used in the sculpture are joined together with slip, a mixture of clay and water about the consistency of thick cream. To weld the parts together, the edges to be joined are scored lightly with a knife, filled with slip, and joined by firm pressure. The joints then must be worked together and smoothed with a wooden modeling tool, such as a tongue depressor. Textures may be scratched, scored, or impressed into the clay when it is firm or still in the flat pieces. The dried finished piece can be fired under the supervision of the art teacher and glazed.

MODELING

MATERIALS Dough mixes, moist clay, plasticine, papier-mâché, plaster of Paris, copper, and aluminum foil.

SUPPORTS Wire, wood, rolled and formed newspaper.

Approaches to modeling

Dough Modeling dough is made from sawdust mixed with wallpaper paste or from salt mixed with flour or cornstarch. These mixes are inexpensive and easily obtained, have interesting texture and color, and can be used for modeling directly or on an armature. The salt and cornstarch mix dries very hard and often is referred to as salt ceramic. All these mixes are easy to work with and can be used successfully at all age levels.

PREPARATION OF THE SAWDUST AND PASTE MIX Wallpaper paste is mixed according to the directions on the package, and sawdust or zonolite is added until the mixture is of a doughy consistency.

PREPARATION OF THE CORNSTARCH (OR FLOUR) AND SALT MIX For this mix, 1/2 cup of cornstarch (or flour) is added to 1 cup of salt and 3/4 cup of water in the top of a double boiler. The mix is cooked slowly, while enough water is added to make a pliable, doughy mixture. This is worked into a ball of plastic material which is used for modeling.

Plaster gauze   This surgical plaster is built up over a wire or wood support. If it is allowed to stiffen, the gauze can serve as an armature on which plaster or other gauze strips can be added.

Papier-mâché   Torn   newspaper,   newsprint,   or discarded paper toweling, soaked and mixed with wallpaper paste to the consistency of clay, makes an inexpensive modeling material. In the primary grades, it can serve as a substitute for clay, since it is just as pliable and will harden. In the upper grades, strips of paper or gauze, treated in the same manner, are useful to overlay crushed-paper forms or to overlay modeled clay to make a form on which to create such art products as masks. Strips of papier-mâché can be molded over an armature made of tightly rolled newspaper or heavy coat-hanger wire to develop animal and figure forms. Parts of puppets or marionettes can be made with papier-mâché.

PREPARING THE PULP   Several sheets of newspaper are torn into pieces about 1 inch at the longest measure, in a bowl with enough water to saturate the paper, and kneaded. The preparation may be left until the next day or immediately mixed with wheat paste until the pulp is doughy. This mixture may be used as clay or built up over an armature. It is well to let the first layer of pulp dry before it is very thick, and add coats over the dried base. When the pulp is thoroughly dry it can be painted with tempera and shellac or with acrylic colors and medium.

Strip modeling   A base of clay, rolled newsprint, wood, or wire is prepared in the general shape of the object to be formed. This base can be shaped further by tying wadded newspaper in place with string. Torn strips of newspaper, dipped in wheat paste, are applied to the basic form. Using alternate layers of colored and white

newsprint facilitates even application. If details are needed, cardboard cut to the shape can be glued to the surface and the paper formed over it. Finer details can be modeled from tissue paper mixed with wheat paste. Every other layer of paper can be applied dry so that the work does not become messy with paste. It is well to let the object dry after every few layers of paper. The finished product should dry for several days. After the drying period, the modeled form may be decorated as suggested for the pulp material.

Clay   Clay is a significant material because it is plastic and can be pulled out, pushed in, squeezed, pinched off, rolled, and otherwise manipulated. Often a child can express in clay modeling what he cannot manage in graphic materials. Modeling in the round is effective at all age levels; modeling in relief, making simple coil or slab pottery, and working in ceramic are more suitable after Grade 2.

In the lower grades decoration may be done with underglaze color or acrylic color and then coated with shellac (white) or a clear polymer medium. At the upper elementary and middle school levels, underglaze overpainted with a transparent glaze may be used, and a one-fire process in a kiln completes the work. For specific instructions about firing, the art teacher should be consulted.

MATERIALS FOR CLAY MODELING   Clay, slip, rolling pin, form, oilcloth, pan of water, cloth, cutting knife, underglaze, clear glaze, tempera, shellac, acrylic polymer medium, brush, sieve, petroleum jelly, mixing bowl.

PREPARING THE CLAY   Air bubbles must be worked out of the clay so it will have a smooth, plastic consistency. The process is called wedging. A piece of clay is cut by pushing it over a taut wire. The halves of the original piece are put together in a different position and dropped lightly (throwing process) on a plaster of Paris or an absorbent wood surface. This procedure is repeated until the clay is free of bubbles and is plastic. The clay now should be kept covered with a moist cloth or be put in a damp box when the child is not working with it. The desk or table surface should be covered with oilcloth when clay is being used.

THUMB BUILDING After the child has rolled the clay into a ball, he places the ball on the oilcloth-covered surface and works a hole into the center with his two thumbs, keeping his fingers on the outside surface of the ball. As he works the clay, gradually applying pressure while turning the ball, he can shape a bowl or dish. This approach can be used to develop slablike forms for ceramic sculpture.

COIL BUILDING The clay is rolled under the heels of the hands until it is of even thickness—about as thick as a child's finger. The base may be prepared as a slab (see under Sculpture) or by winding coils of clay in a spiral. Slip (a thick mixture of clay and water) is placed between each coil and the coils pressed together firmly. The sides of the shape are built up with coils, and slip is used between each layer to weld the clay together. This should be done with care so the coils will not crack apart after the object has been formed. The coils are blended together by rubbing the inside and the outside surfaces. The thumbs must be on one side of the surface and fingers on the other so that the form will not be pushed out of shape. This blending process should be done after the application of each coil layer.

Plasticine Plasticine (and other oil-base modeling materials) will give the child the same experience of modeling as will clay, but these materials cannot be fired. After use, the plasticine can be balled, wrapped in a plastic bag, and placed in a metal container for future use. Plasticine may be used in place of clay to model pieces to be cast in plaster. It can be used as a foundation for papier-mâché, particularly when making puppets and marionettes.

Thin-gauge metal Orangewood manicure sticks, popsicle sticks, shaped tongue depressors, tin snips, pliers, steel wool, and small wooden mallets are used to work with metal.

Thin-gauge metal is suitable for the child in late elementary and middle school; its use carries some risk, however, and it should not be used in the lower grades or in any situation where children may be careless.

The tools are used to shape, cut, bend, and model the metal. Parts may be soldered on or attached with epoxy cement to make more complicated forms.

Thin-gauge tooling copper and aluminum are available commercially and may be used for repoussé work. In repoussé work, the surface is decorated with a pattern formed in relief by impressing it gradually with a wood tool over a layer of soft, resilient material such as a pad of newspaper. After the child has developed a design or picture the same size as the foil he will use, he should place the foil on a pad of newspaper, lay the drawing on the foil, and trace the lines of the drawing with a sharp, firm pencil so that the image of the drawing is impressed on the foil. The foil should then be modeled on both sides by pressure with a wood tool. The foil is then polished with steel wool and lacquered. With the assistance of the art teacher, liver of sulphur can be applied to the surface of the metal to give it an effective tone. After the liver of sulphur has dried, the foil can be buffed lightly with steel wool and lacquered.

CONSTRUCTION

MATERIALS Cardboard boxes (all sizes), wire, adhesives (epoxy, milk-base glue, vegetable glue), cardboard, balsa wood, string, plastics, various discarded items.

TOOLS Pliers, scissors, X-acto knife, tin snips, stapler.

Approaches to construction

Cardboard-box construction In the early grades, the children can build a houselike structure out of a large cardboard carton into which they can walk or crawl. The exterior of the construction can be painted and areas of the cardboard cut away. The final construction may be abstract or realistic.

In later grades, large and small boxes may be fastened together to create more challenging constructed forms.

Mobiles and stabiles   A mobile is a construction made of wire, cardboard, or thin wood and developed on a hanging armature. The child can form an armature and suspend it by means of heavy twine from a wire or rope stretched across the room. The child cuts out various shapes from materials which seem to go together and which relate to the shape of the basic form, and hangs these from the armature and from other attached pieces so that they move freely. From this experience, the child learns about the relation between the physical and visual balance of materials.

A stabile is built up from a base set firmly on a surface. Usually, the base is the only part of the construction which touches the surface. However, as in contemporary sculpture, other forms may spring out from the base and come in contact with the surface for the purpose of enhancing the work.

Space boxes   The child can collect materials and parts of objects such as dowels from the back of an old chair, lids of jars, spools, etc., and arrange them inside an old wooden box. The box and the arrangement may be painted one color or various colors as the work progresses. If a cardboard box is used and scenes are developed with natural or constructed simulated materials, the work is a diorama.

Block construction   Old blocks of wood collected from a finishing mill or the school shop are glued together to make interesting forms. This construction experience is suitable for a child in the lower grades. An older child can develop challenging block sculpture. *It is a technique which intellectually, visually, and physically limited children find most rewarding.*

Another type of block construction suitable for the late elementary and middle grades, uses various items of junked materials that can be hammered, altered, and arranged to form a new image. A completed junk construction should not look like junk. If toothpicks are used in a construction, the finished product should not look like a collection of toothpicks, but like a new form in which toothpicks have been used to develop a textured surface.

FILM AND TRANSPARENCIES

MATERIALS   The newest challenges for elementary school art programs today are in the areas of the film arts. Materials include discarded movie film, clear movie film, clear and developed black-and-white and color film, transparent cellophane, colored and clear acetate, gelatin for theater spots, screens, paint, oil in water, colored ink, a Polaroid camera and film (colored and black-and-white), glass for slides, an overhead projector, bromide or chloride photography paper, paper developer, and hypo photographic solutions.

TOOLS   Brushes, sharp instruments for scoring, scraping, and scratching, transparent adhering materials.

Approaches to film and transparencies

Photograms   Working in a ventilated room with a yellow paper safelight, the child can place various objects over photographic printing paper and flash the surface of the paper rapidly with a flashlight from different angles. The paper is put in a bath of slow (diluted) photographic developer solution until an image appears. When the dark areas are black and the lightest area is white, the paper is quickly rinsed in water and then in a hypo solution. After the paper has been in the hypo for the required time (*observe directions on the can or package*), it is washed in running water for 15 minutes. The children must wear a rubber apron and rubber gloves. *A child with a history of skin allergy should never use photographic chemicals. Whenever photographic materials are used, the teacher should explain to the children that they should never touch their faces until they have washed their hands with soap and water.* This experience is suitable for children in Grade 5 and over if they respect advice and are self-disciplined.

Film production   Old film may be scratched, scored, or scraped with a sharp instrument. Clear film may be painted with transparent colors. Following these experiences, the length of film may be spliced, placed in a movie projector, and viewed. After an evaluation of the effect, changes are made and the film reshown until the total result is satisfying. Usually, in the beginning of this experience, film is created on a purely experimental basis. This experience is recommended for the grades beginning with the sixth; however, if the art program is especially rich, it can begin earlier.

Slides   Colored transparent and paper-thin materials may be glued to the surface of glass for slides and the results viewed by means of a slide projector and photographed with a Polaroid camera.

Polaroid prints   Using an inexpensive Polaroid camera and black-and-white film, children early in their school life can search for new shapes and textures in the things around them and develop a sensitivity to aesthetic visual relations in two-dimensional space.

Overhead projection of visual imagery   Flat dishes of water are placed on the table of an overhead projector, and insolvent materials such as oils and colors are put in the dishes. The light from the projector throws the image on a screen or a white surface, creating a design. Devices such as placing a piece of window screen on the projector, using more than one screen, using transparent colored materials may enhance the image. The visual image may be recorded as a color print with a Polaroid camera. This experience with the overhead projector may begin as early as children learn how to manipulate the equipment. If they are permitted to use a piece of equipment in the early grades and are oriented to respect it, this material can be presented as early as the third grade.

HAND ARTS

The term "hand arts" describes a visual arts experience in which the child, working with his hands, designs and executes two- and three-dimensional products useful in daily life. The areas of hand arts experiences include basket-weaving; bookbinding; ceramics; enameling; making household accessories; making jewelry; working with stones, leather, metal, plastics; pottery-making; stitchery; textile decoration; hand and loom weaving; and woodworking. Guiding this work requires a more comprehensive understanding of many tools, materials, and approaches than can be presented here. For this reason, only a few introductory experiences for the elementary school art program will be described, and the teacher is referred for further information to the bibliography at the end of these appendixes.

In presenting the hand arts the principles of creative-evaluative teaching should be applied, and the approach is essentially the same as for all other visual arts experiences. Original thinking about experimentation with, research on, and manipulation of craft materials are the foundation for the development of insight and understanding. Craft kits, in which the materials are precut designs and children are made to follow directions, constitute a serious deterrent to creative experience and should not be used.

Weaving

MATERIALS   Paper, string, yarn, grass, plastic, metallic material, seeds, other collected objects.

Approach   Weaving is a process of passing lengths of material (called the weft, filler, or weaver) horizontally over and under vertical lengths of material (called the warp) assembled to equal the desired size of the finished weaving. Traditionally, weaving is associated with thread, yarn, and rags, but any weavable material can be used. In the past, weavers attempted to keep the textures of woven materials in a consistent, tight pattern. Recently weaving has become less tied to tradition and interesting open-work and nubby textures are produced. Children at almost any level of education can weave as long as the concept of the process and the kind and size of the material used are within their ability levels.

Paper-weaving in the early grades is a valuable

initial experience. Variations of color, value, and texture of material used in the warp and the weft give the child experience in controlling the surface pattern and design.

A loom is a frame used to anchor the warp at top and bottom. The frame can be made of paper, cardboard, metal, or wood. In the weaving process, the more devices used in different ways to separate the warp threads at random or systematically, the more complicated the procedure. The least complicated method is to sew the weft material through the warp by an over-and-under process of handweaving. Lifting the warp with harnesses permits the weaver to repeat an order of threads more readily and to throw a shuttle between the separated warp threads; it speeds up the process of weaving, but restricts the weaver to the procedures possible with the harnesses (unless he resorts to complicated handwork or tying up the harnesses to achieve alternative means of changing the warp threads).

To make a frame, heavy cardboard, in rectangular or circular form, can be notched across the edge of the short dimension or on the circumference of the circle. Warp threads can be laced over the cardboard. In circular form, the warp would go from the outside circumference through a center hole large enough so that each warp thread can be placed side by side.

For larger weaving a wooden loom can be constructed by lacing the warp material over a board, box, or picture frame; many commercial frames with and without harnesses are available. The teacher should try weaving before working with it in the classroom. When looms with harnesses are used, the special art teacher should be consulted for details regarding the particular looms purchased for the school system.

Children can weave wall hangings on suspended warps, as the Indians did.

Stitchery and appliqué

MATERIALS Cloth pieces, yarns, string, thread, collected two-dimensional material, mercerized embroidery cotton, ribbon, metallic thread, glue, size.

SURFACES Cloth (burlap, crinoline, netting, heavy cotton, linen, old clean sheeting, lightweight duck, felt); cardboard.

TOOLS Needles, scissors.

Approach Cloth is a useful background for various types of stitches (sewing, flat, satin, bundled, cross, herringbone, back, running, loose, ragged, loop, chain, feather, knot, and free stitches) to create effective and interesting surfaces. For hooking, an open cloth like burlap should be stretched on a frame. For appliqué, the cloth should be strong and colored and textured so that contrast can be developed with the materials applied to the surface. Stitchery and appliqué may be combined to design shapes of many sizes and textures on larger surfaces such as wall hangings and screens.

For the child in kindergarten or Grade 1, cutting shapes and sewing them on cloth are good experiences in manipulating materials. For the older child, learning to cut and combine shapes and colors heightens interest.

Stitchery and appliqués can be combined in the upper grades with block printing, stenciling, and screening processes in the decorating of textile surfaces. Each of these other processes may also be used individually.

Batik and tie-dyeing

MATERIALS Cloth dye, mixing pan, string, wax, wooden stamp.

SURFACES Varieties of cloth materials.

Approach Batik and tie-dyeing are ancient arts from Java and India. In batik, a design is blocked out by saturating certain areas of the fabric with wax. The fabric is then dyed in a vat. The blocked areas resist the dye and remain the original color of the cloth. The design may be varied by blocking out more areas and redyeing in the same or another color or by removing the wax from the first-blocked areas, applying wax to a new area, and dyeing again. The wax is removed by boiling in water; small areas may be removed by placing the material between two sheets of blotting paper and applying a hot iron until all the wax is removed.

In tie-dyeing, the areas may be blocked by wrapping strips of material around areas of the cloth or by knotting the cloth tightly. These experiences are suitable for children at the third-grade level and above.

Puppets

MATERIALS Old sock, tissue, papier-mâché, toilet-paper tube, cotton batting, thread, string, acrylic paint, wool, buttons, beads, felt.

TOOLS Needle, scissors, X-acto knife.

Approach The child can develop interesting puppets to be used over his hands to produce dramatic presentations correlated with his immediate educational and life experiences. The toe-end of a sock serves as the base for the head, and by stitching and papier-mâché applications the features of a head are formed to resemble a particular character. Cardboard tubing is inserted into the sock and the sock is stuffed with cotton to form a head shape. About 4 inches from the toe, the sock is glued or tied to the tube. The tube should extend into the skirtlike remaining lower part of the sock. The remainder of the sock is developed as the costume of the puppet. Armholes are cut and an old glove is inserted so that the forefinger goes into the head and the thumb and little finger go into the arm holes. The fingers are decorated to go with the costume.

A head can also be made by applying papier-mâché to a light bulb and then removing the bulb. The papier-mâché form is used as the base for the head, which is attached to the forefinger of a cloth workglove. A costume is then attached to the glove. For a small child simple puppets can be created by using glue and cut paper to create features on a small paper bag. Yarn makes good hair for the puppet.

The making of puppets may culminate an experience in the class related to creative writing.

Appendix V
BASIC PRINCIPLES OF DESIGN WITH VISUAL MATERIALS IN ART

Design is a process of arranging elements in relation to basic principles to gain a visually expressive and aesthetic form. In the language of visual art the elements include the following:

Line is a mark that maintains a constant width and is some dimension longer than it is wide.

Outline is a line whose ends join to surround an amount of flat surface.

Shape is the quality of an area in terms of the relative position of all points making up its outline or total surface.

Size is the scale of a thing in terms of largeness or smallness.

Form is the particular shape that gives an art object its particular quality, nature, or characteristic.

Value is the quality of lightness or darkness of another element in terms of the scale white to black.

Color is the quality of light and possessing three physical properties: hue, value, and intensity.

Hue is the term used in art which is generally called color. Yellow, red, blue, etc. are hues.

Value (color) is the amount of light present in a hue and determines its lightness or darkness.

Intensity is the brightness or dullness possessed by a hue.

Warm is the impression a color gives visually associated with the sun or heat.

Cool is the impression a color gives visually associated with sky or water.

Recede is the sensation of a visual image going away or being in back of something.

Advance is the sensation of a visual image coming forward.

Light is the total rays from the sun, theoretically waves, that vibrate at different speeds so that some are short and some are long producing different colors.

White is a surface that reflects all of the sun's rays.

Black is a surface that absorbs all of the sun's rays.

Red is the longest wavelength of light.

Violet is the shortest wavelength of light.

Tints are the lightest values of color.

Shades are the darkest values of color.

Texture is the quality of a surface in terms of roughness or smoothness. A single element repeated over a surface produces texture.

Motif is the arrangement of two or more elements in a design.

Pattern is a motif repeated over a surface.

Alternation is the repeat of two or more motifs in a pattern.

In the language of art the principles are the following:

Balance is the quality of an arrangement of elements in a design or picture so that one half of the composition of the picture seems to belong to the other half.

Formal is a symmetrical arrangement that produces a formal quality in a design.

Informal is an unsymmetrical arrangement that produces a free or organic quality in a design.

Repetition is the repeating of elements, motifs, or similar forms in an art object.

Rhythm is the quality of producing a feeling of continuous flow by repeating elements progressively in a design.

Emphasis is a quality which makes one thing stand out from others owing to a contrast.

Contrast is a condition created when two elements of different characteristics are placed side by side.

Dominance is produced when an element or object is made to stand out because of a contrasting difference such as size, value, color, etc.

Subordination is produced when an element is less prominent due to a lack of contrast with its surroundings.

Appendix VI
ART MATERIALS FOR A BASIC PROGRAM OF ART IN THE ELEMENTARY SCHOOL CLASSROOM

All elementary school teachers should be familiar with the types and amounts of art materials needed in each classroom for an adequate program of art education. Following are lists of (1) materials that should be immediately available and stored in the classroom, (2) materials that can be stored in the stockroom of the school building, and (3) materials to be supplied by the special art teacher that can be stored in the central supply room of the school system.

MATERIALS TO BE STORED IN THE CLASSROOM

Crayons
   One box of large crayons per child (Grades K–2)
   One box of small crayons per child (Grades 3–6)
Pencils
   One per child
Scissors
   One pair per child; when used with care, scissors need be replaced only when broken

Brushes
One dozen per room (Grades K–2); when all children use brushes at one time, additional brushes may be borrowed from a reserve shared by all teachers and kept in the school supply room
One brush per child (Grades 3–6); replacements should be needed only when brushes wear out

Watercolor boxes
One metal box with 8 fillers for each child (Grades 3–6)

Paper
One ream of 12 by 18 inch manila (Grades K–3)
One ream of 12 by 18 inch American white (Grades 4–6)

Powder paint
One pound each, primary colors (Grade K–1)
One pound each, primary and secondary colors, black, and white (Grades 2–3)

Tempera paint
One quart each, primary and secondary colors, black, and white (Grades 4–6)

Finger paint
One pint each, primary colors and black (Grades K–3)

Paste
One quart

Containers
One water cup per child

MATERIALS TO BE STORED IN THE SCHOOL STOCK ROOM

Paper
Bogus paper for chalk, mounting, and pasting
Colored construction paper, sizes 12 by 18 inches and 18 by 24 inches
Newsprint, plain sheets, size 18 by 24 inches
Stencil paper, size 9 by 12 inches
Kraft paper, size 24 by 240 inches; one roll per classroom
Project roll (mural paper), size 36 inches by 75 feet; one roll per three classrooms

Clay
Moist clay, one pound per child

Plasticine, one pound per child

Paint
Poster paint reserve
Finger paint reserve
Watercolor refills
Textile paints, one set per classroom

Graphics materials
Block-printing ink (water base)
Brayers
Speedball cutting tools

MATERIALS TO BE SUPPLIED BY SPECIAL ART TEACHER AND STORED IN CENTRAL SUPPLY ROOM

Charcoal sticks[1]
Linoleum, mounted and unmounted
India inks
Pen points and holders

Paint
Enamel
Spatter paint and guns
Oil paint and medium, if necessary
Acrylic polymer emulsions and paint

Paper
Railroad board
Poster board
Colored tissue
Crepe paper

Adhesives
Milk-base glue
Epoxy cement
Fixative and sprayer
Shellac
Wax
Rubber cement
Masking tape

Craft
All special craft items

---

[1] Charcoal is difficult for a young child to master because the sticks are brittle and the lines he draws are easily smudged; this material should not be used in the primary grades.

BIBLIOGRAPHY

Alschuler, Rose H., and W. La Berta, *Painting and Personality,* Chicago, University of Chicago Press, 1947.

Arnheim, Rudolph, *Art and Visual Perception,* Berkeley, University of California Press, 1954.

Art Education (Journal of the National Art Education Association, Washington, D.C.), Vol. 21, No. 6, June 1968.

Baker, Harry J., *Introduction to Exceptional Children,* 4th ed., New York, Macmillan, 1962.

Bannon, Laura, *Mind Your Child's Art,* New York, Farrar, Straus & Giroux, 1952.

Barbe, Walter B., *The Exceptional Child,* Washington, D.C., The Center for Applied Research in Education, Inc., 1963.

Barkan, Manuel, *Foundations of Art Education,* New York, Ronald Press, 1955.

Barkan, Manuel, *Through Art to Creativity,* Boston, Allyn & Bacon, 1960.

Bayles, Ernest E., *Democratic Educational Theory,* New York, Harper & Row, 1960.

Beelke, Ralph G., ed., *Curriculum Development in Art Education,* Washington, D.C., National Art Education Association, 1961.

Beittel, Kenneth R., "The Effect of Self-Reflective Evaluative Conditions on Learning Art," report presented at the convention of the American Educational Research Association, 1964.

Beittel, Kenneth R., and Robert C. Burkhart, *Effect of Self-Reflective Training in Art on the Capacity for Creative Action,* University Park, Pennsylvania State University, (Cooperative Research Project No. 1874, U.S. Dept. of HEW, Office of Education), 1962–1964.

Bennis, Warren G., Kenneth D. Benne, and Robert Chin, *The Planning of Change,* New York, Holt, Rinehart and Winston, 1962.

Bigge, Morris L., *Learning Theories for Teachers,* New York, Harper & Row, 1964.

Bland, Jane C., *Art of the Young Child,* New York, Museum of Modern Art (Simon & Schuster), 1958.

Blumenau, Lili, *The Art and Craft of Handweaving,* New York, Crown, 1955.

Brittain, W. Lambert, ed., *Creativity and Art Education,* Washington, D.C., National Art Education Association, 1964.

Bruner, Jerome S., *The Process of Education,* Cambridge, Mass., Harvard University Press, 1965.

Burkhart, Robert C., *Spontaneous and Deliberate Ways of Learning,* Scranton, Pa., International Textbook, 1962.

Burton, William H., *The Guidance of Learning Activities,* New York, Appleton-Century-Crofts, 1944.

Cane, Florence, *The Artist in Each of Us,* New York, Pantheon Books, 1952.

Cataldo, John, *Lettering: A Guide for Teachers,* Worcester, Mass., Davis Publications, 1958.

Cole, Natalie R., *The Arts in the Classroom,* New York, John Day, 1940.

Cole, Natalie R., *Children's Arts from Deep Down Inside,* New York, John Day, 1966.

Conant, Howard, *Seminar on Elementary and Secondary School Education in the Visual Arts,* New York, New York University, Cooperative Research Project No. V–003, Office of Education, U.S. Dept of HEW, 1965.

Conant, Howard, and Arne Randall, *Art in Education,* Peoria, Ill., Chas. A. Bennett, 1959.

Conrad, George, *The Process of Art Education in the Elementary School,* Englewood Cliffs, N.J., Prentice-Hall, 1964.

Cox, Doris, and Barbara Warren, *Creative Hands,* 2nd ed., New York, Wiley, 1951.

D'Amico, Victor, *Creative Teaching in Art,* rev. ed., Scranton, Pa., International Textbook, 1953.

D'Amico, Victor, *Experiments in Creative Art Teaching,* New York, Museum of Modern Art, 1960.

DeFrancesco, Italo L., *Art Education: Its Means and Ends,* New York, Harper & Row, 1958.

DeLong, Patrick D., Robert E. Enger, and Robert Thomas, *Art and Music in the Humanities,* Englewood Cliffs, N.J., Prentice-Hall, 1966.

Dewey, John, *Art as Experience,* New York, Minton, Balch, 1934.

Eisner, Elliot W., and David Ecker, *Readings in Art Education,* Waltham, Mass., Blaisdell, 1966.

Erdt, Margaret, *Teaching Art in the Elementary School,* rev. ed., New York, Holt, Rinehart and Winston, 1962.

Feldman, Edmund Burke, *Becoming Human Through Art: Aesthetic Experience in the School,* Englewood Cliffs, N.J., Prentice-Hall, 1970.

Gaitskell, Charles D., *Art Education for Slow Learners,* Peoria, Ill., Chas. A. Bennett, 1953.

Gallinger, Osma Couch, *The Joy of Hand Weaving,* New York, Van Nostrand, 1950.

Garrison, Karl C., *The Psychology of Exceptional Children,* rev. ed., Ronald Press, 1950.

Gesell, Arnold, *Child Development,* New York, Harper & Row, 1949.

Harris, Dale B., *Children's Drawings as Measures of Intellectual Maturity,* New York, Harcourt, Brace & World, 1963.

Hastie, W. Reid, ed., *Art Education* (Sixty-fourth Yearbook of the National Society for the Study of Education), Chicago, University of Chicago Press, 1965.

Heilman, Horace F., *An Experimental Study of the Effects of Workbooks on the Creative Drawing of Second-Grade Children* (doctoral dissertation), University Park, Pennsylvania State University, 1954.

Henrickson, Paul R., and E. Paul Torrance, "Some Implications for Art Education from the Minnesota Studies of Creative Thinking," in *Creativity and Art Education,* ed. W. Lambert Brittain, National Art Eduction Association, Washington, D.C., 1964.

Henry, Edith M., *Evaluation of Children's Growth Through Art Experience,* Washington, D.C., National Art Education Association, 1963.

Henry, Nelson B., ed., *The Psychology of Learning* (Forty-first Yearbook, Part II, of the National Society for the Study of Education), Chicago, University of Chicago Press, 1942.

Heyne, Carl J., Florence W. Nicholas, Margaret M. Lee, and Mabel B. Trilling, *Art for Young America,* Peoria, Ill., Chas. A. Bennett, 1967.

Hils, Karl, *Crafts for All,* Newton Centre, Mass., Branford, 1960.

Hurlock, Elizabeth B., *Child Development,* 4th ed., New York, McGraw-Hill, 1964.

Hurwitz, Elizabeth A., *Design, A Search for Essentials,* Scranton, Pa., International Textbook, 1964.

Jefferson, Blanche, *Teaching Art to Children,* 3rd ed., Boston, Allyn & Bacon, 1969.

Karasz, Mariska, *Adventures in Stitches and More Adventures, Fewer Stitches,* New York, Funk & Wagnalls, 1959.

Karel, Leon C., *Avenues to the Arts,* Kirksville, Mo., Simpson Publishing, 1966.

Keiler, Manfred L., *Art in Teaching Art,* Lincoln, University of Nebraska Press, 1961.

Kelly, James J., *The Sculptural Ideas,* Minneapolis, Minn., Burgess Publishing Company, 1970.

Krevitsky, Nik, *Batik Art and Craft,* New York, Reinhold, 1964.

Kubler, George, *The Shape of Time,* New Haven, Conn., Yale University Press, 1962.

Landis, Mildred, *Meaningful Art Education,* Peoria, Ill., Chas. A. Bennett, 1951.

Lanier, Vincent, Final Report of the Uses of Newer Media in Art Education Project, Washington, D.C., National Art Education Association, 1966.

Lansing, Kenneth M., *Art, Artists, and Art Education,* New York, McGraw-Hill, 1969.

Lantz, Beatrice, *Easel Age Scale,* Los Angeles, California Test Bureau, 1955.

Lark-Horovitz, Betty, Hilda P. Lewis, and Mark Luca, *Understanding Children's Art for Better Teaching,* Columbus, Ohio, Charles E. Merrill Books, 1967.

Linderman, Earl W., *Invitation to Vision,* Dubuque, Iowa, William C. Brown, 1967.

Linderman Earl W., and Donald W. Herberholz, *Developing Artistic and Perceptual Awareness,* Dubuque, Iowa, William C. Brown, 1964.

Lindstrom, Miriam, *Children's Art,* 5th ed., Los Angeles, University of California Press, 1962.

Logan, Frederick M., *Growth of Art in American Schools,* New York, Harper & Row, 1955.

Lowenfeld, Viktor, *Your Child and His Art,* New York, Macmillan, 1954.

Lowenfeld, Viktor, and W. Lambert Brittain, *Creative and Mental Growth,* 4th ed., New York, Macmillan, 1964.

Lowenfeld, Viktor, and W. Lambert Brittain, *Creative and Mental Growth,* 5th ed., New York, Macmillan, 1970.

Luca, Mark, and Robert Kent, *Art Education: Strategies of Teaching,* Englewood Cliffs, N.J., Prentice-Hall, 1968.

McFee, June King, *Preparation for Art,* Belmont, Calif., Wadsworth Publishing, 1961.

Mattil, Edward L., *Meaning in Crafts,* 2nd ed., Englewood Cliffs, N.J., Prentice-Hall, 1965.

Mattil, Edward L., Kenneth R. Beittel, and Robert C. Burkhart, "The Effect of Depth versus a Breadth Method of Art Instruction at the Ninth Grade Level," in *Studies in Art Education,* Charles M. Dorn, ed., Washington, D.C., National Art Education Association, 1961.

Mendelowitz, Daniel M., *Children Are Artists,* 2nd ed., Stanford, Calif., Stanford University Press, 1963.

Merritt, Helen, *Guiding Free Expression in Children's Art,* New York, Holt, Rinehart and Winston, 1966.

Moholy-Nagy, Ladislaus, *The New Vision,* New York, Norton, 1938.

Montgomery, Chandler, *Art for Teachers of Children,* Columbus, Ohio, Charles E. Merrill, 1968.

Moseley, Spencer, Pauline Johnson, and Hazel Koenig, *Crafts Design,* Belmont, Calif., Wadsworth Publishing, 1963.

Packwood, Mary M., ed., *Art Education in the Elementary School,* Washington, D.C., National Art Education Association, 1967.

Pappas, George, "An Analysis of the Process of Beginning and Developing Works of Art," *Research in Art Education,* Jerome J. Hausman, ed., Washington, D.C., National Art Education Association, 1959.

Pappas, George, *Concepts in Art and Education,* New York and London, Macmillan, 1970.

Ragan, William B., *Modern Elementary Curriculum,* New York, Holt, Rinehart and Winston, 1961.

Rainey, Sarita, *Weaving Without a Loom,* Worcester, Mass., Davis Publications, 1966.

Read, Herbert, *Art and Society,* New York, Macmillan, 1947.

Read, Herbert, *Education Through Art,* New York, Pantheon, 1949.

Read, Herbert, *To Hell with Culture,* New York, Schoecken Books, 1963.

Richey, Herman R., ed., *Theories of Learning and Instruction* (Sixty-third Yearbook of the National Society for the Study of Education), Chicago, University of Chicago Press, 1964.

Rucker, W. Ray, *Curriculum Development in the Elementary School,* New York, Harper & Row, 1960.

Rueschhoff, Phil H., and M. Evelyn Swartz, *Teaching Art in the Elementary School,* New York, Ronald Press, 1969.

Sawyer, John R., "The Ability of the Mentally Retarded Child for Graphically Representing Spatial Relationships" (unpublished research paper), Durham, University of New Hampshire, 1953.

Sawyer, John R., "Convergent and Divergent Instructional Procedures Used in the Preparation of Teachers of Art" (doctoral dissertation), University Park, Pennsylvania State University, 1966.

Sawyer, John R., "Television Goes to Elementary Art Classes," *Journal of Education,* Boston University, Publisher, Vol. 136, No. 6, March, 1954.

Schaefer-Simmern, Henry, *The Unfolding of Artistic Activity,* Berkeley, University of California Press, 1948.

Schinneller, James A., *Art: Search and Self-Discovery,* rev. ed., Scranton, Pa., International Textbook, 1968.

Schultz, Josephine B., *Planning Facilities for Art Instruction,* Washington, D.C., National Art Education Association, 1961.

Shultz, Harold, and J. Harlan Shores, *Art in the Elementary Schools,* Urbana, University of Illinois Press, 1948.

Shumsky, Abraham, *Creative Teaching in the Elementary School,* New York, Appleton-Century-Crofts, 1965.

Smith, B. Othanel, William O. Stanley, and J. Harlan Shores, *Fundamentals of Curriculum Development,* New York, Harcourt, Brace & World, 1950.

Smith, James A., *Creative Teaching of the Creative Arts in the Elementary School*, Boston, Allyn & Bacon, 1967.

Sowards, G. Wesley, and Mary-Margaret Scobey, *The Changing Curriculum and the Elementary Teacher*, Belmont, Calif., Wadsworth Publishing, 1961.

Steveni, Michael, *Art and Education*, New York, Atherton Press, 1968.

Tannahill, Sallie B., *Fine Arts for Public School Administrators*, New York, Columbia University Teachers College, 1932.

Taylor, Calvin, ed., *Creativity: Progress and Potential*, New York, McGraw-Hill, 1964.

Torrance, E. Paul, *Constructive Behavior: Stress, Personality, and Mental Health*, Belmont, Calif., Wadsworth Publishing, 1965.

Torrance, E. Paul, *Education and the Creative Potential*, Minneapolis, University of Minnesota Press, 1963.

Torrance, E. Paul, *Guiding Creative Talent*, Englewood Cliffs, N.J., Prentice-Hall, 1962.

Wachowiak, Frank, and Theodore Ramsay, *Emphasis: Art*, Scranton, Pa., International Textbook, 1965.

Wankelman, Willard F., Philip Wigg, and Marietta Wigg, *A Handbook of Arts and Crafts for Elementary and Junior High School Teachers*, Dubuque, Iowa, William C. Brown, 1968.

Weitz, Morris, *Problems in Aesthetics*, New York, Macmillan, 1963.

Wickiser, Ralph L., *An Introduction to Art Education*, New York, Harcourt, Brace & World, 1957.

Williams, Helen, *Puppets Go to School*, New York, Holt, Rinehart and Winston, 1955.

Winebrenner, D. Kenneth, *Jewelry Making as An Art Expression*, Scranton, Pa., International Textbook, 1955.

Zechlin, Ruth, *Complete Book of Handcrafts*, Amsterdam Internationale Vitgeoery Duphare, 1959.

INDEX

INDEX

Designed by Rita Naughton
Set in Optima
Composed by Progressive Typographers
Printed by Halliday Lithograph Corp.
Bound by American Book-Stratford Press, Inc.
HARPER & ROW, PUBLISHERS, INC.

71 72 73 74 7 6 5 4 3 2 1

6 7 5 7